Fast-Forward and Reverse

For over 15 years I made my living sitting behind a large pane of glass. It's the glass you see in a recording studio, the one that separates the performer from people like me: the engineer and the producer. I have worked with hundreds of recording artists in this way, cutting their demos and seeing the hope in their eyes, right through the final mixes of tunes that became huge hits for them. Through it all, I have always found this "separating glass" the perfect analogy for a business that works so hard at separating the artist from their money. Conjure this image: the novice performer sits blissfully in a darkened booth, while on the other side, protected by soundproof walls and expensive machinery, bean counters and executives decide their fate.

Over the years, and in the dim, smoky light of a 2 A.M. recording session, many artists have confessed to me, "If I'd only known better when I signed my first deal." In this moment of crisis, when their manager isn't returning their calls, their girl- or boyfriend is angry with them, their sidemen are getting wasted, the producer is on the phone, and the label won't give them more money, they have turned to me, the unassuming technician, in hopes of a sympathetic ear. They spoke and I listened. This book is the result.

It probably comes as no surprise that these artists feel taken advantage of by the very companies they've made millions for. Are they paranoid, or were their expectations perhaps too high? You will decide for yourself as you learn every trick, scam, and lie they were told—and told back.

What separates this book from the scores of other books on this business is the fact that most other books are written by attorneys and discuss the music business in theory. Certainly there's value in that. But unfortunately attorneys are not always in the best position to speak openly about their clients' business practices. I'm not an attorney. I have no allegiances to protect. I won't bore you with anal interpretations of how things are supposed to work. Here you will only read how things *did* work when applied to real-life situations. Plus, you will see *real dollar numbers* showing what everyone makes at the end of the day, from the record company to the recording engineer.

Every account in this book is *real*. They're designed to illustrate strong examples of how money can slip away from the artist who is not savvy to the way things really work, and give the artist strong ammunition to help them preserve their assets.

The first part of this book looks at the typical recording deal from three distinct points of view: (1) the artist, (2) the producer, and (3) the record label. After reading each section, you will understand why record deals are so complex, and thus whatever phase of the business you're thinking about entering, you will be well–armed for a negotiation.

The second part of the book can be thought of as an encyclopedia of skullduggery—the first volume ever assembled that catalogues every known way to swindle artists, producers, and even labels out of their hard-earned cash.

It's my guess that most of you reading this book are thinking about a long and successful career in the music industry. Will this book make you paranoid? Well, hopefully it will make you cautious, but will it try to discourage you from getting into the business? Absolutely not. This book is no more than a tool. It's designed to empower you to go forward and deal from a position of strength. Ultimately, it's your talent, passion, and determination that will push you toward a life in music, and that passion will be the beacon for your success.

Within these pages I address the concerns and frustrations of many in this industry—an industry once mired in corruption, but which in the last decade has traded its "family" ties for ones with multinational conglomerates. The trade-offs are sometimes less noticeable than one might expect.

Tomorrow's music industry has the potential to be the most spiritually powerful business in the world. It is my hope that this book can be part of its growth as the industry moves through the new millennium and on to realize the spiritual image it so realistically feigns.

It is my sincerest wish that this book will someday be obsolete.

❯ Who the Hell Am I?

I entered the business in the early '80s as an engineer in a small 8-track studio. Back then, there were no tell-all books the way there are today. All we had were gossipy stories about people like Morris Levy and the founder of Motown Records, Berry Gordy—paranoid tales of how entrepreneurs swindled naive musicians and songwriters out of their money.

As is common among engineers, after several of the records I worked on charted, I became a producer. I quickly realized that all I had heard as the artist's confessor was true. And, I'm sorry to say, I had become part of that very system, employing many of the same values that I had disagreed with years earlier.

I recalled something a client had told me. He was a successful producer for whom I engineered for years. He said, "No one wants to rip off anybody. Everybody is just doing what they think is right for their client."

Self-serving? Maybe, but I have seen enough over the years to know that in the arena of music, karma often takes a backseat to leverage. What you'll see, after we dissect the pros and cons of major record deals, is that who the good guys and bad guys are is largely a matter of outlook.

❯ Introduction to the Second Edition

Truth rings the town bell, someone once said, and in a business where sleaze runs rampant like a Satyr in a brothel, the truths expressed in *Confessions* seem to be resounding through our community.

Confessions of a Record Producer

How to Survive the Scams and Shams of the Music Business

By Moses Avalon

Backbeat
Books

San Francisco

Published by Backbeat Books
600 Harrison Street, San Francisco, CA 94107
www.backbeatbooks.com
Email: books@musicplayer.com
An imprint of Music Player Network
United Entertainment Media, Inc.

Distributed to the book trade in the U.S. and Canada by
Publishers Group West, P.O. Box 8843, Emeryville, CA 94662

Distributed to the music trade in the U.S. and Canada by
Hal Leonard Publishing, P.O. Box 13819, Milwaukee, WI 53213

Text Design: Richard Leeds
Typesetting: Chris Ledgerwood
Cover Design: The Visual Group

Library of Congress Cataloging in Publication Data:

Avalon, Moses, 1962-
   Confessions of a record producer: how to survive the scams and
   shams of the music business / by Moses Avalon.—2nd ed.
      p. cm.
   ISBN 0-87930-660-2
   1. Sound recording industry—Vocational guidance. I. Title.
ML3790 . A93 2001
780'.13'73—dc21   2001052701

Printed in the United States of America
03 04 05   5 4 3

Since the release of the first edition, readers have sent me in excess of 1000 e-mails with stories that parallel the ones in *Confessions*. What started out as a subversive alternative to starchy manifestos on the music business has become an established and accepted text in colleges and seminars. *Confessions* is now quoted by reporters in newspapers and in the press releases of hit-makers; its examples have been used by major stars to leverage their labels into better deals.

This is the good news. However, there is some bad. When the publisher requested updates for a second edition, it was my hope that substantial alterations would be necessary due to the raised awareness. Unfortunately, after looking over each chapter, the only thing that required serious updating was the math to reflect adjustments for inflation. This book is, sadly, still far from obsolete.

What you do have in this edition is an update to reflect the recent mergers and the addition of several sections to incorporate issues regarding the Internet. You will notice that chapters like "Airplay" have been changed to "Airplay and Webcasting." Stuff like that. Also, due to the unparalleled growth of the Latin music scene, I have sprinkled information that those in the Latin community will find eye-opening.

One interesting irony that I noticed when scouring through the pages that deal with budgets for albums, is that major label recording budgets have not changed enough to warrant updating. Meanwhile, the price of CDs has increased about 20% since *Confessions*'s first printing. This means that labels have succeeded in widening the spread between cost and profit while artists' representation has failed to keep pace and capture some of this new booty. To add insult to injury, labels are now collecting money from new revenue streams created by the Internet. Evidence suggests that none of this new money is, as yet, being passed on to the artist. In fact, were it not due to endorsement deals with major advertisers many artists might even find themselves in a deficit position from five years ago.

Let's hope that by the third edition of *Confessions*, the true creators of our industry can learn enough to regain some ground. That is the goal of this book.

❯ How to Use This Book

Being a musician (and VCR owner) myself, I am very sensitive to the fact that we already have far too many manuals to digest about our equipment to labor through instructions on how to use a book. So I'll be brief.

Why does this book need a "how to use" section? Couldn't you just read it front to back? The answer is yes, and you would probably get the most out of it that way. But this book has been designed to help you find the answers you need easily, without rummaging through many pages. Simply use the table of contents to find the subject that fits your inquiry best, and turn to the page. Each section of the book is self-contained. (The trade-off for this convenience is that some information is repeated in more than one section.)

To help make this book even more user-friendly, the footnotes can act like a magic tour guide. They contain side comments and supporting facts for the text as well as references to other parts of the book with related information. So, whatever page you open to, you will never be lost.

Part 1, "The Game," is the main component of *Confessions*. It deals with the record deal itself and the people who make it happen. The first section of this part, called "The Players," dissects every person you will have to deal with, their background, what they do, their actual agenda, and how much they get paid for doing it.

Understanding what the other person wants and needs from a deal builds powerful and successful negotiating techniques. The second section of Part 1, "The Deal," breaks down the record deal by looking at both major and independent label deals as well as "baby" production deals. We'll look at the deals from three main points of view: artist, producer, and label/production company. Each faction has its own set of concerns. Here also are the money numbers that you can expect to make from these deals.

Part 2, "Scams and Shams," is a collection of 15 years of stories and rumors about how everyone got ripped off by everyone else. The first section of this part deals mostly with the copyright laws and how the strong prey upon the weak to steal material—and what you can do about it. The final section, "Miscellaneous Myths and Untruths," is basically a Q-and-A that will dissolve many of the B.S. rules that you may have heard in your quest for enlightenment about this business.

❷ A Word About the Sidebars

Don't skip them! Not only did it take me a long time to write these things but they contain some of the most valuable information in the book. Everything has been designed to make what may be the most complicated business in the performing arts simple enough that even your cat will understand it (provided your cat can read). Sometimes a short example can be more useful than pages of detailed explanations. The sidebars tell stories that illustrate the text with a real-life scenario. So take the time to read them.

By the way, if your cat can read, don't waste your time in music—get an agent and call Disney, fast!

❷ Disclaimer No. 1

Every effort has been made to provide the most up-to-date industry information available. It must be noted that the music industry is a constantly changing environment. New laws are changing the way artists will be paid, and companies are sold, resurrected, and merged every day. This book is a guide only, not a road map.

❷ Disclaimer No. 2

Nothing in this book should be misconstrued as legal or professional advice.

Enough boring stuff. Let's get to it.

TABLE OF CONTENTS

The Game

Capitalism is convincing somebody that you own something.

—Henry David Thoreau

⊖The Players

As in any business, before you get in over your head, it is important to understand what type of players you'll be dealing with. Those who invest in the music business are an unusual breed of gambler. A lawyer friend once explained it to me this way: "The entertainment industry is like a big casino. Motion pictures are the backroom baccarat tables for the millionaires with the $10,000 gold chips. Television is the $100 table for the yuppies, theater the $25 table, and the record biz is the $2 table, essentially for the bargain shopper."

This is not intended to demean musicians, or the other players in the game. On the contrary, to be a player and win at the record game, you have to place many high-stakes bets, and because you'll have to place a lot of them, they'd better be cheap and shrewd ones. Nor is the above to say that the $2 table is not worth playing; many a large fortune was built on small, carefully thought-out wagers.

In this section we are going to examine the various types of players, both artists and professionals—their roles, agendas, and incomes. But for those of you who've never sat at the $2 table, I can tell you straight out, most of us got our clout from being shrewd, conniving, and in many cases, lawless.

Welcome, brother.

CHAPTER ONE

⊝The Pros

No matter what aspect of the business you pursue, over time you will find yourself talking to more nonmusicians than actual music makers. Even if you are an artist, as you become more successful, the creative end of music will occupy less and less of your time and you will be dealing mostly with lawyers, accountants, managers, business affairs people, label promotion personnel, distributors, and more lawyers.

There is a natural feeling of dread many of us experience when dealing with high-priced professionals. We often believe that because they went to a fancy school, or have framed degrees on their wall, they must be more astute than we are. In the music business, this does not always apply. Here's a big secret:

Most music industry pros, at one time or another, dreamt of being some type of performer.

I remember a piece of advice I received from a successful friend. He said that when meeting important or intimidating people he would try to imagine them naked; all their grandeur would instantly wilt. Building on that advice and looking at the line in bold above, try to imagine the pompous pro in front of you playing in a rock band, arguing over chord changes and how he should wear his hair tonight.

Though not all industry professionals were artists, you should be cautious about the ones that were. Even though they've given up the spotlight, their heart may still be there. The best pros are the professionals who love music and may even be musicians but have made peace with the path they have chosen. They are centered and secure with their station in life. These pros are worth their weight in gold. Even these, however, may have a hidden agenda, as we'll see in the upcoming chapters. The key, when dealing with them, is to relax, listen carefully to what they say, and don't panic. No matter how impressive they try to make themselves out to be, remember that they too are sitting at the $2 table.

❷ Lawyers

Let's start with everyone's favorite target, the lawyer. As stated earlier, until recently most books on the music industry have been written by attorneys. As a result, these books tend to overlook the lawyer's contribution to certain problems in this business. Whether this is done out of convenience or naiveté is anyone's guess. Consider what follows as equal time.

Before any record deal is done, it must go through a lawyer, usually several in fact. The reason: if both sides of the deal are not properly represented, the entire contract may be disputed down the line. That's the actual law! (As practiced by lawyers.)

Because lawyers are centrally placed on all sides of the deal, they have the ear of every important person you will need to know.

Fees for attorneys normally range anywhere from $125 per hour to $600 per hour, although sometimes the lawyer will work for a percentage of the deal instead of an hourly fee. The size of the deal—whether with a major label, a small indie, or a production company—will usually determine the size of the lawyer's fee.

Lawyers typically come from educated upper-middle-class backgrounds and earn anywhere from $60,000 to $500,000 a year. The cream of the crop have been reported to make $1,000,000 per year and up. Clive Davis started out as an attorney and became the president of Arista Records. In 1995, his contract was renewed for $5 million per year (but that's minus a bonus).

However, you shouldn't think that just because the lawyer you've been speaking to has platinum records and framed law degrees on his wall he or she has great knowledge of the law. Many music biz lawyers are more salesmen than litigators. The mainstay of their day revolves around meetings and lunches to rope in business. They are often called "rainmakers."

Behind them, kept well out of sight of the clients, are what I call "the worker bees."

They stay in the office well past 9 P.M., drafting the contracts and making sure the rain-makers, who promised the world to the client, can actually deliver. The worker bees aren't slick like the rainmakers. They get less glory, but they are the ones who really know what's going on and what you can and can't get away with. One way I can always tell a rainmaker from a worker right off the bat—workers wear less jewelry.[1]

[1] This is not a hard-and-fast rule, just an observation.

One other type of lawyer is one I call "the crusader." Crusaders tend to be young attorneys just starting out in business. They've picked up all the book smarts in law school but have yet to learn how to apply it to real life. As with most people who are new, they tend to be somewhat idealistic about how things actually work. The result can be that they over-negotiate a deal into nonexistence. Afterward they will justify their actions by saying it was a lousy deal anyway.

New attorneys tend not to understand that business is about people, not clauses, especially in the music business. It's about relationships. Keeping an eye on the bottom line can be shortsighted in a business where most people are not initially making a huge living. Unfortunately, lawyers are trained to see things in an arbitrary fashion, so sometimes they can do more harm than good, especially when negotiating small money deals. My friend Larry, who is a music industry attorney, says he would never hire a lawyer who wasn't, at some time, in business for himself. I agree, but this isn't always practical.

Some crusaders mature into excellent lawyers; some don't. Until you can determine which way they will go, my advice is to steer clear of the crusader. A typ-

LAWYER LOGIC

It is all too easy for a lawyer to simply say, "Forget this deal."

Consider the lawyer's logic: If he tells you to sign a contract and something goes wrong, you will likely blame him, but if you never do the deal, he can remain forever wise.

Unlike your best friend or family member, lawyers are accountable for the advice they give. Bad advice can lead to a lawsuit against them. So it is in the lawyer's best interest to lean away from a deal (usually after they've racked up a few billable hours examining it). This is not to say that every deal the attorney tells you to pass up is a good one, but you have to always consider the source when asking for advice.

ical example of how crusaders can muddy the waters is illustrated in the sidebar, "My Friend Don."

Conflicts of Interest

An important point about lawyers is to understand their career goals. For example, if you were negotiating a contract with Atlantic Records, would you hire an attorney who was thinking about working for that company soon after your contract was completed? Would this make you a bit suspicious? Would you wonder how hard your lawyer was going to push for you, knowing that he was trying to suck up to the label?

Many attorneys dream of being executives of major labels and see representa-

MY FRIEND DON

Don came from an affluent family and had been working in the music business for several years when he decided to start his own production company. He hired a lawyer to draft a standard production agreement for him to use when negotiating with his clients. The contract, which was very professionally done, was about nine pages long, with lots of fine print. It cost Don a small fortune, too.

I had been operating my own production company for several years, and I tried to warn Don that his contract would never work. He said to me, "But it's a very good deal for the artist."

It *was* a very good deal for the artist. The problem is that the artist usually wouldn't read it because it was too complex and intimidating. I suggested that he do what I did—a simple three-page agreement in plain English. Don's attorney complained that my agreement was unprofessional and left many things out that should be addressed; he insisted that Don keep the agreement that he had drafted. Don did just that.

For about a year he produced no one. No artist he came in contact with had the patience or the money to have a lawyer explain the meaning of the nine-page novel. Out of frustration, his prospective artists chose to look elsewhere rather than deal with Don's business practices, *even though it was a good deal for them*. After 15 months and no new business, Don threw the contract out and Xeroxed mine.

tion of artists, producers, and managers as a mere steppingstone. Other attorneys' main mission is to represent the biggest artists in the business, negotiating against the corporations. Which side of the fence your lawyer is on is important.

But besides this, there is one other oddity that is unique to the music business: it is not uncommon to have attorneys from both sides of a lawsuit working *at the same firm*. By the letter of the law, this is in fact illegal. But in the music business, it happens every day. How can we trust that we are being represented fairly when opposite sides of a dispute sometimes literally share a file cabinet?

We can't. The only answer is to be very cautious about who you get in bed with. Don't go just on instinct that you are being well served. Almost all attorneys who work in large firms ask their clients to sign a document that makes the client aware that conflicts of interest do occur. The client, by signing the contract, agrees to give up their right to have any recourse against the firm if it causes a problem. If a situation arises where the closeness of the two attorneys could bias the outcome of a case, then the ethical attorney would, at that point, tell their client to seek a different lawyer. But not all attorneys are ethical.

A few humbling facts about lawyers:
1. Most lawyers in the U.S. don't earn much more per year than the average sanitation worker.
2. Most lawyers have never taken anyone to court.
3. The most ethical entertainment lawyers make the least money.
4. Most lawyers are not as ethical as they think they are.

⊘ A&R

The A&R people work for record companies and are paid by them to find and sign talent that will record hit records for the label. Today, they are not generally supposed to dictate the creative content to the artist; however, this was not always the case. First, some history:

A&R stands for *Artists and Repertoire*. Up until about 1960, A&R men[2] were the "producers" of the records. They spent time with the artists, developed the material, and were responsible for the *sound and quality* of the record. The A&R person would, more often than not, cowrite the songs and assist with the arrangements, yet they would not receive a single royalty because they were employees of the record company—it was part of the job.

As the business went through its first major consolidation in the 1960s, labels

[2] There were no A&R women at the executive level until about 1965.

began to cut expenses and farm out various functions, one of which was the producing of the record. With this element no longer part of the A&R responsibilities, those A&R persons who excelled at production became "independent producers." Record companies hired them on a project-by-project basis, giving them a fee for producing and a percentage of the profits (usually 3% after recoupment of expenses). With the creative part of the job now filled by an independent contractor, the role of staff A&R was reduced to that of buyer for the record label.[3]

A typical day for an A&R person consists of arriving at the office around 11 A.M. and taking phone calls and meetings (including lunch) until about 6 P.M. Then they go to a club to see an act they are interested in (often called a showcase). They will spend the better part of the evening talking to band members, managers, and producers, all in an attempt to put a deal together between the band and the label they work for. This can go well past midnight.

A&R people make a starting salary of just under $30,000 at most large labels, and this can go up to $150,000 at the executive level, once they've survived in the game for a while. On rare occasions, an A&R person may prove so vital to the label that his combined salary and bonus exceeds $500,000 a year.

The position of assistant A&R, which leads to an A&R executive position, seems to be the most nepotistic job in the industry. Most people who get these jobs are in some way related to the higher echelon of the label's management, or they have parents who know someone high up in the label's holding company. This is starting to change as the industry consolidates much of its middle-management and smaller indie labels start to seem more efficient to the majors. Smaller labels, who don't have any room in the budget for waste, prefer to hire producers, managers, or people who have worked in the industry as A&R rather than the nephew of a CEO.

It is not uncommon for an A&R person—even a successful one making a six-figure salary—to leave a label after a year because they have fallen out of grace with the higher-ups or get a better offer from another label. The A&R position is a rather tenuous one. They become an easy target for blame in the failure of many projects. It's a worthwhile risk, however, because if the band is a success, the A&R person gets a lot of recognition for his/her forecasting.

Often the most successful A&R people will try to get their own label spun off of the major label they were working for. (This is important information. Remember this when we're talking about the recording deal in the section called "Super-Duper Cross-Collateralization" in chapter 12.)

[3] Unfortunately, somebody forgot to tell many of today's A&R people that this transfer of duties took place. Today, A&R people who have the clout to muscle in on the creative process sometimes do so under the title of "executive producer" (EP). They can, and sometimes will, attempt to dictate the sound of the record. This is not always a bad thing. Some A&R people have built excellent reputations as having "golden ears."

A&R at the Indie Level

At smaller labels, the A&R person is usually the owner of the label. Chances are they once worked for a major label and have now grown their own legs. To do so, they've found an investor who is, in essence, investing in the A&R/owner's judgment as to what is going to sell.

Many of these little labels don't last long. But if an A&R/owner can survive the first two years, they have good potential for success. Some examples are Rick Ruben, founder of Def Jam Records (who released the Beastie Boys and Run DMC), and Steve Gottlieb of TVT, who discovered Nine Inch Nails.

A few humbling facts about A&R:

1. Despite their alleged expertise, 90% of all acts signed by A&R people fail to sell enough records to turn a profit.
2. The average tenure of an A&R person at a major label is two years.
3. A&R people are rarely welcome guests at recording sessions.
4. In fact, they're rarely welcome anywhere near the creative process.

➌ Managers

Yes, yes, managers. What exactly do they do, and how valuable are they in the grand scheme of things? This is complicated, because managers seem to come from every corner of the business. Almost anybody can qualify to be one, because the role is a bit nebulous. So, let's say you're a recording artist (or hope to become one) and you're looking for a manager. What will he or she do for the 15% to 20% that they will take off the top of your gross earnings? Well . . .

- Managers shop and negotiate the deal between the artist and the record label. *But wait, doesn't the lawyer do that?* Well, yes.
- Managers make sure that the artist gets their proper royalty payments. *But wait, wait, doesn't an accountant do that?* Well, yes.
- Managers help the artist select material for the record and help develop the sound. *But wait, doesn't the producer do that?* Well, yes, he does.
- Managers make sure that the venue conditions are the ones agreed upon in the tour contract (i.e., that there's enough beer backstage and the instruments are in tune). *But don't we have tour managers and stage managers for that?* Yup, we do.

- Managers get the act great gigs on the road, like opening up for a national act. *But can't a booking agency do that for 10%?* Uh, yeah.
- Managers supervise the artist's interviews and press releases. They make sure that nothing too negative leaks to the press (unless they want it to). *But don't we have publicists for that?* Most definitely.
- Managers help mold the artist, like with the proper look. *But can't you get a stylist or image consultant to do that for a few hundred bucks?* Sure.

Give up? Well, if you're confused, welcome to the club. It is difficult to place exactly what managers do. One thing that everybody agrees upon is that you need one if you're going to get ahead.

Here's my definition of a manager: He's someone who pays attention to how things get done. Managers are like toll booth attendants. You could bypass them and take a longer road to get to where you want to go. But if you want to get there faster and safer on a nice paved interstate highway, you have to pay the toll. Managers keep everyone talking to each other. They are master schmoozers, and because there are only two qualifications for the profession—(1) that they are good talkers, and (2) that they have lots of contacts—many people from many backgrounds call themselves managers.

SUPER MANAGER

Legendary record man "Swervin'" Irving Azoff once managed the mega-group the Eagles. During a tour at the height of their career, one California hotel was unable to provide adjoining suites for the "Hotel California" songwriters. Swervin' Irving drove to a hardware store, purchased a chainsaw, went to the hotel, and turned two separate rooms into one suite by sawing down the wall between them.

Being prudent and realizing that he would not be able to be there whenever the Eagles needed on-site remodeling, he had a carrying case made for the saw so that the group could take it on tour with them.

Now that's hands-on management.

This description may, on the surface, seem negative, but it isn't meant to be. A manager is a classic example of the whole being greater than the sum of the parts. Each function could be dissected and delegated to one of the other pros. But the manager has his or her hands in all of these areas and, if he or she's a good one, keeps the machinery oiled with funny stories, rounds of drinks, free tickets, and the three "R's" of the record industry—relationships, relationships, and relationships.

Some unfortunate facts about managers:
1. Most managers hide valuables when their clients come to their house.
2. Managers spend less than 6% of their waking time at their primary residence.
3. It can take a manager up to an average of three years to develop and sign a new artist.
4. Managers are often dumped by their clients after three years.

❯ Publicists, Booking Agents, Tour Managers, and Image Consultants

See above.

CHAPTER TWO

➢The Creators

T he other types of players are the creative entities who make the music. I divide them up into five categories: *musicians, songwriters, engineers, artists,* and *producers.*

Don't let the word "artist" confuse you. In general, the use of the word "artist" in the music business is much the same as the use of the word "talent" in the film industry. It is a description of the person's role and not a reflection of the quality of their work. As used in this book, it refers to a career recording artist.

➢ Musicians

The people in the music business that I have the most profound respect for are the musicians. They work the hardest and, as a group, get paid the least. As I said earlier, almost everyone in this business started off as a musician, but after a few professional (or less than professional) encounters, many opt for something more steady. The ones that stay with it seem to do so for one main reason: they feel a burning passion to create. They did not choose music, *music chose them!* It's a dedication that is often underappreciated by labels.

Musicians fall into two general categories: *The Survivor* and *The Jobber.* (Note: It's important to understand that this book is about the pop record industry. Therefore, the comments about musicians in this section don't necessarily apply to other genres like classical or jazz. Also not included in this section are *singers*, whom I have classified under "Artists," below.)

The Survivor

Typically, this musician is a male between the ages of 17 and 29. He has a day job that pays him $15,000 to $35,000 per year before taxes. After his survival expenses, he spends most or all of his surplus income on musical equipment. He reads some trade magazines but mostly the ones that cater to his particular instrument, like *Keyboard, Guitar Player,* or *Modern Drummer*—rarely *Billboard, Variety,* or any business-oriented trade mag. He plays in at least one band and maybe as many as three, gigs out at least one to three times a month, and makes about $25 per gig. Many

MY FRIEND STEVE

Steve was a singer and cowriter in a five-piece band and was about to sign a major record deal. It had been agreed that Steve would share the publishing of the songs with the entire band. The label recognized Steve as the driving force in the band's material and wanted him to sign a copublishing arrangement with them—a common request from major labels (for the reason why, refer to "Publishing Deals," page 69. Steve and the rhythm guitarist, who cowrote most of the material, had no problem with this, but the drummer, bassist, and lead guitarist, who started the band and whose connections brought Steve to the label, didn't feel comfortable giving up half of their publishing. The issue became a deal-breaker.

So one week later, Steve and the guitarist quit the band (effectively firing the others) and regrouped. Within a few days, they had a new rhythm section. The new players were excited just to be in a band that was going to be signed. They didn't care about the publishing. The deal went forward and everyone was happy, except for the now-out-of-a-gig drummer, bass player, and lead guitarist, who undoubtedly felt screwed.

It's important to keep in mind that record companies are primarily interested in singers and songs. To them, the rhythm section is replaceable. The side players in Steve's band felt the need to assert their power, not realizing that *their hand was weak.*

survivors play with a wedding band on the weekends, which could gross $400 or $500 per gig for them. Occasionally he or she gets session work, usually on the recommendation of a producer/engineer friend who believes in them.

This type of player is easy prey for those looking for a bargain on talent. Because this musician doesn't involve himself in the industry, he's at a disadvantage when it comes to negotiating a good pay rate or copyright share, so he will often be hired to work for little to no money. The trade-off for this exploitation is the hope that the job will lead to something bigger. Long odds for these little gigs, even on a good day.[1]

Ninety percent of the people who call themselves musicians are covered by the above description. A small percentage of them will be attached to an act when it gets signed to a deal with a good label that pays on its contract. About a year after the deal is signed they may, if the record is doing well, start to make enough money to quit their day job.

But the survivor often doesn't grasp the concept that getting a record deal is the beginning of the race, not the end. Most bands break up after three albums, and then the survivor is often back to square one. If they have songwriting credit, then at least they will get publishing royalties (see "Publishing Deals," page 69). But for various reasons the survivor rarely contributes to the actual copyright of the songs on the record and so has little to show for the experience save the box of complimentary CDs in the corner of his basement.

Most survivors that I know move into other areas of the business. Some try to get their own deal as an artist. Some go on to be producers and/or managers. There are several who have found bigger success as A&R people than they did on the road as a musician.

[1] The survivor could try to assert him- or herself and say something to the producer/ friend who's hiring him, if he knew exactly what to say. But then again, from the producer's point of view, he probably wouldn't have hired his buddy, the survivor, if he had a budget to pay people. Instead he would have gone with a jobber (described next).

THE ULTIMATE SURVIVOR

After penning and performing the megahit "U Can't Touch This," rapper M.C. Hammer just couldn't seem to bounce back. His next album sank to the bottom of the charts faster than lead in a swimming pool.

Husband and father to three children, Hammer declared bankruptcy in 1996 and went to work as a telephone salesman.

He once was worth $30,000,000.

The Jobber

At one point in their career this musician looked a lot like the survivor. But they hung around a few more parties, or read music better, and eventually got a break on an album as a side player or on a jingle or some high-profile gig that earned them a reputation. This break can come at any time, but usually happens when they are about 27 or 28 and generally occurs after they have been hanging around the scene for some time. When the break does come, they quickly become *session players*, getting hired often, usually with language like, "We have to get so-and-so, he's hot now."

Jobbers have no day job. They sleep during the day, sometimes do a session in the afternoon, and play with a heavy act that's in town at night. Or they're on the road with a national pop act, or playing in the pit band of a Broadway show or with a big orchestra. They often make as much as doctors, from $60,000 to $300,000 per year. If they're vocalists, they can make even more by doing national radio spots. Obviously, the supply-and-demand factor here is much different than for the survivor, and the competition for these jobs is murderous.

A subcategory of this same group is the writer/producer. This person is a heavy jobber but also writes songs and/or jingles. Because they are meeting and interacting with the top performers in the industry, they are in a choice position to hawk songs to them. As mentioned above, typically these same jobbers also write jingles and soundtracks whenever they can get the work. They rarely commit themselves to a single scenario, like a band, because they make too much money by staying uncommitted and floating around from situation to situation. They always have a pet project that they're developing,[2] and I have yet to meet one who wouldn't chuck all the money for a good offer from a record label to do an album of their own stuff with themselves as the artist.

But these offers are rare to none. Ironically, the jobber is too overexposed to be of interest to labels, who mostly look for artists that are younger and are discovered under serendipitous circumstances.[3] Jobbers, however, will often network themselves into a producing position because they're good musicians, personable, and have a lot of studio experience.

> **Some ironic facts about musicians:**
> 1. Most musicians can't read music.
> 2. Many successful musicians never took a formal music lesson.
> 3. Up-and-coming musicians often live with their girlfriends.
> 4. Successful musicians usually don't allow their girlfriends to live with them.

[2] This is usually an artist that they have signed to a production deal (see "The Baby Record Deal," page 123).

[3] See "Gigging a Lot Is Good Exposure to the Industry," page 210.

⊘ Songwriters

Although it is easy to lump songwriters in with musicians or artists, I prefer not to. Songwriters have a unique place in the creative process in that they make the

WHO IS THE SONGWRITER IN RAP MUSIC?

In rap, the question of who writes the "song" is a bit more complex. Rap usually has no melody. Since the Copyright Act requires a melody, the rapper artist agrees to share writing credit between the writer of the rap and the arranger of the music bed, which is called "the beats."

Rap is not the only area where the definition of "songwriter" becomes unclear, but it is the most common. Consider the following scenario: You write a musical arrangement using only instruments and sampled loops. You arrange and, if you're using a computer, program the drums, bass line, and chords. But when it comes to the lyrics, you give it to a partner to write the words and a melody that fits into your composition. Who does the law recognize as the writer of the song? The answer is your partner, not you. If push comes to shove, your music bed, unless it is very unique, can be reproduced by another arranger. You get nothing, *nada,* no rights, no money, not even the home version of the game, and there will be little you can do about it[4] (unless you enjoy taking people to federal court—this is a subject we will revisit in several forms throughout the book).

Obviously this is unfair. The reason it works this way is because of left-over loopholes in the copyright law, which has yet to deal with the fact that songwriting often involves the scenario I just described. But people in the know recognize that the arrangement of a song can be, and often is, as important as the lyrics and melody. In fact, many arrangers have argued that since most lyrics in pop songs are unintelligible—the melodies buried under a wave of electric guitars, drums, loops, and synthesizers—what people are really hooking into when they buy a song *is* the arrangement, the sound and the production.

Hopefully the law will soon be updated to recognize the importance of the arrangement. Until then, lyric and melody writers will have the lion's share of the leverage when cutting their deals with arrangers.

[4] See "Sound-Alikes," page 171; and "Sample Rights," page 72.

foundation for all other creative work. Plus, it is a misconception that most recording artists write their own material—most do not, particularly in the R&B area.

Also, many songwriters are not traditional musicians. Some don't even play an instrument; instead, they will collaborate with arrangers by humming the melody to their lyrics. An arranger/cowriter figures out the chords and composes the accompaniment that makes up the musical bed. This is an exception, though. Many writers play one if not several instruments. These days, computers have made it possible for one person to play many instruments without having to go through the trouble of learning to read music.

Most writer/arrangers who share ideas with lyricists agree to split the writer's credit 50/50 regardless of who wrote what. It seems to be a simple way to end nasty arguments and keep the marriages friendly.[5]

If figured in dollars per hour, songwriters are the highest-paid professionals in the business. Songwriters who are *not* recording artists can make anywhere from zero to millions of dollars per year. If a writer has a song on an album that goes platinum in the U.S., he or she stands to make about $65,000 on record sales alone, even if the song is the worst one on the record.[6] If their song is the hit single, then in addition to record sales they can look forward to royalties from the radio airplay. A typical hit song plays for six weeks, many times a day, on hundreds of stations throughout the country. It will earn an average of $150,000 for that year, depend-

[5] The producer is often responsible for arranging the songs, and yet gets no cowritership. For this service he or she is generally compensated with an arranger's fee separate from their producer's fee, but it is a pittance if the song becomes a huge hit. (See "The Major Label Deal from the Producer's Point of View," page 75.)

[6] See "9-to-1 Publishing," page 181, and "Publishing Deals," page 69.

SO YOU THINK YOU WROTE A SONG?

Think again. Ironically the word "song" is never mentioned in the Copyright Act, so there is no legal definition for it. So if the law can't define a song, how can we, as writers, copyright it? Remember, you can't copyright something that can't be held in your hand or duplicated (like a piece of paper or an audio cassette). So a song is really a *"work" that is the embodiment of a "literary work" accompanied by a musical composition "fixed" in a tangible medium in its "best edition."* Not too sexy. Imagine approaching the spotlight with, "Thanks for the encore. And now for our next fixed sound embodiment . . ."

To make things simple, the word "song" as used in this book is exactly what you'd think it means.

ing on which Performing Rights Organization the writer is affiliated with.[7]

If you are a working songwriter and you manage to get even one average-sized hit a year, you can look forward to $200,000 to $300,000 for the year. If you're a superstar writer like Andrew Lloyd Webber, Babyface, Billy Joel, or the artist now once again known as Prince, you can multiply those numbers by ten.

[7] See "Performing Rights Organizations," page 34.

These figures can be deceiving, though, because most writers have deals with publishing companies, agents, and managers, all of whom take a cut, but still it's not too bad for a profession that doesn't even require a high school diploma.

In 1997 the artist Sting signed one of the largest publishing deals in history—$32 million. Included in the deal were his rights to his older hits with the Police and several future albums. Also included was the money earned from sampling his hit "Every Breath You Take" for the rap hit "I'll Be Missin' You"—an estimated $600,000.

Some ironic observations about songwriters:
1. Most songwriters don't sing well.
2. A successful songwriter will earn more money in one year than the President of the United States will earn during his entire four-year term in office.
3. Almost no songwriters know the words to "Louie Louie."
4. Both Ronald Reagan and George W. Bush knew the words to "Louie Louie."

❷ Engineers

This is a category close to my heart, because it is the group from which I came.

WRITE ME A KILLER TUNE

Serial killer/songwriter Charles Manson earned an estimated $66,000 on songwriting royalties when the '80s rock group Guns N' Roses used his lyrics for a cut on one of their albums.

Manson never saw the money. Authorities forced him to donate the cash to the families of his victims and the state for the cost of his prosecution. He wouldn't have much use for the money anyway.

Engineering is both a fantastic and a thankless task. Producers usually get the credit for the engineer's good work, and paying dues is murderous. But the engineers often are the hub of the entire creative process, like the lawyers are the hub of the business process. Engineers sit in on a lot of different projects, and they hear what everybody is working on well before the public does. They will often be asked their opinion by a producer for this reason. By way of this dynamic, the engineer will often become the psychiatrist of every person on the gig, especially the producer (who is usually pulling his or her hair out because of some insurmountable problem that could only be fixed if there was another $50,000 in the budget or by rewriting all the choruses in all the songs).

Usually, if there is no designated producer on hand, the engineer, by default, will end up in control of the session. Two or more band members may get into a dispute over a part, and in order to settle the argument the engineer will be consulted. Once requested, his opinion is rarely challenged.[8] It's easy to see why many engineers go on to be producers, but this was not always so.

In the '50s and '60s an engineer was someone who had a background in electronics and worked his way up, first spending time as a maintenance assistant for a number of years. Then, gradually, they were booked on sessions by studio managers, and—here's the important part—engineers were *employees* of the recording studios.

Today, studios don't generally employ engineers. They retain, on an independent contractor basis, studio assistants. Producers bring their own engineer, whom they are comfortable working with.

Most engineers today, especially remixers, have only basic electronic knowledge. They rely on the studio maintenance technician to know the internal workings of the machinery. An engineer's main responsibility today is to concentrate on keeping the session happening.

While successful engineers can make over $200,000 per year, the average working engineer makes about $40,000 if he works studio gigs regularly in New York or Los Angeles, $90,000 if he's out on the road three quarters of the year. Many engineers started out by investing anywhere from $5,000 to $10,000 in audio school to learn the techniques of engineering and then interned in a studio for little or no money. After a year or so, they became assistants and earned about $6 to $10 per hour before taxes.[9]

Almost 85% of the engineer interns/assistants are men, and they take home about $375 per week. Because they usually live in the major cities, it's easy to see that they must have some financial assistance, beyond studio work, to pay their bills. While it's true that there are many young interns and assistants who work

[8] An important note: The engineer, unless he is close to the group personally or has clout, will *never* get credit or points for his coproduction advice.

[9] Something that you may want to consider before embarking on the career path of engineer: The retail price of CDs, tapes, and so on, has increased over 100% in the past 15 years, while the price of recording an album has gone down substantially. As people invest in home studios, the need for engineers decreases, while the supply of them increases with each graduating class from dozens of audio engineering schools.

hard and live frugally while paying their dues, the reality is that most come from middle- to upper-middle-class families who support their offspring during this hazing. And then there are those who, unfortunately, supplement their income by acting as a procurer of controlled substances for their clients. I don't condone this, but I have known it to produce good results for some of my peers.

Another important point about engineers—they lead a *very* high-stress existence. They are constantly getting fired—usually for political reasons, but it's to be expected when you consider that the engineer usually gets the job *because* of political reasons. In order to attract clients, up-and-coming engineers often discount their work enormously, or give large commissions to the producers who hire them.[10]

[10] See "Kickbacks," page 82.

Some ironic facts about engineers:

1. In general, recording engineers know more about electronics than airline pilots.
2. The most important part of a half-million-dollar recording project, aligning the tape machine's electronics, is often done by the engineer's apprentice, who makes little more than minimum wage.
3. Many engineers are addicted to *Star Trek* or *Dungeons and Dragons*.
4. Almost all engineers are heavy smokers.

❥ Artists

Since this book is by and large very pro-artist, I'm going to take this opportunity to dissect some of the artist's more controversial qualities. Those who have had frustrating experiences with artists may want to pull up a chair.

I have, on more than one occasion, heard an A&R person say, in confidence, "This business would be so much easier if we could just make records without artists."

This statement is echoed by many in the industry. But why? If it weren't for the artist, we would have no music to enjoy and profit from, yet many pros roll their eyes in frustration or hide under their desks at the mere mention of "the artist."

To get an idea, we should consider all the problems that artists face.

Although there are the Britney Spearses who come from affluent families, I believe most artists come from working-class backgrounds. If they did come from money, they have divorced themselves from their families and are now self-reliant. I base this belief on the fact that many of them enter record deals with poor representation and accept amounts of money that wouldn't impress people who are financially savvy. The facts would indicate that most recording artists are living in situ-

11 For the reasons why, skip to "The Major Label Deal from the Artist's Point of View," page 53.

ations where they can be easily compromised into signing deals that give away a lot of their rights. In a moment of drunken weakness, most record execs will admit that a disenfranchised artist is often a cooperative one.

Most artists start trying to get a record deal when they are about 20. Although in recent years we've seen several superstar artists who are younger than 18, most don't generally sign a deal until roughly age 24 if they're women and 27 if they're men. Since it's often their second or third album that puts them on the map, they don't start to make a decent living until they are in their late twenties.[11]

Artists also face other complications that are dissuading. Because the industry has become so visual, artists often have to emphasize their looks to gain the attention of the pros. Many artists find these values distasteful as it instills the axiom that though love may be blind, *lust is surely deaf!* Compromise, to the artist, seems to translate as "selling out." Sometimes they're right, but often they're shooting themselves in the foot. (See "What Are the Odds?" in the sidebar below.)

I do, however, have a lot of sympathy for the artist's position. That's one of the reasons I've written this book. Often artists *are* being asked to compromise, and often it's for a deal that doesn't pay as much as they think (which we'll discuss in more detail in later sections). However, every person in a cutthroat business should understand where they sit in relation to their competition. Many young artists

WHAT ARE THE ODDS?

Consider the following fact: The average major record company receives between 10,000 and 12,000 demo tapes a year. Depending on the size of the annual A&R budget, each company can only sign between 5 and 40 acts a year.

These are not very good odds—1 in 300 under the best of circumstances. One might think that with so much working against them, artists would be willing to play ball with a record label *at any cost*. Many aren't. Stubborn artists will hold out for better terms, usually overstaying their welcome in the loop of people that they're dealing with. If the artist isn't willing to give up something, they will not get a first deal. Since the people who are shopping them only get paid if a deal is consummated, they will quickly lose interest in a temperamental artist. (See the other sidebar in this chapter, "Arrogance and the Record Deal.")

have embraced the business side of music with a fervor and understand the trade-offs that are inherent when art meets finance. These artists, for better or worse, stand the best chances for success.

How Much Do Artists Make?

When it comes to artists' income, it is difficult to speculate, because it fluctuates quite a bit during the course of their career. I'll be discussing different examples throughout the book, but if you need to know now, see "Wrap-Up" on page 147.

A revealing fact about artists: Despite their tendency to express gratitude to God at award ceremonies, most artists can more readily quote the Beatles than the Bible.

❂ Producers

"Producer" is a confusing term, and often I am asked exactly what a producer does. It can be hard to explain to someone who has not sat in on the recording process.

The producer guides the artist through the recording of their record. They help select the material and determine which takes are keepers and which are losers. Sometimes they compose the arrangements and do the engineering, and they usually supervise the final mix of the record.

Although the average record buyer thinks that the artist—the person whose pic-

---

THE YUPPIE ROCK BAND

I have some friends who formed a successful club band called Everyone's Hero. Each person in the band was a professional: there were three lawyers, one real estate broker, and an accountant. They asked me if I could help them get a deal. They had a good following, and their music was as good as anything else out there on the radio.

I ran down the numbers as to what they could expect to get in the best-case scenario. I foresaw an artist development deal with $100,000 to start and an "all-in" recording fund of $350,000. (See "The All-In Deal," page 78.)

The total advance for the entire deal wouldn't have equaled the yearly salary of any two members of the band.

If you read the liner notes on pop records, you will see that artists rarely use the same producer for their second albums. Usually it's because the artist can now assert the creative control they gave up in order to get their first record deal. This is especially true if the artist signed a "production deal" with the producer. See "The Artist/Producer Production Deal," page 124.

ture is on the record jacket—is the one making all these decisions, they almost never are. The producer is responsible for the sound and quality of the record. If the mix is terrible, it's the producer's fault. If the performances are weak, it's the producer's fault. (There are exceptions to this, as you will see later.)

A good analogy is to think about the artist as being like a movie actor. The producer is like the film's director and editor. He or she tells the actor how to play the scene and the best way to communicate the message. More often than not, the producer will have veto power over a first-time artist's creative decisions.[12]

In rock, the members of the band are the songwriters and the instrumentalists, and the producer has a more passive role, but in R&B and rap, the dynamics of the producer's role are more intricate. They usually write all the music and do all the arranging of the rhythm tracks. Then they find a vocalist, who will be the artist, to sing the lyric track. In this arrangement the artist/singer almost never has any say

ARROGANCE AND THE RECORD DEAL

I remember one group I produced back in 1987, a band that we will call Penny Whistle. They had a sound that was raw, heavily distorted, but with contemporary pop overtones. This sound would, in 1990, be labeled "alternative rock," but in 1987 it was noise to most.

I produced the band in my basement studio and took the tape to my lawyer. He liked it and started to pass it along to some of the people he was doing business with. Eventually one of them, Sony Records (which at that time was CBS), became interested.

My lawyer suggested to me that now would be a good time to secure a contract between myself and the band. He gave me a standard management/production contract from the firm's computer. It was nine pages long. The contract had language in it that obligated the band to fulfill a recording contract that I would negotiate for them, it secured me a 15% commission for all services rendered, and it lasted for three years.

The leader of the band decided that he wasn't going to be bound by any agreement that wouldn't let him quit when he wanted to. I explained to him that there was no way a record company, especially one the size of in the arrangement or the sound of the final product. They are entering into, basically, a "work for hire" agreement.

In terms of income, producers that are successful make over a million dollars a year during the peak of their careers, but these are rare exceptions. A typical producer gets a fee of anywhere from $25,000 to $75,000 per album that he or she produces and will produce about three to four albums a year. In addition to this, they will get an override on the records (about 3%) if the record sells big.

Many producers come from an engineering background. These producers often do remixing (the final process where all elements of the sound of the record are fine-tuned and balanced). The going rate for this service is between $10,000 and $25,000 per song. If a producer is a remixer, he can do many such jobs a year. It has to be remembered, however, that producers have phenomenal overhead—mostly their special equipment that they use to create their sound. This equipment will

Sony, was going to invest in them if they didn't make a commitment for at least a couple of albums.

The band leader, Jimmy, who wrote all of the songs and was the lead singer, decided no. And so the deal was officially dead. Jimmy then quit, broke up the band, and moved out of town, stiffing me on his thousand-dollar production bill.

Last I heard, Jimmy was delivering pizza in Pennsylvania. One year later, a band with the same sound and look as Penny Whistle hit MTV as a buzz clip on *120 Minutes*. Their name—Nirvana.

I tell this story because it is typical, and it's my hope that you, the reader, can extract some lesson from Jimmy's example. Hold out for a good deal, but don't forget that the record business is just that—a business. Everybody involved needs to see some prospect of being satisfied financially in order to make the deal work. Some artists have difficulty understanding that. They often promise points to people helping them get signed. But if they haven't been through an actual record deal, they probably don't know what they're talking about. And when they see how much the percentage they promised really costs them, they will generally try to renege. We'll discuss why this happens in much more detail throughout the book.

get carted around from studio to studio, wherever the job takes them. In cartage alone a producer can spend over $50,000 a year. The equipment and insurance are many thousands more.

Two observations on producers:
1. Many producers have somehow mastered the knack of supervising several projects at once without attending a single recording session.
2. Producers never have anything positive to say about recordings they didn't make.

❷ Last but Not Least: Control Freaks

Have you ever had the displeasure of working for someone who distracted you while you were doing the very task they employed you to perform? If you don't acknowledge what they're babbling about, they become offended; if you screw up the job, they become indignant. You may not know it, but you were working for a control freak: someone who must, usually because of neurotic need, control every aspect of every situation all the time.

All right, in truth there is no specific person called "a control freak." I wish they did have labels; that way you would know who they are before you get involved with them. Rather, control freaks go by many more common names: egomaniacs, arrogant pricks, unproduceable, uncompromising, sleazebags, and my favorite, "someone with a bad vibe." But no matter what you call them, their presence in the music industry is so pervasive that this particular player warrants his own section in this book.

It's important to point out that not everyone who wants their own way is a control freak. Some individuals are true perfectionists, and their persistence is for legitimate artistic reasons.

I'm not a psychologist, so I wouldn't presume to comment on why these people seem attracted to the music business. Perhaps the music industry's lack of official structure is an invitation to the control freak to "be their own boss." If you've ever found yourself threatening to sue someone because they owe you money for a job, and they say, "Go ahead!," you probably have a control freak on your hands and will in all likelihood never see that money. Control freaks are much happier paying their attorneys twice what they owe you.

In the following sidebar are some of the telltale signs of a control freak. If you find that the person you're working with fits more than four of the examples, start looking for new work.

Counteracting the Effects of the Control Freak

If you are trying to work with this type of person, you must be careful. What they really think of you could depend on how useful you are to them at that moment.

CONTROL FREAKS...

- Ask many questions at inappropriate times.
- Won't let you off the phone when you are talking to them.
- Interrupt you when you're speaking.
- Want to do everybody's job (write, produce, manage, engineer, etc.).
- Tend to be argumentative and unwilling to compromise.
- Tend to have little professional training at anything.
- Will fire (or ignore) anyone who can outperform them.
- Will fire (or ignore) anyone who disagrees with them and is proven to be right.
- Order an extra dessert when someone else is paying the dinner bill.
- Relentlessly complain about how much things cost.
- Often employ simple-minded and incompetent help.
- Often complain that they have been ripped off.
- Owe money to many people, especially their lawyers, and construct brilliant rationalizations for not paying them.
- Consult expert after expert until one tells them what they want to hear.
- Make deals they have no real way to honor.
- Think they know everything.
- Will overcomplicate situations with misleading and esoteric information.
- Harbor paranoid suspicions towards other people and often generalize with terms like "they," "them," and "those people," without ever clarifying who "they" are.
- Believe that everyone is entitled to hear their opinion.
- Will usually take credit for anything that they can get away with.
- Often sport mustaches.

Some typical examples are the following: an artist who thinks the whole industry is full of shit, but you are the one person they will trust; the producer or manager who insists on contracts with long terms attached to them; people who are interested in establishing their irreplaceability in a project before it is even off the ground; lawyers who want to manage as well as produce an artist but have little experience with anything other than law. I think you get the point.

So how do you deal with someone like this? It's not easy. The first thing I would suggest is to accept that there will be times when you will have to button your lip and play the cards the way that they are dealt. Aside from that, there are a couple of techniques that come to mind for coping with this person.

First, always let them think that you agree with them. You can't change their mind anyway, so just play along. Time and circumstances will usually prevail over their stubbornness. Second, never allow yourself to be caught up in their dogma. Always have a plan when you enter the employ of a control freak. Focus on why you are there and what you are getting out of it. As soon as you've achieved your goal, don't hang around one minute more than necessary. And, as a reformed control freak myself, I can tell you the cardinal rule for this type of person: Make them right. Even if it kills you. Acknowledge them and agree, no matter how absurd what they're saying seems. Remember an old Yiddish saying: "Never try to teach a pig how to sing. It wastes your time and annoys the pig."

CHAPTER THREE

Companies, Companies, Companies

So one afternoon you sat down and wrote a simple four-chord song and made a rough recording on your cassette player. You sent it to a friend who liked it, and the next thing you know a top artist heard it and fell in love. They want it for their next album. A few months later, the song is on the radio and it's a hit. You've won the jackpot. Suddenly, as if from nowhere, your mailbox is being stuffed with large, thick envelopes from various companies. Who are they? What do they want? My god! There seem to be hundreds of them and they all have thick forms and legal documents for you to fill out. You're hearing from record companies, performance rights organizations, publishing companies, promotion companies, the Musicians' Union, publicity companies, rights clearing houses, and some guy named Harry Fox. At what party did you meet this Fox person, and how did he get your address?

It is staggering how many companies are associated with a marketable song—often referred to as "product."

All right, so the above example is a bit oversimplified, although I have seen songwriters with successes almost that dramatic. The point I'm making is that most artists are at first unaware of the staggering amount of paperwork and legal documentation that goes into the simple four-chord song they wrote and produced in their living room. Here is a basic list of the main types of companies and what they do. They are the entities we speak of when we speak of "the music industry."

❯ Record Companies

Record companies are in the business of making bets. Every band they sign requires an outlay of cash. If it's a major label or a major-owned indie, it could be anywhere from $200,000 to $1,000,000 per act. If it's an independent, the tab is usually no more than $50,000. In essence, record companies are really banks that specialize in lending money to musicians. Continuing with this analogy, one could compare the A&R person and the business affairs person to investment bankers. The idea that a record company *gives* an artist money is the most common misconception among new artists. In reality, record companies *loan* the artist money.

When you read about an artist getting a one-million-dollar recording contract, it means that the record company loaned that artist a million dollars. The artist is expected to pay it back out of the royalties that their record earns.

Aside from loaning money, record companies offer promotional and distribution services to a recording artist. These services can range from merely distributing an already finished record, usually for about 25% of the artist's profit, all the way to the other end of the spectrum of financing the recording of the record and then promoting and distributing it. For this, the take is generally up around 90% of the proceeds from record sales.

Tour support and music videos, contrary to popular belief, are not a prerequisite in a record contract, although many new bands may get them. Whether tour support and video money must be paid back out of royalties, or whether they're an outright investment by the record company, is open to negotiation, and depends on the clout of the artist.

❯ Production Companies

These operate *exactly the same way* as record companies, except they do not have a specific distribution contract to get their recordings shipped to stores. This is no small exception—if you can't get the records to the store, you usually can't sell very many of them.

Production companies, which I sometimes call "vanity labels" or "three-deep labels,"[1] are usually owned by producers or recording studios. They sign artists and

[1] See the chapter "Vanity Labels," to get a complete understanding; I define this term a bit differently than others.

produce demos and shop them in hopes of getting the artist a record deal.

Many production companies dream of being record companies and often seek an affiliation with a major label to distribute them. But don't be fooled. Unless the production company *has secured a distribution contract*, they are no more capable of selling records in a national chain record store than you or I.

❷ Publishing Companies

The role of the publishing company is easy to comprehend, even if publishing deals themselves are not. Simply put, publishing companies collect the money that is due to the songwriters they represent. They also shop your songs to various other companies to use in movies, commercials, TV shows, and so on. In exchange for these services the writer agrees to share a percentage of the copyright of the song with their publisher, resulting in the publisher receiving 25% to 50% of the monies they collect for the song.

If you've written a song that is going to be released on a major record label, you are going to make money. Because the Copyright Act of 1976 requires record companies to pay for the use of a song on a record, the major labels have agreed to pay an amount of money called a "statutory rate" to each person who writes a song that's

DISTRIBUTION DIATRIBE

I have known of several situations where XYZ Records (a fictitious example) had a distribution deal with a major label. Thinking that the major would get the record to the store for them, XYZ signed artists and went into production. Then the major's president was fired. The new president decided to trim the fat and let go of the "little labels" (sometimes called boutique or vanity labels) that they had been distributing, including XYZ Records. Now, overnight, XYZ is reduced in status to just a production company. If you are an artist and you are signed to such a company, watch your back. Your "record company" may lose their distribution. If it does, you might want to consider trying to get out of your agreement with them. Better still, when signing a contract with such a company, try to get language included in the contract that will give you an out should this situation arise.

2 This 8 cents is ap-
proximate. The ac-
tual figure is based
on a complex roy-
alty formula (see
"Publishing Deals,"
page 69).

on any record they distribute. As of January 2002 the rate will go up to 8 cents per song for each record distributed.[2]

So, to continue our mock example, you wrote a song that will now be on a big record. The record company must pay the owner of the copyright a compulsory licensing fee of 8 cents for each song on a record, for each record sold. (See the sidebar, "What Do Doctors and Songwriters Have in Common?") A million-seller has huge potential.

The publishing company sees an opportunity to collect some easy coin, so they will try to make a deal to collect writers' royalties, since writers seldom want to go to the trouble of pounding the phones and hiring accountants to do this nasty work themselves. The publishing company will also collect the synchronization license fees for a song. A synchronization license is the fee that a movie or television company pays for the right to use the song as part of the soundtrack in a film or TV show. These fees can be quite high. For the use of Sonny and Cher's "I Got You Babe" in the movie *Groundhog Day*, the film's producers paid the song's publishers $80,000. Not bad. In recent years publishing companies have found new sources of revenue in "clearing samples." Samples are the small sound bits used mostly in rap and R&B to make up pieces of the groove of a song. The publishing company owns the rights to the songs embodied in the samples, so they can negotiate a fee for use of the sample in a new song.

As an artist or writer, you may be asking yourself, "Why do I need this?" Well, you may not. Starting in the '60s, many artists who wrote their own material realized that they were giving up 50% of their money to a service that they didn't require, because they were the artist recording the material. Why hire a company to sell the material to others? They began to make publishing arrangements directly with the record companies. In order to compete with this new trend, publishing companies started handing out big advances to new artists, as high as $1,000,000 for a new act. In fact, this still is not an uncommon practice. But still, why would an artist accept any amount of money to give away 50% of their music when they don't have to? For the answer to that and other perplexing questions, you will have to wait for chapter six, "Publishing Deals."

❯ Performing Rights Organizations

The one type of revenue that publishing companies do not collect for the writer are performance royalties—that is, the royalty that the writer of the song gets for each time their song is performed publicly on things like radio or network TV. In the music business, "perform" has a unique definition that goes beyond the normal use. When you see a musician play a song on TV *live*, you're obviously watching a performance. But did you know that when a DJ spins a record in a club, what you're hearing is a performance as well, even though it's originating from a machine?[3] This also goes for cover bands playing at weddings, as well as jukeboxes in bars, VHS tapes, DVDs, CD ROMs, turntables in nightclubs, and any other type of music that is experienced *in public*. So, yes, the common interpretation of law says that each time a radio station plays a song for their hundreds of thousands of listeners or a DJ spins a mix in your favorite dance club, the writer should get paid a few pennies for the "performance." If the song is a hit, this can add up to quite a few pennies. But how can you ever know how many times each station or club plays a song, or how many wedding bands are turning your cool hit into "the bride cuts the cake"?

Enter the PROs, that is, the Performing Rights Organizations: ASCAP, BMI, and SESAC. In the United States, they represent the writers, the little guy out there trying to make a buck in the super-duper Big Brother environment of the broadcast industry. They stand for:

ASCAP: American Society of Composers, Authors, and Publishers

BMI: Broadcast Music Inc.

SESAC: Doesn't stand for anything. (They bought the name from a European company. The acronym doesn't translate into English, but they kept the letters anyway.)

These three companies monitor clubs, venues, theater, and the airwaves and keep track of who plays what and how many times. They collect performance fees (which vary according to the approximate listenership of each station or size of each venue) and distribute this money to the writers who are registered with them.

Since you cannot belong to more than one PRO at a time, and since hit songs earn a ton of cash, these organizations compete fiercely for membership. The rivalry between ASCAP and BMI has filled the pages of several other books, all worth reading before you venture into joining either. To attract members, each sometimes offers cash advances to a new artist/writer who just signed a big deal (although they "officially" deny this practice), and each also boasts about its unique monitoring system. BMI's pitch is that they have the largest membership in the world. But is this a good thing? Here's some statistics to chew on that may put the whole game in perspective.

[3] This should not be confused with a "mechanical royalty." See Publishing Companies, page 33, Harry Fox Agency, page 41, and Publishing Deals, page 69, for what that is.

Society	Number of writers	Number of publishers	Total membership	Total annual revenue in 2000	Average annual (mean) earnings per member
ASCAP	40,242	18,727	58,969	$508,000,000	$8615
BMI	140,000	60,000	200,000	$455,000,000	$2275
SESAC	5000	—	5000	$5,000,000	$1000

The above chart uses crude math and does not take into account each society's annual cost for doing business.[4] It's just designed to show that more members does not necessarily mean more payment to those members. It also does not take into account that some writers earn millions a year through the societies, while others (the majority) get little to nothing. ASCAP and BMI claim complex secret formulas that they apply to figure out how much money each member makes. They hire people to listen to the radio all day and make logs of what songs are being played. SESAC has a more high-tech approach: They use an on-air monitoring service called BDS (Broadcast Data Systems) that recognizes the recording's digital wave when it's played over devices (like a radio). Regardless of claims by each, writers on all services seem to make about the same amount of money.

There is currently much debate over how fair the systems for ASCAP and BMI are because to some it seems as though the payouts favor certain writers or types of music. SESAC has managed to dodge this bullet for the moment, since they use an "objective" computerized monitoring system—but it is likely that they, too, will be under scrutiny soon as their membership grows.

One other dark note about ASCAP and BMI: Although they are *not-for-profit organizations*, they somehow manage to pay their CEOs over $200,000 a year. SESAC is their *for profit* competitor. But this does not mean they are less motivated to make money—only that they are not bound to reinvest a portion of their profit back into the company (which is all that "nonprofit" really means).[5]

There are other PROs in other countries. In fact, each European, Asian, and South American country has its own versions of ASCAP, BMI, and SESAC, but you need not concern yourself with them unless you plan to market your records in those countries. For those with international hits originating in the U.S., the three main PROs mentioned above will attempt to collect from each of the smaller ones in the individual countries.[6]

⊘The Musicians' Union

Unless you are the producer of the record, you will probably not have to deal much with the union (the American Federation of Musicians). The union wants to

[4] There is no dispute that at present BMI's overhead is more than AS-CAP's. BMI is famous for sponsoring large showcase events to "shop" their members, whereas AS-CAP prefers more intimate workshops and salons where pros come to speak.

[5] Originally, SESAC was interested only in classical music and royalties from European broadcasting, but recently they have been aggressively pursuing more members in the U.S. pop arena. To date they are still the underdog and remain in a distant third place to AS-CAP and BMI.

know if the players on the recording were union musicians, and if they were paid standard union wages.

If the musicians were not Union, then the AFM. will try to get them to join and pay dues. Joining is a good idea for any musician who plans to play on a lot of big records or jingles, the reason being twofold. One, the musician is entitled to collect a performance royalty for each new use of his or her work—for example, if you

WHAT DO DOCTORS AND SONGWRITERS HAVE IN COMMON?

The law protects writers in a way that no one else in the music industry is protected. It guarantees that you are entitled to be paid. The only other professional in the United States who has a law guaranteeing a specific payment is a medical doctor. Behold . . .

[Excerpt of the 1976 Copyright Act, Section 115:] ¶c-3 . . . the royalty under a compulsory license shall be payable for every phonorecord made and distributed in accordance with the license. For this purpose, a phonorecord is considered "distributed" if the person exercising the compulsory license has voluntarily and permanently parted with its possession. With respect to each work embodied in the phonorecord, the royalty shall be either two and three-fourths cents, or one half of one cent ($.005) per minute of playing time or fraction thereof, whichever amount is larger.

In English, this means that if you make a CD and give it to someone and have no intention of getting it back (even if you gave it away for free), then you, as the party who parted with it, must pay this fee for each song on that record. Since most pop tunes are about 3.5 minutes, the compulsory license fee is more than the fee calculated by playing time (.005 x 3.5 = .0175). Because of increases in the fee after the 1976 act, the compulsory fee is now a minimum of 8 cents, not 2.75 cents. Oh, yeah—"phonorecord" is an antiquated bit of legal mumbo-jumbo for CDs and tapes.

This fee is often called a "mechanical license," and it must be paid to the writer within a few months of the record's distribution.

[6] From previous page. Unfortunately, it seems that PROs in other countries are not as heavily regulated as the ones in the U.S. and sometimes don't pass on the money they collect to the writers. In some countries, like Spain, the only PRO is a company called SGAE: Society of General Autores (Authors) and Editoriales (Publishers). This company also distributes records and functions as a publishing company. This triple hat has many wondering if there are conflicts of interest within the organization.

[7] That's why produc-
ers normally re-
quire their non-
Union musicians to
"sign off" their
rights before the
player enters the
session. This does
not mean the play-
ers don't get paid;
they still get their
union-scale ses-
sion fees, which at
the time of this
writing start at
about $100 an
hour.

play on a record and it ends up in a movie. (Yes, even if you are responsible for play-ing the two-bar pennywhistle solo.)[7]

The second reason, and I believe that this is the more important of the two, is that no major label will give you credit on a record unless you are a member of the Musicians' Union, even if you are a featured performer. (See "Getting Credit Where Credit Is Due," page 225.) Major labels also pay a small royalty (several cents per record sold) to the union for a "special payments fund," which goes to all musicians who worked on the record. Why are the labels so generous? The law requires labels to negotiate with unions, and because musicians are not only laborers when they play on records but also "authors," the AFM—according to the Copyright Act—is entitled to extract (although some would use the word *extort*) far more money from labels than they already do. The current label/union agreement is a compromise born out of a conflict between copyright law and labor law. But, *how much* of the money for the "special payments fund" actually gets passed on to musicians is de-batable.

Recently, in Latin music, the majors have been taking advantage of a loophole and not paying the minimum union scale to musicians who record for their Latin division. Labels claim that the Latin components of their family of labels are sep-arate companies and therefore not bound by the agreement reached between the AFM and the parent label. So for example a label pays union wage, but its Latina label does not. The AFM has championed this cause and fought to get musicians (even non-AFM members) more money for their work when recording for the Latin subsidiaries of these majors. Meanwhile, labels often wonder what the union does for them in exchange for the money they *are* required to pay. The AFM claims that their members are the highest quality of performer available. But the AFM currently does not maintain a program for quality control of its members' skill or professionalism level, as other unions that service the arts do. Also, many musicians feel burdened by the AFM, as they are required to pay several hundred dollars a year in dues. The organization also does not secure employment for them, nor does it create a stan-dard contract for recording artists like other unions, such as SAG or AFTRA. Recently the AFM has indicated that it plans to take steps to address these issues.

[8] MCA is now
owned by Vivendi
Universal.

❧Publicity Companies

If your song is getting airplay and being nominated for a Grammy®, you will at some point be approached by a publicity company. What do they want from you? Information. Your background, your influences, your next work, your former lovers, whatever they can get from you. This information is valuable to them because they *sell* it. You might be thinking, who would want to pay for this kind of crap? The only safe answer I can give is, you'd be surprised who wants to know. Magazines, news companies, competitors, and so on. If you become famous and your information starts to become very valuable, you will then hire a publicist to handle incoming requests and outgoing responses to any and all inquiries. A publicist is sort of like a press agent, except that they are not actually making statements of "fact" directly to the papers. Therefore they can get away with being "creative." Publicists work mostly for PR (public relations) firms, although many are independent.

❯ Independent Promotion Companies

Usually, record companies have their own promotion departments that handle their records, but the trend, for the artists that can afford it, is to hire an outside promotion company to support promotion of a new record.

The promotion company contacts radio stations and begs them to play a single off the artist's new record. Since airtime is limited, they have to beg hard. It is not unheard of for these companies to offer the program director of the station a "gift" if he puts the song in what's called "heavy rotation" (frequent play on the air). Many a hit has been "bought" in this way. (See "Airplay & Webcasting," page 101.)

❯ Distribution Companies

The distributor's job is to ship the records, keep track of how many are selling, collect the money from the record stores, and pay the label. Sounds easy enough, right? Most people think that a record company actually ships the records to the record store, but they don't. The record company sends the master recordings to a duplication factory with instructions on how many units to manufacture and which distributors to send the thousands of CDs, cassettes, 12-inch platters, and so on, to. The factory ships it all to the distributor's warehouse and the distributor sends the records to the record store on the record store's request. If the record store doesn't request the record, then it will stay in the warehouse.

Now here's the catch. All records are classified as a *consignment item*. This means that if you own a record store and you ordered a record that didn't sell, you can ship it back to the distributor for a full refund. Good news for the store, bad news for the artist.

As you can imagine, the potential for corruption and the tendency toward kooky accounting is great in such an environment.

Because the records can be returned, distribution companies keep what's called a "reserve" against artist's royalties. Even though they shipped 50,000 units to the record store, the distributor is not going to pay the label its share until they are sure that those records are not going to be returned. (To understand how this affects the artist and producer, see "Returns, Reserves, and Cutouts," page 61.) The label then in turn keeps a "reserve" against the artist's royalties and does not pay the artist their full amount due until the distributor pays them. An example of this is WEA/Maverick. WEA is a distributor that ships records and collects money from the retail stores for the sales of the records produced by artists signed to Maverick Records. WEA holds a portion of the money before passing it on to Maverick. Maverick then, in turn, withholds a portion of that money before passing it on to their artists.

HOW DOES THE RECORD STORE KNOW WHAT TO STOCK?

Well, about two months before the record company is ready to release the record, the independent promoter and the record company start to advertise it to the buyers who are employed by the record store. That doesn't mean that the store will definitely order it. Once again a bit of inducement from the promotion department at the label and a push from the distributor will be required. Often both will give the record store an incentive (read: kickback) in the form of free units: Buy two boxes and they get one box free. This is why only the distributor and the record company know exactly how many records *really sold*.

◉ Rights Clearinghouses

This is a relatively new branch of the industry. If your song is going to be used in a movie or TV program, the producer of that show will have to get the rights to do so. In order to facilitate this process, he or she will probably hire a "music supervisor" to handle the negotiating for all the popular music used in the film.

These supervisors act as clearinghouses for the rights and compensations to use the music. Almost without exception, they deal directly with the publisher of the song that has been requested. If you publish your own songs and you want them in the movies, be prepared to talk to the rights clearinghouses.

❯ The Harry Fox Agency (the HFA)

Remember the 8 cents mentioned above in "Publishing Companies"? Well, how do we know that record companies are paying the songwriters their total required royalties and mechanical license fees? The Harry Fox Agency is a for-hire policeman that periodically checks up on record companies to make sure that they are living up to the provisions of the Copyright Act of 1976, which requires record companies to pay the 8 cents, called a "compulsory mechanical license" to songwriters and their publishers. The HFA charges publishers and writers affiliated with them a commission of 4.5% on any royalty money they collect. They also issue the license to labels that want to put a cover song on their record, and they are supposed to make sure the label pays the original writer his 8 cents per record sold.

The concept of the Harry Fox Agency is a noble one, but since its inception the record industry has evolved from several major record companies to over ten thousand smaller ones. Since HFA earns money on a commission basis, their priority is not in the small profits to be gained by auditing little indie labels. And so, unless you are an artist signed with a large company, Harry Fox is a white elephant. In fact, many smaller indie labels don't even bother to get a license from the HFA if they are going to put a cover song on their release. They just do it and let the chips fall where they may.

HOW MANY RECORDS CAN SLIP THROUGH THE CRACKS?

In 1983 ABC Records was sold to MCA.[8] When the accountants went through ABC's old warehouse, they found over nine million backlogged records collecting dust. These were sold to a "shady" distribution company for 35 cents apiece. No writer or artist was ever paid a royalty on this sale. MCA made close to $3 million in cash and barter.

[8] MCA is now owned by Vivendi Universal

The HFA has been jockeying for position recently in some important negotiations regarding online music. Regardless, I feel the future of this company becomes more tenuous as the digital landscape develops and new forms of untraceable distribution (like downloadable music) become more common. There are also several Harry Fox competitors that, for some reason, you never hear about. The main one is the AMRA (American Mechanical Rights Agency), located in Los Angeles. They work the same way and charge the same amount.

❷ The RIAA

Three years ago, when the first edition of *Confessions* was released, there was little reason to mention the RIAA when discussing the companies a musician would have to interact with. RIAA stands for Recording Industry Association of America. They are a trade organization or "club," so to speak, that represents the major labels (and their affiliate labels) in various legal matters. They also issue the Gold and Platinum record awards when sales of a particular album reach a certain level (only to their members, though).

Recently the RIAA has scored some big ink for leading the pack of lawsuits that have belabored the online file swapping "service" Napster. The RIAA feels highly justified in this action by claiming that the companies they represent lost an average of $1,000,000 a day to piracy in the year 2000.

But don't shed a tear for the majors or the RIAA too quickly. In 2001, the RIAA successfully positioned itself as the middle-man collection agent for massive amounts of new revenue intended for record companies, artists, and musicians. This is due to a new law that creates a royalty for the "performance" of music when it is digitally transmitted, such as streamed through the Internet. (Yes, streaming is now a "performance" under law.) Those eligible to receive this new royalty are the authors of the "sound recording" (the record, in other words). That would be the label, the lead singer, the song writer, and the musicians.

There is some debate as to why the RIAA should be trusted to collect all of this money, which some experts say will amount to tens of millions per year, instead of just the portion intended for their members. The RIAA says they are the most qualified candidate because their members distribute 85% of the music in America. However, this number is a self-postulated reality. According to industry trade magazines, major labels released about 83,000 records in Y2k, while independent labels in that same year were responsible for a little over 200,000 releases. Unfortunately, the RIAA's statistics are not measured by releases, but by *sales*. And since the five major distributors—the key participants in the RIAA—control *all* the major sales channels in the western world, the 200,000 releases on independents are not likely to be tracked with any degree of accuracy. So a small indie that distributes 5,000 to 10,000 CDs per year through local mom-and-pop record stores and nets about $150,000 per annum would not show up on the RIAA radar nor qualify as a "real" record company. When you account for all of this "under the radar" music, a more likely estimate of the RIAA's US representation is about 34%.

The RIAA says that after they deduct a "reasonable" administrative fee, they will divide this money up fairly, giving 50% to record companies (that is, the companies they recognize as real record companies—read: their members and their member's affiliates), 45% to featured vocalists (artists, in other words), and 5% chopped up between side players, background singers, and band members. Since at present the RIAA seems unopposed in this collection service, let's hope their method of dividing up the money is better than it is at deciding who is and is not a legitimate label.

⮞The Deal

I have on occasion compared the record industry to a football game. Imagine that you're trying to explain the rules of football to someone who never even heard of the game. Sure, the basic concept is fairly obvious, but sometimes it's the finer rules like offsides and holding that hold the key to the game's strategy. Without an understanding of the subtleties, a football game would just appear to be a bunch of people running back and forth willy-nilly as they chase a pointy brown ball.

This section breaks down the scrimmage of the record deal. As you'll see, the comparisons to football are more than incidental.

CHAPTER FOUR

⊘Understanding Distribution,
or Why Are There So Many Logos on the Record?

⊘ The Big Five

Before we can talk about a deal with a major record company, we must first define exactly what a record company really is. If we think of a record company as a company engaged in the production, manufacture, and distribution of records, by this definition there are only five record companies in the entire free world (ignoring China and the former Soviet bloc countries). They are BMG, EMD, Sony, UNI, and WEA.[1]

In fact, one could define a "major label deal" strictly as a deal to create a record that will be distributed by one of these five companies.

To help create a picture that makes this clear, think about it as five trees with one distributor as the trunk of each tree. At the first branching off of the tree trunk, you would have each of the distributor's major affiliates. For example, WEA's main companies are Warner Bros. Records, Elektra Records, and Atlantic Records. These three companies make up the first three and largest branches of the tree. From these branches come the smaller twigs—the other labels. (For a more complete picture of how the industry is structured as of this writing, you can refer to the "Family Tree of Big Five," page 251.)

[1] Starting in the mid-1980s, independent avenues for sales tightened and labels merged. By 1987 most significant independent labels had joined one of the six main distributors. Arista joined RCA. RCA joined BMG. Chrysalis went to EMI. A&M merged into PolyGram, making 90% of the national product controlled by six companies. At the end of 1998 PolyGram became part of Seagram's, who owned Universal Music as well. They then sold it only two years later, in 2001, to the Vivendi Company, making it an almost neck and neck tie with Warner Bros. Records (WEA) as the largest music distributor in the world. WEA was bought by Internet giant America Online in 2001. AOL/Time Warner and Vivendi Universal are now the two largest distributors on the planet.

2 Recently the trend is for major-distributed "indies" that have shown an ability to create a unique voice to assert their autonomy. In the future you'll be seeing fewer multiple label names on videos and records. So, for example, Motown and Mercury, although both are distributed by Universal, don't feature the Universal name on some of their product.

Here are a few examples:

1. From the Island/Def Jam branch of UNI comes Mercury Records.
2. From the Warner Bros. Records branch of WEA comes Maverick.

Sometimes it can get confusing, because a Big Five distributor can have the same name as one of their record divisions:

3. From the BMG Records branch of BMG Distribution comes RCA Nashville—not to be confused with the RCA Records Group, which is also distributed by BMG Distribution.
4. From the MCA distribution branch of UNI comes MCA Records, from which comes the famous classic label Chess Records.

A family tree of the distribution channels expands every day, with more and more offshoots of labels splitting the branches thinner and thinner until you get to what I call "vanity labels"—small labels that have only one act on them. (See "The Vanity Label," page 131.)

When you look at a CD you'll notice that there are several logos on the mirrored surface. These logos make up the pipeline of the act's distribution. These same names appear at the base of the TV screen when you watch the group's video. Some examples are "PolyGram/Mercury," "BMG/Arista," and "Sony/Epic/Crescent Moon."[2]

3 This might be because PolyGram's actual corporate parent name used to be Groeilampenfabrieken N.V.—known in America as Philips Electronics—and they make most of their money selling computer circuits. How many recording artists would care to boast that they're employed by a Dutch components conglomerate? They were bought in 2001 by the Vivendi Corporation. Vivendi does healthcare and waste management. Most of their money comes from construction and selling bottled water.

❯ What Is a Real Independent Label?

The independent label enjoys a certain freedom that majors do not. They are not managed by a multinational conglomerate so they don't have the pressure of annual financial reports to live up to (see "The Big Picture," page 237). They are owned and operated usually by one or two people with a love of music and a brash entrepreneurial spirit. But these days there seems to be an underlying desire for many record companies to market themselves as "independent" when in fact they are controlled wholly or in part by one of the majors. PolyGram, for example, had almost 100 smaller labels under them at one time, some of whom would refer to themselves as independent.[3]

The term "production company" is often misrepresented as an indie label. For example, consider Shady, a "record company" owned by the artist Eminem. It's displayed like this: Shady/Interscope/UNI. The first label in the distribution chain,

Shady, is, in reality, only a production company. They sign the artist and develop the act. The next label in the chain, Interscope, usually markets and promotes the act, and the last label, UNI, one of the Big Five, distributes the record.[4] (Use of Shady as an example is not meant to imply that they are trying to misrepresent anything. It's only an example.)

It starts to get confusing as to whether a label is a *true* independent. Logic would simply define independents as labels that are not distributed by one of the Big Five. But consider this example: Gotham (considered by many to be independent) is distributed by independent distributor ADA (Alternative Distribution Alliance). But ADA, one of the largest independent distributors in the world, is 60% owned by Time Warner, which also owns WEA. Does that mean that Gotham is no longer an indie label? Time Warner claims it's a silent partner with ADA, allowing them to maintain their own clientele of mom-and-pop record stores. Of course, this might change in time.[5]

To add to the difficulty in defining "independent" is the fact that a single indie label could have several distributors. For example, at one time, the indie distributor Vernon Yard was partially distributed by another indie distributor, Caroline, and partially by its parent major label, Virgin. Yet parts of Caroline are also distributed by Virgin, and all of Virgin is distributed by EMI. Confused?

In the early part of the 1990s the industry saw a serious readjustment: the sale of MCA to beverage behemoth Seagram (makers of the famous vodka). Following this was the forming of DreamWorks with record industry guru David Geffen. Both had rippling effects throughout the industry that resulted in a great deal of consolidation.[6] Because of this consolidation, nowadays it's common to find labels that are not controlled by one of the Big Five, yet have some of their product distributed by them. These labels have crossbred the family tree of majors with independents to become what some have called "the major/indie."

God help us.

So who's left? If every label is somehow tied to the Big Five in some way, what alternatives do we have? Well, there are many small labels that are not distributed by the Big (Brother) Five but rather by smaller distributors such as Dutch East India. These distributors function just like Big Five labels in that they shift the burden of warehousing and shipping the records to stores off of the label and charge them a fee of about 25%. Indie volume demands are also much lower. An indie distributor would be happy to ship from 5,000 to 50,000 or more records a year from one label. These numbers would be a joke to a Big Five company.

By strict interpretation there is only one company that is presently indepen-

[4] Part of the confusion of major vs. indie has roots going back to 1975, when major labels were appalled by a new brand of music called punk. Punk's violent anti-social lyrics offended the sensibilities of major label A&R, but small labels recorded these bands and were able to sell millions of records through little mom-and-pop stores. Many of these labels, called indies because of their non-mainstream taste and because they had no direct distribution ties to major distributors, were literally run out of people's bedrooms. Majors eventually caught on and bought out many of these "bedroom labels," but by then the trend had faded. The bedroom labels, now clearly extensions of the corporate machinery that bought them, still called themselves "independent," perhaps as wishful thinking and in keeping with the political climate of the time.

[5] In fact it already has. Massive consolidation in 1998 has dissolved many of the indie distributors.

6 (from previous
page) The MCA
sale sparked a
huge restructuring
at Warner Bros.
Records and EMI
Records. Both of
these giants con-
solidated, letting
go hundreds of
people. The Time
Warner Corpora-
tion eliminated
many of their sub-
labels, allowing
smaller companies
direct contracts
with the parent la-
bel/distributor,
Warner Bros.
Records. EMI fol-
lowed by dissolving
several of its mid-
dle management
divisions and be-
came EMD (which
stands for EMI Mu-
sic Distributors).

dent and has annual sales equivalent to a major label—the Walt Disney Company. They produce, manufacture, and distribute everything themselves. But we don't
think of them as an independent, for obvious reasons.

⊘ One-Deep & Two-Deep Labels

Rather than get all hung up about who is and is not a true indie, I'm going to in-
vent my own jargon. For the purposes of this book, I'm going to call *all* record deals
for which the records end up being distributed *directly* by one of the Big Five, "major label deals," and all the parent labels that are wholly owned by them "major labels." So, for example, some major labels would include Elektra, MCA, RCA, Mercury, and so on.

The labels that are branched out from major labels will be called "one-deep labels." Take Bad Boy Entertainment, which is owned and marketed by Arista but distributed by BMG. The chain would read "BMG/Arista/Bad Boy ." But since Bad Boy
is one step away from the actual parent distributor, I'm therefore going to call the
deal on Bad Boy a "one-deep label deal."

As you've probably guessed by the way the proverbial distribution tree branches, there will be two-, three-, and four-deep label deals as well. For example the alternative "indie" label called Flip is actually administrated by Geffen, marketed through
MCA, and distributed by UNI. The chain would look like this: UNI/MCA/Geffen/Flip.
A deal on a label like Flip I will call a "two-deep label deal."[7]

Anything that falls outside of Big Five distribution will then be called "indie distribution," or "indie deal." Bear in mind that there are many indies who actually
do take their records to the store themselves in a van or a car. We have to admire
this kind of determination, because it is these individuals who discover and culti-
vate most of the best music. These people look at talent first and the bottom line
second. Therefore, we shouldn't begrudge them the few dimes more that these records
cost, because a world without indies would be a gray world indeed.

However, the odds of making any serious money with this self-delivery method
are long odds indeed. Since most artists want to make a lot of money, they invariably look to the major labels, thinking that should be their first way to go. In many
cases this can be exactly the wrong approach. To understand why, let's look at how
a major label record contract works.

7 Since the contract
with Flip will read
very much like one
with its parent la-
bel, MCA, I there-
fore classify Flip as
a major label,
though the A&R
staff there might
take issue with me.

Flow of Ownership

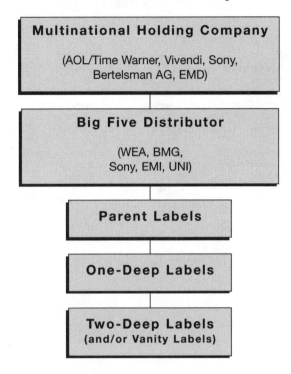

Multinational Holding Company

(AOL/Time Warner, Vivendi, Sony, Bertelsman AG, EMD)

Big Five Distributor

(WEA, BMG, Sony, EMI, UNI)

Parent Labels

One-Deep Labels

Two-Deep Labels
(and/or Vanity Labels)

Sample Family Tree

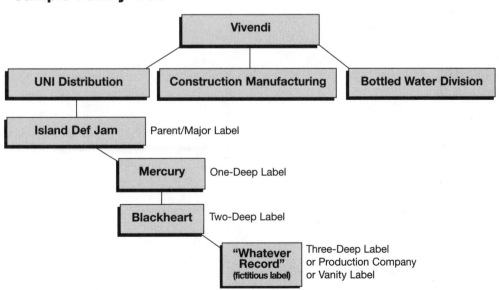

Vivendi

UNI Distribution — Construction Manufacturing — Bottled Water Division

Island Def Jam — Parent/Major Label

Mercury — One-Deep Label

Blackheart — Two-Deep Label

"Whatever Record" (fictitious label) — Three-Deep Label or Production Company or Vanity Label

		BMG Music		

Arista

Bad Boy Ent.
Arista UK
Grateful Dead

BMG

BMG Classics
  Bluebird
  Catalyst
  Conifer Classics
  Deutsche Harmonia
   Mundi
  ECM
  Greatest Hits
  Living Stereo
  Melodiya
  Novus
  Buddha
BMG U.S. Latin
  AME
  Ariola
  Arista Latin
  Barco
  Milan Latino
  NCR
  Palma
  Premium
  RCA

RCA

RCA
  Nashville
Arista
  Nashville
BNA
RCA
  Nashville
Windham Hill
BNA
RCA
  Nashville

Zomba

Battery
Benson
Brentwood
Dangerous Mu-
sic
Essential
Jive
Music For Na-
tions
Reunion
Sickwidit
Silvertone
Sound Mex
Verity
Volcano

Various other labels

CMC International
Damian Music
Dancing Cat
J Records
  Y Clef
Logic
Milan/Jade
  MusicMasters
  New Amer. Music
  Push
  Razor & Tie Ent.
Continental
ATO
Babylon
Blue Dog (UV Records)
Iron Music Group
Melisma
Sanctuary
Records Group
Beyond
Restless
Robbins Ent.
Time Bomb
Trauma
V2/Gee Street
White Label Music
Wind-up Ent.

CHAPTER FIVE

The Major Label Deal

from the Artist's Point of View

L et's say you're in a rock band and your manager calls and says that he has wonderful news: he's negotiated hard with Pacific Records, a huge label distributed directly through one of the Big Five, and he's got you a great deal—the kind you dream about, the kind that will make you famous (Pacific is a fictitious label for the purposes of the example; don't go looking for them).

First off, he's got you a full-color album cover and full-color printing on all promotional materials (Pacific only wanted to give you black and white at first). He's also persuaded them to give you a five-album contract instead of only three, plus the company has agreed to manufacture 100,000 units in your first printing. And, you're gonna make at least one video. You're gonna get $200,000 for the first record and $300,000 for the second, with a sliding royalty scale that goes up with each album you record.

Sounds amazing. Where do I sign?

Well, before you get too excited, remember the football analogy. You need to understand some things about offsides and holding. In reality, a good manager would never let you sign a deal like the one above unless the advance money was so big that no one cared how many records you were going to sell. Are you surprised? Then you're reading the right book.

There is an allure surrounding the major label record deal that seems to have many new artists mesmerized. So much so that they rarely ask the important questions about how the deal really pays off.

On the surface, the concept seems simple enough. A group is "lent"[1] money by a record company to record songs. When the recording is finished, the company markets it to the public and waits to see if the record sells. If it does, they pay the group or artist a percentage of the profit, known as a royalty. If it doesn't sell, then the record company and the group go their separate ways.

Obviously, it's not that simple, or we wouldn't need the pros. What most lawyers, producers, and managers won't tell you (unless you ask) is that a deal with a major

> [1] Many lawyers object to my use of the word "lent," because "advance" has a more precise legal definition. They're being anal.

MATCHING TIE AND AX

When you sign a major recording contract, you are in effect signing an employment contract. The band, or artist, will become an *employee* of the label. You will perform where they ask you to perform, record when they ask you to record, and re-record if and when they ask you to re-record. They own your work, and they own whatever they can get that your contract lets them have. Most pros won't tell the artist this for the obvious reason—most artists are looking to *avoid* employment. The idea that if they sign a major record contract they are becoming a "company person" will be an instant turnoff, so it's not generally mentioned. Even though there is language that specifically states that the recording agreement is not an employment contract and that the artist is an independent contractor, this is semantics. The recording contract functions as an employment contract no matter what they call it, except you don't get the health and pension benefits that you would if they called you an employee.

Most large companies compensate their employees with retirement plans, like 401(k) plans. No record company that I've heard of in the United States gives their artists any means of squirreling away their earnings (except by recommending "financial planners"), yet they treat their artist like an employee by controlling the quality and frequency of their work.

label is, in effect, *an employment contract* (see the sidebar "Matching Tie and Ax").

Even if you express concern over this, a pro will still steer you in the major label direction because, they will say, that's where the most money is, and the best opportunity for success. What they leave out is that that's where the money is for *them*, not necessarily for you, the artist. Pros usually work on commissions and fees, not royalties. An attorney negotiating a major record deal will bill between $5,000 and $75,000 dollars for that negotiation. The manager gets 15% to 20% of the advance (which might typically come out to about $100,000 for him). The accountant or business manager gets 5%. Since their payoff is directly tied to the size of the advance, their main incentive is to get as much money as possible *up front*. Producers are of the same mind: the bigger their budget, the bigger their fee.

So what's wrong with commanding high fees and getting a lot of money from a major label? Well, nothing if the artist is popular enough to justify a big advance. But if you are starting out and no one has heard of you yet, it can be disastrous. You're about to see why.

❷ Recoupable Financing— The Moving Goal Post

As mentioned earlier, record companies do not give away money, *they loan it* in the form of an advance against future royalties. The only difference between a record company and a bank is that with a bank you have to pay the money back regardless of the success of your venture. With a record company, the artist doesn't usually have to pay back anything if the record is a flop. In the finance world, this is called "forgiven debt," and for this privilege record companies feel that they have the right to ask for a disproportionate split of the proceeds. For a new artist, typically the split is 12% artist, 88% record company.

The really sucky part is that the artist pays back the big advance (i.e., loan) out of *their 12%*. Meanwhile, the record company is recouping their expenses from their 88% end of the stick.

You don't have to be a math genius to figure out that long after the record company has recouped its initial investment, the artist is still trying to recoup out of the 12%. Eventually, if the record sells, the artist will make additional money, but where is that threshold? You'll see soon. (If you're impatient, fast-forward to the Egghead Box.)

Unfortunately for the artist, the above example is only the start. Out of the

[2] In some situations, an up-and-coming producer may have to wait for the recoupment of the recording fund before he gets his money. It's the same amount of money, he'll just get it later.

artist's 12%, 25% goes to the producer. Producers, if they are in demand, traditionally get paid their royalty up front, from record one, meaning that they get paid from the first record sold and not after the recoupment of the artist's advance.[2] In other words, if you owe your label $500,000 and the producer gets paid 50 cents from the sale of each record, and you are paid one dollar from each sale, then if you sell one record a dollar is subtracted from your debt and 50 cents tacked on. You now owe the label $499,999.50. If you sell two records you owe the label $499,999.00. And so on and so on... If this doesn't make sense now, it's okay. Continue reading. The important thing to grasp is that the record company tends to pay the producer's royalty *first* with each record sold and tacks what they pay the producer onto the artist's bill.

In addition, in most contracts 50% of the money spent on videos, tour support, promotions, and the cost of full-color record jackets also gets added to the artist's recoupable account.

❯ The Big Five Deal with Real Deal Numbers

Let's apply some real-life numbers to this example. A typical major label deal would include giving about $200,000 to the artist for the production of the album and setting aside another $300,000 for promotion, making a total bill of $500,000 to the artist. This bill is called by accountants "the aggregate sum" or "the Schedule of Standard Costs" (SSC). Another, more common name for it is the "recoupment fund." They are all more or less the same thing. Try to remember these terms as they'll be used over and over again.

Out of the $200,000 sent to the group for production, the manager takes 15% of this, or $30,000. The lawyer takes about $5,000 for services rendered in negotiating the deal. Let's say that the producer takes only a $10,000 fee (this is very conservative, believe me). This leaves the artist $155,000 to make a record and live on while they are in production. Production could be anywhere from three to five months.

[3] See "The Major Label Deal from the Producer's Point of View," page 75.

I know many artists who spend the entire $155,000 in the studio and have nothing left over for themselves. The producer will try to persuade the artist to do this, because he makes more money.[3] But let's say that the artist holds him down to a $100,000 budget and decides to save $25,000 for unanticipated expenses. This leaves $30,000 left over for the artist. If there are four players in the band, then that will be split four ways, leaving $7,500 for each member of the act—before taxes.

This is all the money that the artist will see from the label on that record until the label has recouped the entire $500,000 advance![4]

So How Long Till I See Some Money?

In our example, the artist's deficit to the label is $500,000 for recording and promotion expenses. They will pay the company back through their royalties. Let's say that the CD's suggested retail list price (SRLP) is $17.00. For each record that sells, the artist gets 12% of that (or $2.04) deducted from their recoupment fund. But remember, for each CD sale the producer gets paid their 3%, or 51 cents, *first*. This 51 cents gets deducted from the $2.04 above, so only $1.53 actually gets deducted from the artist's debt to the label. Rather than teach an accounting lesson here, I'll give you the break-even number. Using these figures, the artist will have to sell 326,797 records before the record company is required to give them any more royalty money on album sales.

EGGHEAD BOX #1

Let x = the number of records to break even.

Artist's & Producer's share		Aggregate sum (SSC)		Producer's share
$2.04x	*=*	*$500,000*	*+*	*$0.51x*

$1.53x = $500,000

x = 326,797

➋ Packaging Deductions and Giveaways

But the fun doesn't stop there. In all record contracts, major or indie, there are two things to look out for. The first is the now-famous packaging deduction, also called a *container charge*. This is the cost of the actual case that the CD or cassette or 12-inch vinyl record is wrapped in.[5] The amount usually charged to the artist is 25% of the retail sales price of the CD, or about $4.25, which is deducted off the re-

[4] In some cases the label will spend additional money on tour support. But even if they do, this money is invariably recoupable from the artist's royalties. There is also additional income from publishing advances, if the artist is also a writer, but we'll deal with that later.

[5] With CDs this is called a "jewel box."

tail sales price *before* the artist's and producer's royalties are computed. This means that even though the artist is supposed to get 9% of $17, they will really only get 9% of $12.75. Snag. The way this is usually phrased in the contract is a "25% container charge on CDs and a 15% container charge on cassettes and 12-inch phonorecords."[6]

The second pitfall is the "giveaway" clause, also known as "free goods." The record company will argue that in order to promote a new artist they will have to give away many CDs. The distributor of the record will want latitude with "giveaways" as well, in order to induce a record store to pick up a new artist—like, buy two boxes and get one free. For this reason the artist will agree that a royalty will only be paid on *actual records sold* and not on records that are shipped or are given free as promotion. The programs for giveaways are often called "special goods programs."[7] This deduction is usually another 25%.

[6] We all know that it doesn't really cost the record company $4.25 to package the album. It probably costs about $1, but it is an accepted "give" that artists deal with.

[7] When you reach star status, you can usually negotiate this out of your contract. There is not as large a need to seduce a record store to carry, or a radio program director to play, someone like Garth Brooks.

[8] This also includes Minidiscs, and anything else new.

❯ Breakage—The 90% Rule

Even within the actual sales (called "bona fide sales" in most contracts) the record company will only pay you on 90% of them because of "breakage." This is an old tactic left over from the time when records were made of brittle vinyl and had a tendency to break during shipping. The record company's rap is that the artist shouldn't be paid for broken records.

This was bogus even back then. Now that most records are CDs made of polycarbonate, one of the strongest synthetics in the world, this clause is beyond ludicrous. But it's still in many major label contracts.

So now we have a royalty base of $12.75, which is only payable on 90% of the sales. (I have seen contracts where the breakage clause is as stiff as 80% of sales.)

❯ The ³/₄ Royalty

We're not quite done yet. Record companies rarely pay the full royalty promised. On the sale of tapes and 12-inch records they sometimes pay the full royalty, but generally only pay to a ¾ royalty (that is, three quarters of the 9%, or 6.75%) on CD sales, because CDs are still considered "new technology" (even after more than a decade).[8] Uh-huh. So the alleged research and development cost is passed on to the artist. Artists' representatives have become savvy to this scam, so the "new technology" deduction is slowly falling by the wayside. But record companies have found clever ways of reinserting it. Of late they call it a "new configuration" deduction and are applying it to records sold as MP3s, DVDs, and any kind of Internet download, which will likely account for many U.S. sales in the future.

The ¾ royalty has several other manifestations —"budget records," for example. If a record doesn't sell for the full $17.00 (which it rarely does), the artist is not entitled to their full royalty but rather only ⅗s (or sometimes ½) of it.

Still yet another manifestation of the ¾ royalty is the "special TV and advertising deduction." In this one, the record company decides that since they are spending "extra" money on your promotion around the time of your release, they will pay the artist only between ¾ and ½ of the normal royalty during these times.

All the above together basically means the only way to earn the full royalty promised is to sell tapes or 12-inches at full price starting at six weeks after the record's release. Best of luck. Hopefully lawyers and managers will soon be able to get the ¾ royalty clause out of the contract forever.[9]

When we add all this together, we see that the artist must sell over one million records before they break even. Let's do the math:

To make it simple, I averaged the cassette sales and the CD sales together, because history has shown that to date an artist will usually sell an equal amount of CDs and cassettes under normal circumstances (aside from the 1% hedge mentioned earlier). The box below shows the equations for calculating the artist's and producer's royalty base.

[9] Had car designers made the decision to switch to CD players as standard features in economy cars instead of sticking with cassette players, recording artists might have seen a drastic reduction in their income. Three cheers for the global economy.

ARTIST:

Cassettes

SRLP $10.50 – $1.57 (packaging) = $8.93@ 9% = $0.80

CDs

SRLP $17 – $4.25 (packaging) = $12.75 @ 6.75% (¾ rate) = $0.86

$$\frac{0.80 + 0.86 = \$1.66}{2} = \$0.83$$

PRODUCER:

Cassettes

SRLP $10.50 – $1.57 (packaging) = $8.93 @ 3% = $0.26

CDs

SRLP $17 – $4.25 (packaging) = $12.75 @ 2.25% (¾ rate) = $0.28

$$\frac{0.26 + 0.28 = \$.54}{2} = \$0.27$$

And now let's plug the numbers into the final equation.

EGGHEAD BOX #2

Again, let x = the number of records to break even.

Artist's & Producer's share		Aggregate sum (SSC)	Producer's share
$1.10 x	=	$500,000	+ .27x

$.83x = $500,000

x = 602,410 divided by .75 (75% of sales for "giveaways") = 803,213 divided by .9 [90% of sales] = 892,459

And if the artist is lucky enough to actually sell close to a million records, look how the numbers work out. Remember, break-even is 892,459. Only sales above this number become actual dollars back in the artist's pocket.

◉ Deep in the Hole

Here's the score after 1,000,000 records have sold:

Producer: $270,000
Record company gross: $6,000,000 (approximate)
Artist: $60,250[10]

The record company's average profit per unit is $4.50, meaning they broke even on their "mean cost" after only 111,000 records.[11] But the artist is barely recouping even after 1,000,000 records sold.

What if the record sells 2,000,000 units? After 2,000,000 records sold:

Producer: $540,000
Record company gross: $12,000,000 (approximate)
Artist: $620,500

[10] Here's the math for those who care: .83 (1,000,000) (.75) (.90) – 500,000 = $60,250

[11] This equation is based on the assumption that labels average about $6 profit per record. This number is then divided into the artist's advance of $500,000. For the complete breakdown of record company profits, refer to page 248, or review "The Major Label Deal from the Record Company's Point of View," page 87.

Finally the artist gets some significant coin. But before you go putting a down payment on a house, there are a few deductions: 15% for the manager and 5% for the accountant leaves the artist with $496,400. Split that four ways for each member of the band, and you've got $124,100 before taxes. Which is enough to buy a nice car and live well for about a year.

It's about time you made some money. But wait, there's more. I've saved the best part for last.

⊜ Returns, Reserves, and Cutouts

Without a doubt the most Byzantine point of all in the record agreement is the reserve clause.

Records are a consignment item, which means that a store can get a full refund on records that they don't sell. So, just in case the unsold records ship back to the distributor, the label holds the artist's royalties for up to four pay periods (two full years), so that if records ship back, they can make return and shipping *deductions* from the artist's account. This is no small matter. The reserve clauses tend to be for 20% to 40% of gross sales!

Remember at the beginning of this chapter when the manager told the artist that the record company was guaranteeing a 100,000 minimum run on the first pressing of the album? Well, that's fine if the artist's market warrants it. But most new artists rarely sell more than 60,000 units on their initial release. If the record doesn't sell all 100,000, the remainder will be shipped back *at a charge to the artist.* The returned stock will then be sold as "cutouts," and no royalty will be paid on these units (see the sidebar "Getting 'Cutout' of Royalties").

Based on a 20% reserve, if the artist sold two million records and is owed $620,500 for the first year, the company will apply only $496,400 (80%) to the artist's account. The balance of $124,100 will remain in the label's bank for another two years, gathering not dust but *interest.* At average prime rate (5%), that works out to about $6,200 worth of interest per year—*none of which gets passed on to the artist.* So, even though the artist should get about $600,000, they get only 80% of that. The rest they will have to wait a year or two for. And during that time they are loaning it to the record company, which gets to make money on it and not pass a dime of that extra profit back to the artist.

It would be easy to understand the record company holding back the royalties and keeping the interest if they were still owed money, but after two million records sold, they have long since recouped and are well into the black. Why hold the artist's money? The cold hard truth is, because they can.

Was I right? Isn't the football game more interesting to watch when you know about offsides and holding? While the record company nets millions, the musicians are surviving on the few thousand dollars they saved from their recording budget. And remember the full-color CD jacket the manager promised? The artist pays for that as well. The more the cover art and liner notes cost, the more money gets charged to the artist's recoupment account for packaging and container fees.

Back in the '60s, rock and roll managers would neglect to tell their clients that all the goodies that the label was promising the band, like color cover art and big

GETTING "CUTOUT" OF ROYALTIES

Almost all new artist recording agreements with major labels insist that the artist will not be paid a royalty on "cutouts." Cutouts are the backlogged records that didn't sell and remain in a warehouse where eventually they will be shipped back to the label for a refund. They are called cutouts because the label cuts out the album from the company's catalogue of inventory. Basically, a dead record. You've seen them in the discount bin at places like K-Mart.

Record companies traditionally sell cutouts at fire sale prices (sometimes they sell for as low as 60 cents apiece) to companies who broker them to the "offbeat" retail chains, record clubs, and little mom-and-pop stores or sell them to recycling plants for scrap plastic.

Obviously a record company can't pay the standard royalty to an artist when they're selling the merchandise at below cost. However, when cutout sales topple mainstream sales, it starts to smell fishy. In the 1980s, the major labels sold an estimated 200 million records *a year* as cutouts! It makes you wonder how hard they pushed to sell the record in the initial release.

Artists get angry when they read royalty statements claiming they still owe the label money when their record is selling in the hundreds of thousands. This leads to audits. But these audits usually conclude that the uncredited sales are cutouts and therefore royalty-free.

It's a tough bind. As an artist, it's nice to know that your record is in hundreds of thousands of homes, but it sure would be nice to get paid for it. There is no easy way to solve this problem. Good managers know the game and should always be aware of exactly how much real revenue their client is worth to the label and press heavily in negotiating their next advance.

psychedelic black light posters and limousines, were being paid for out of the band's advance and would be applied to their royalties.

Oops!

Keep in mind as well that all the above is what's in the standard "boilerplate" recording contract. Your best hope is that many of these ridiculous clauses can be negotiated out of your deal.

I know what you might be thinking: There's always the second album. Remember how your manager said that the budget for the second album would be more than the first? Maybe you can keep some of that money this time around. Except for one thing—the record company insisted that all the records on the contract be *cross-collateralized.*

Cross-what?

◗ Cross-Collateralization, or Robbing Peter to Pay Paul

"Cross-collateralized" (or as it's sometimes relabeled by lawyers, "offsets") is one of the most important phrases to be on the lookout for in a record contract. Put simply, it means that the debts you run over the course of your deal will be repaid out of any profits from future records or publishing. So even though one of your albums may have gone double-platinum, if the others lost money and those losses are more than the profits from your hit album, guess what—you still owe the label money. Debts from one album can be recouped from the profits of the others. (For an astounding and sobering explanation of cross-collateralization, read Donald Passman's book *Everything You Need to Know about the Music Business* [Simon & Schuster]. Or my book *Secrets of Negotiating a Record Contract: The Musician's Guide to Understanding and Avoiding Sneaky Lawyer Tricks* [Backbeat Books].)

But there are other versions of this. If you went over budget $100,000 from the first record and they promised you a $300,000 advance for the second—guess what? You're getting advanced only $200,000 to make the second record, and now you owe them $300,000. The record company takes its $100,000 first. This can get really ugly if the contract states that you're supposed to get an advance of, say, $500,000 to produce your fifth album. Here you are, looking forward to getting a huge check after working your butt off for four albums, and then the record company says, "Sorry, but you went over budget on your last three records by $400,000, so we're only advancing you $100,000 for your fifth record." With this pittance, they will now expect a pop group with a good enough track record to warrant a fifth album to produce a quality recording under low-budget conditions.[12]

12 $100,000 an album is considered low-budget by major label standards. See the sidebar "Typical 'Official' Album Production Budget on a Major Label," page 79.

So much for scraping some money off your next record's budget. Well, there's still the sliding scale royalty they promised you. Maybe, maybe not. It depends on your deal.

Atlantic Records in the '70s and '80s had a clause in their standard contract that promised the artist the standard 12% royalty on the first record, a 13% royalty on the second, and then a whopping 15% from the third on. The catch was that the artist had to deliver the finished masters of each record no later than eight months after the last one. Anyone who's been in the industry could tell you that between touring and recording and writing, there is little chance of this happening. In the Atlantic contract, if the artists didn't deliver in time, they were kept at the old royalty rate. Nice. (See "Decoding of an Actual Warner Bros. Record Contract," page 198.) And there are still more severe versions of the deal "offset" that would allow the record company to take money the artist owes them out of any source whatsoever—including publishing, touring, merchandising, or anything they can think of. We'll get to that stuff later. But if the artist is smart and has learned from experience, they'll manage their second record advance much smarter their first one.

❯ A Major Label Deal Is Like Having a Credit Card at 66% Interest

So, what have we learned thus far? We see that the artist is borrowing $200,000 with the understanding that they are going to have to pay back $500,000 ($300,000 going for promotion) and that the $500,000 is a *moving goal post,* meaning that the record company can spend more at their discretion and charge it back to the artist. Since the initial contract period of these deals lasts about two years and it is within that time that the advance money must be paid, the artist, in effect, is entering into a loan agreement at an interest rate of 66.3% per year. And even after they pay back all this money, they don't own the rights to their master recordings—the record company does.

When a lawyer, manager, or producer is talking about shopping you to a major record label, this is the type of deal they are talking about—a short-term loan at 66.3% interest with a forgiven debt clause. They won't mention that this will be the situation, and they usually won't explain about the moving goal post unless you ask them. This is because long after the artist's record is in the discount bin, the pros will have taken their commissions off the top of the deal, and the producer will have started to collect his or her 21 cents from the first record sold.

But all this funny accounting is only an issue if your record actually gets released. No one says the label *has to* release your masterpiece debut record, as you'll learn in a moment.

➢ Drop-Kicked from the Roster

The frigid reality of the major record deal is that, in spite of the fact that a label will sign about 20 to 30 new pop acts a year, it may only have the budget to market about six of them effectively. This means that there are going to be several unhappy campers at the end of the fourth quarter when the vice presidents make cuts to their roster.

In my opinion and experience, these decisions are rather arbitrary and often based on politics rather than the quality of the record. Yes, it is important that the artist produce good material, but what if all 30 acts signed that year produce good material? *Several will still be cut for economic reasons.*

One factor in this decision is the "A&R revolving door." If the A&R person who signed the act is no longer with the company, all the acts that he or she signed that year stand a good chance of being dropped. Since A&R persons tend to label-hop with great frequency these days, the odds of getting dropped are better than not.[13]

13 See "A&R," page 9, for the reason.

For many acts this is disastrous because it means starting all over again. Most artists focus on the getting of the deal as their main form of competition. They don't recognize that once they are on a label's roster they are still competing with other acts for position on the release calendar and promotion money. For this reason it is important that the band have a manager who is well-connected to the inner sanctum of the label.

Aside from politics, marketing departments look at the changing needs and whims of the public. Herein lies what is probably the single most frustrating part of major record deals: the timing of the release, or what I call "time warp."

➢ Time Warp: How Long Till the Record Comes Out?

Typically, a manager shops an act to several labels. When one takes an interest, the manager and the A&R person sit down and smoke fat cigars and discuss the deal. When they reach an agreement (and that could take several months), then they "do lawyers" for $50,000. The lawyers argue and debate the finer points of the agreement, ultimately producing a document 50 to 75 pages long. This is the record agreement, also referred to as "The Thick" or "The Long Form." This process can easily take up to six months, and has been known to take as long as 15 months before the thick was finished.

When this is done, the act will go into the studio and record a single or an album. If they are well-prepared, this will take an average of about two weeks to six months. After the album is done, it sits on the shelves of the A&R person and the marketing department for another few months while the political wheels turn and decide whether the act will be drop-kicked or move on to be marketed.

By this point, about a year has passed since the label agreed to sign the artist they thought was so special. There's just one problem—that was a year ago, and by now the industry trends may have changed, or the A&R person may have been fired and his or her replacement doesn't want the old A&R's dirty laundry.[14]

There are at least 500 ways for a label to say "no" to a potential contract signing or a release. The artist or their representation must try to cut down that number. What this really means is that artists competing for a deal or market attention must become like televangelists—they are in the believer business. They must make believers out of all who come in contact with them. This is what is often called a "good vibe"—one that instills confidence in the record company. It starts not with the vice president who makes the ultimate decision, but with the lowly secretary, who often has the ability to get you past security.

Some artists manage to do this with pure arrogance, and some with humility. Whatever works, use it. Because when the record is done, the battle isn't over. There is still the marketing department to contend with, and the publicity department, and the promotion department. You will have to make friends with all of them if you want your record to be a success. (See "Image Molding," page 91.) Remember:

Artists are in the believer business.

❯ Need and Greed: Be Careful What You Wish For

Do you still want a major record deal? Are you sure? Your lawyer told you it was a good deal, and your manager agreed. Even the producer thinks it's the best thing for you. Can they all be wrong?

Yes.

As we've seen, pros and the producer get paid by different schedules than artists. But to be fair to these folks—whom we do not want to alienate—let me state in their defense that there is another reason why nobody mentions all the pitfalls of major label deals to the artist. That is because the artist rarely wants to hear about it.[15]

Most people agree that the standard major label recording contract is unfair, but pros will tell you, the artist, that it's the only real money game in town. They will also bolster their opinion with rationalizations like, "Long before you are supposed to start collecting royalties on your first record, you will be receiving your larger advance for the second record." They'll also tell you that once you become a big star you can negotiate almost all of these pocket-picking clauses out of your contract. You can get bigger royalties payable on 100% of sales with no special goods programs. You can get the record company to pay for the video and other promotion costs instead of passing their cost of doing business on to you.

All that is true, but until you prove yourself with a successful record, you'll be facing the standard deal that most new artists live with. Maybe now it's easier to understand why so many artists "sell out" when they sign to major labels.

But if at the outset you are only getting a few thousand dollars to close the deal and then, two years later, $95,000 *if* you sell two million records, how can you survive? What advice do the pros have for you? What do you have left to sell that is of any worth? (Besides instruments and vital organs.)

Well, how about the right to collect your songwriting royalties? Sounds promising, so let's take a closer look at "the publishing deal."

[15] I've tried on occasion to persuade an act that I was producing to go with an indie label over a major. They look at me cross-eyed. The advance money is drastically smaller on an indie. I try to show them that despite the large advance they will probably never see royalties. It's futile.

CHAPTER SIX

⊜Publishing Deals
The 200% Pie, or 100% of Something Is Better than 200% of Nothing

I f you are signing with a major label, then in all likelihood a publishing company will want to be involved with you as well. Here's why.

While the record is still in recoupment hell, the authors of the songs on the record are vacationing in Boca Raton. Unlike recoupment negotiating, which inhabits the realm of twisted legalese and creative accounting, writers get paid because the law recognizes their contribution as intellectual property. In other words, there are laws that dictate how and when a writer gets paid.[1]

The Copyright Act of 1976 establishes a minimum payment that must be paid to the writer of a song that appears on any CD, tape, or 12-inch phonograph record that is distributed in the United States. The payment, called a "compulsory mechanical license," has a special rate set by the Act called the "statutory rate."

To keep things simple, let's just say that since the average pop song runs four minutes, the current industry-accepted statutory rate is 8 cents for each song on an album for all records distributed. Let me repeat that: *for all records distributed.* The Copyright Act defines "distributed" as *"if the person exercising the compulsory license has voluntarily and permanently parted with its pos-*

[1] See "What Do Doctors and Song-writers Have in Common?," page 37.

session." In laymen's terms, "sold." Since it would be hard for a record company to argue that they manufactured records without the intent to sell them, it would follow that all records manufactured would require that a royalty be paid. But you will only be paid on the ones that actually sell through normal retail and wholesale distribution.[2] So if you're the writer of all the songs on your record, let's see what the record company owes you just for the turnkey expense of mass-producing your CDs.

You'll get 8 cents per song x 10 songs on a record x 100,000 units (the first run in the hypothetical contract we've been discussing). That's $80,000. But in case you haven't caught on, nothing is as simple as it seems in this business of music.

❷ Three-Quarter Rate

First, record companies will make the artist agree to only charge them three-quarters of the statutory rate of 8 cents (or 6 cents per song) if they want the deal. This is called the *three-quarter rate.* Second, they will limit the artist to a total of ten songs at this rate per album for an "all-in" mechanical license of 60 cents per record sold. But with a million-selling record, the three-quarter rate can still spell real money for the writers: 75% of 8 cents = 6 cents x 10 songs x 1 million records = $600,000.[3]

No wonder there are publishing companies that want to collect this money for you. If the deal looks big enough, they will even offer you a recoupable advance against future earnings of your mechanical license. For a new act on a major label, the advance can be anywhere from $25,000 to $500,000. That's a lot of cash for the artist who desperately needs something to live on while the record company holds royalties in reserve.

But nothing is for free in this world. That advance money is in exchange for the right for the publishing company to control 50% of the song's copyright.

Now here is where it can get confusing. First of all, let's turn the pie we are about to split up into a 200% pie. It's just like 100% inflation. Everything that would normally be 10% is now 20%. You can think of the song's pie as a 200% pie that is divided up 100% for the writer and 100% for the publisher. So when you hear people talking about 100% of the "publisher's share" they are talking about 50% of the total money the song earns. Before you go on, reread this paragraph over and over again until it is clear.

But why should you want to give 50% to a company to collect the money that should be paid to you by law? The publishing company's argument is a good one: They sell the idea that you, the artist, don't want to go to all the trouble of going around collecting money from all the sources that owe you for the use of your song,

2 It's a forgone conclusion that you never see a dime of publishing royalties from cutouts and special goods programs. See "Getting Cutout of Royalties," page 62.

3 Instead of $800,000, which would be the compulsory license at full rate. You're already saving your record company $200,000 on a big hit by agreeing to this. You're quite a sport. For reasons why they do this, see "Deductions," page 88.

like radio stations, movie companies, movie soundtracks, other artists who do cover versions of your song, and most recently, sample rights.[4] (In case you were wondering, this statutory rate of 8 cents is chargeable whenever anybody else records the song or uses a sample of the song.) The main reason you sell 50% of your proceeds to a publishing company is to have them market the song to commercials, movies, TV shows, and so on. You just have to sit back and be creative. They handle all the business, for a cut of every dollar the song makes. Seems reasonable.

There are, as always, a couple of catches. Let's deal with the recoupment clause first.

[4] A sample is a piece of a recording usually taken off a record and incorporated into the arrangement of a new song. The act of getting the right to use the sample is called "clearing." See "Sample Rights," page 72.

➔ Publishing Advances and Their Deductions

This tends to be a bit confusing, so let's go slow. Example: The publisher loans the songwriter(s) of the record (who is usually the artist, on a first record) $100,000 against the money he will earn from record sales. The recoupment formula should be about the same as for record sales, right? Each album sold equals 60 cents of revenue, which means the advance will be recouped when you've sold 166,666 records. (Refer to Egghead Box #3.)

EGGHEAD BOX #3

$$.60x = \$100,000$$
$$x = 166,666 \text{ records}$$

But it doesn't work out that way, for two reasons.

Administrative Expenses

The first is that many deals have a clause built in for administrative costs; these can be as high as 20%. This comes out of the *writer's percentage*.

If the publisher takes only half of the *publishing share*, then in effect they are taking 25% of all the writer's mechanical royalties. (Remember, it's a 200% pie. So a 75%-25% split becomes a 150%-50% split.) Let's say that the copyright of the song earns $1,000 from sources like record sales, radio play, or a movie soundtrack. In this case, 25%, or $250, goes to the publisher and the remaining $750 gets applied to the recoupment of the writer's advance.

But publishers usually charge administrative costs, which average about 10%. These are deducted *first,* before the split. So, $1,000 minus 10% equals $900. Once the publisher subtracts its cut (25%), the artist is left with $675. By this account, the artist must earn $148,148 to pay back an advance of $100,000. This is roughly the same as borrowing money at 48% interest.

But this isn't so bad, really, especially when you compare it to the record deal in the last chapter. My only real complaint is that a publisher's overhead is nowhere near as massive as a record company's, and their risk is much lower because they usually don't give advances unless there is a distribution deal in place, thus minimizing their risk. They can be wrong about how successful a new artist will be, but it won't cost them anywhere near what it costs a label to take that gamble. Yet they still take a large chunk of the writer's money.

The only dangerous thing to look out for here is the cross-collateralization clause. If you have signed a record deal with one of the Big Five, then they will want you to give them your publishing contract as well. Many managers and pros recommend against this, but I say it can be a good thing for the first album because it will give the record company an extra incentive to work the record for you. *But if the contract cross-collateralizes your record deal with the publishing deal, then any money that you earn as a writer will go toward recouping your record deal.* This *sucks—always,* all the time. Don't let them try this one on you, or you will be forever in a bottomless pit of recoupment hell.

Sample Rights

The second way the writer/artist gets gypped out of their money is with sample rights. This is a new form of publishing revenue born in the past decade or so.

Most early rap and R&B records "borrowed" bits and pieces from other recordings to make up the arrangement of their new recording. For a while they got away without paying for these, but eventually publishing companies caught on and started asking for a portion of the copyright on the new song. A famous case that comes to mind is the song "Ice Ice Baby," by the artist Vanilla Ice. To make the main groove of his hit recording he used a portion off of a David Bowie record. Bowie's publisher asked for 50% of all the publishing on the recording and the full statutory rate of 5.5 cents in exchange for the right to sample his recording.[5]

Today samples have found their way into almost every form of modern music.

[5] 5.5 cents was the rate at the time. The rate has since been increased to 8 cents.

Clearing the rights to use the samples is a matter of course and courtesy. If you steal a sample, the consequences can be costly litigation that you are likely to lose.[6] But remember, in the "three-quarter rate," the label made the artist agree to an "all-in royalty" for all mechanical license fees of 60 cents per CD. So who pays for the right to use it?

Nowadays the record company charges the sample rights back to the artist in a clever way. They deduct it from the statutory rate that they pay on album sales.

So, for example, if you are supposed to receive 60 cents for the ten songs on your record, but you use a sample and the publisher of that sample wants you to pay the full 8 cents to them for the right to use it, guess what? The record company will deduct this 8 cents from the 60 cents they were going to pay you. If you know anything about music production, you know that songs that tend to use samples rarely use just one to compose the arrangement of a song. Over the course of a typical rap or R&B record, it is not uncommon to find 15 to 50 samples being used. So if this is the case, you can kiss your statutory, guaranteed-by-law, licensing fee good-bye.

What makes this really evil is that even when an artist is signed to a major label and they are using samples that come from their own label's publishing catalogue, the above conditions will still exist. (See "Sample-Alikes," page 173, for a way around this.)

❷ The Workaround for Recoupment Hell

How does one beat this system? Answer: forget royalties. The name of the game is advances! Get as much money up front as you can, then administer it wisely. Assume that you may not get any more money from the label or the publisher. If the first record does well, renegotiate firmly for a larger advance on the second record. It's better to have the label owe you money than vice versa.

❷ Collecting Money in the "New Economy"

The buzz word at the start of this millennium was "new economy," spawned largely by the growth of the Internet. Dot-coms, as they have come to be known, sprouted up like weeds offering the promises of new and cheaper distribution methods

[6] Publishing companies hire listeners called "sample police." These people do nothing all day but listen to new records in search of unlicensed samples.

and the ability for anyone with a home computer and a phone line to own entire catalogs of music for *free*. "They" called it "a revolution that would change the music industry forever." It lasted exactly 13 months.

Almost as quickly as you could say "ISP," record companies and publishing companies were just as quick to say the word "lawsuit." Within months, the big payers in the dot-com game were all but dot-*gone*. The ones that remained were absorbed into Big Five oblivion. However, the dot-com wars left in its wake a new distribution channel: music sales via downloading records directly into a home computer. Record companies initially turned their noses up to this idea, but they gradually began to see it as viable.

Many technical and legal glitches still need to be worked out before it will be possible to get entire catalogs of old favorites and new releases with just a mouse click, but publishing companies are now fighting for their share of the download pie. As this goes to print, lawyers from labels, publishing companies, and the Copyright Office are negotiating a fee, much like the 8-cents-a-song fee discussed above, for downloading music. Whatever this fee is, the income to songwriters should increase substantially in the next five to ten years—provided they ever get around to figuring out what the fee will be. (Remember that it took Congress 67 years after the invention of the record player to create the first statutory rate and to agree that a recording should be protected by copyright.)

An important point to keep in mind is that there is nothing really "new" about the new economy. There have been and always will be new ideas for making money, as older, perfectly good systems fade away. And the art of collecting money hasn't changed much despite all the new bells and gadgets, either. The economy is the economy is the economy. However, we tend to be less cynical about things that are new, because despite our skepticism, deep down we would like to believe that "new" means "improved." If the dot-com wars taught us anything, they taught us this is not necessarily the case.

CHAPTER SEVEN

◉The Major Label Deal
from the Producer's Point of View

The word "producer" is often associated with someone who raises money and puts a deal together. This is most true in the theater, film, and TV world. But in the record industry, the producer is more like the director of a feature film than a financier. The producer will often play a very creative role in the production, directing the musicians the way a film director would direct actors.

The producer on a major label record sits in a very different position than the new artist. Usually they already have a track record of delivering quality product to the label and are commanding high fees for their participation in important records.

Before one can grasp the agenda of the producer, one has to understand exactly who hires him or her. And the conflict that comes with the job.

◉ The Artist/Producer Conflict

Starting out as a producer is not cheap. Producers are very much like artists. Many, in fact, started out that way. Maybe not as full-fledged recording acts but as a main member of a band or the chief writer for a band. Other producers come from engineering backgrounds. Often, to get his or her business off the ground, a new producer will buy thousands of dollars worth of equipment for making demos (demonstration recordings) of the artists they will contract and shop to record labels. As you can imagine, the investment in equipment and time can be enormous. This is why new producers often think more like businesspeople than like artists.

But this bottom line attitude often makes artists leery and fosters an attitude that producers are out to rip off their songs and hijack their publishing rights.[1] Because of this, artists can be less than respectful of the fact that a producer will invest thousands of dollars in time and resources developing the artist's sound. Instead they tend to see only that what they bring to the table is irreplaceable, that they are "the talent" and therefore deserve immediate respect and recognition.

Producers can be equally suspicious of artists, fearing that after they do all the work (usually on spec) the artist will break ties, leaving them out of the windfall loop.

Things would be easier if artists were in touch with the reality that 90% of new acts lose money. But, given the headstrong position of both parties, it's easy to see why the process of record deal-making can be a small miracle in itself.

When a major label does eventually sign an artist and plops down a half a million dollars to launch their careers, the posture of the producer/artist relationship changes radically. Experience has taught the label that most new artists can't be trusted with a large budget, and since in all likelihood they do not have the studio experience to produce the record themselves, the label will stipulate in the contract that the artist will, *at the artist's expense*, hire a producer.

The phrase "at the artist's expense" is somewhat misleading. Since the producer will be paid out of the artist's advance and the producer's royalty will be carved out of the artist's share of 12% (see "Recoupable Financing—The Moving Goal Post," page 55), the artist is the one who hires the producer in the legal sense. But it's the record company that puts the food on the producer's plate, since without the label the artist wouldn't be able to afford the recording.

The artist may or may not do well, but the record company is here to stay.

Add to this the fact that once a major label is involved, the producer has a lot of emotional leverage. As an old expression goes, "If you pay a doctor for his advice and you ignore him, who are you hurting?" This is the position that most producers will take with a reluctant artist who wants to do something avant-garde or non-commercial on major label money.

[1] Most artists are young and inexperienced with business, so it is not surprising that they perceive all forms of authority—producers, record companies, and so on—as "the establishment," hungry for the millions that can be made off their music. The recreational drugs that many artists indulge in do not help to eliminate their paranoia, either.

Artist: "Nah, man, we don't like that thing you had us do in the chorus, it's too commercial."

Producer: "Well, okay, it's your record. I don't want to ruin your vision."

Following this dialogue, in all likelihood the producer, who almost always has a close relationship with the A&R person, will tell him that the group isn't being co-operative and he has doubts as to whether they will be able to deliver a hit record. The A&R person will, in turn, talk to the group's manager (with whom he also has a good relationship), and the manager will tell the group that they had better shape up and listen to the doctor.

This is an extreme case, but it does happen often enough to be a realistic example of how the producer's allegiance and leverage works. The band hires a producer more often than not at the insistence of the label and then pays him to protect *the record company's interests*. Nobody likes to talk about this small conflict of interest, but everyone knows it exists.[2]

On the point of who should have final say over a creative choice on a record, I side with the producer. If you think this is self-serving, remember why a producer is hired in the first place. If artists wants to make "art," they don't need a producer or a record company. Anyone can produce a record if they don't care how commercial it is. But when artists sign with a major label, they are signing a contract that says, "Yes, we want to make records that sell in large quantities." The producer is hired as the expert consultant toward that goal. If an artist is not in touch with that re-ality, they are wasting their time and the record company's money.[3]

The producer also has knowledge that the artist probably does not. They've been around the industry and see how long things take. They know that the time between an artist's signing and an album release could easily be over a year. In that time the fickle market can change direction. To combat this, the expert producer must be somewhat of a fortune teller. He might try to influence the band to incorporate new elements into their music so that when the record comes out it will sound fresh. The new band almost never understands this concept. They create in the vacuum of their self-contained environment and often don't concern themselves with how they will be perceived after one or two years against the vast tapestry of new re-leases.[4]

Herein lies the fundamental dilemma of the producer: how to make a commercial record and still be original and faithful to the artist's sound. It's a delicate tightrope to walk. But remember, if the record sells a million copies and the band hates it, that producer will work again. Period. Even if the artist is upset at the way the record turned out. With that established, let's look at the different types of producer deals and their ins and outs.

[2] *Unless* it's a pro-duction deal where the producer and the artist were signed as a pack-age. For more info on this subject see "The Baby Record Deal," page 123.

[3] Given enough time and money, the artist will probably come to the same or similar solutions that the producer comes to. The only difference is that the artist rarely has unlimited time and money. That's why the producer was called in in the first place. So if you pay someone for their expertise and you don't lis-ten to them . . . . You get the point.

[4] The label of course has a great deal of foresight since they know all the other artists that they have on their roster, as well as a good idea of what's on other label's rosters.

Note: In this chapter we discuss the elements of the major label deal that the producer will be most concerned with. However, for the up-and-coming producers reading this book, still looking for that breakout deal, you might also want to cover the chapter called "The Baby Record Deal" (page 123), as that chapter addresses more specific issues that arise between the artist, the producer, and the smaller label/production company.

❷ The All-In Deal

A new producer being contracted by a group signed to a one-deep label[5] will ask for and usually receive a $50,000 fee for producing a rock, pop, country, or jazz album. This fee is for overseeing the record and working with the artist on the arrangements. However, sometimes they will be paid by the song in what's called an "all-in budget," meaning that the record company gives the producer a chunk of money to produce one song.[6]

The producer with an "all-in budget" pays all the vendors involved, the recording studio, the engineer, everything. The budget also includes a sum that the producer "pays" to himself or herself. But if the producer can complete the project for less than the budget allows, then whatever is left over is his or hers to keep. The producer's total advance from the record company, including the amounts to be paid to the various vendors, is usually about $35,000 per song. If the producer is clever and thrifty, he can usually keep about $22,000 of this. While all the money for the recording fund is recoupable from the artist's side of the equation, only the portion that is considered to be the producer's fee is recoupable from the producer's side of the royalties equation (see Egghead Box #1, page 57). This is the factor that gives the producer the incentive to bring in the project for as little as possible. Whatever he doesn't spend, he gets to keep—free of recoupment.[7]

The all-in deal can be very tricky. Most producers prefer it because they can juggle money around and the record company won't know exactly how much things cost or how much the producer actually keeps.

There is one major drawback for the producer in an all-in deal—that's when the record company decides that it wants a remix or re-edit of the final version of the song and expects the producer to pay for it out of his recording fund. Unless the producer has good management or clout, these changes can continue ad infinitum until the producer has gone into his own pocket to complete the record. Generally, the record company will reach a compromise with the producer and offer to pay some or most of the expenses involved in remixes.

[5] See "One-Deep and Two-Deep Labels," page 50, if you don't know what this means.

[6] "All-in" funds can be distributed for entire albums as well, and, while they are most common in the R&B, hip-hop, and rap fields, they can be found in the rock and pop fields as well.

[7] I know several producers who record everything in their home studios and then charge the label the same rates as professional large studios (about $150 per hour). They even go to the trouble of printing bogus invoices. So out of $50,000 they net almost all of it.

TYPICAL "OFFICIAL" ALBUM PRODUCTION BUDGET ON A MAJOR LABEL

E ven in an all-in deal, the producer must submit a plan for the recording, but there are still all kinds of ways to hide money in a budget. If the producer is clever, neither the artist nor the label will ever find it. Below is what two normal budgets look like to the untrained eye.

	New artist	Mid-level artist (or one that is in demand)
Basic trax		
Three weeks at major studio ($2,500 per day "card rate") discounted[8]	$15,000	$32,400
Engineer ($400–$1,100 per day)	$8,400	$23,100
Tape (2-inch 24-track) 20 reels @ $150 per reel	$3,000	$3,000
Union scale—musicians' fees for the backup band—$350 per player per day (four players)[9]	$29,400	$58,800 (dbl. scale)
Overdubs		
Smaller studio ($1,000 per day) for four weeks discounted	$20,000	$30,800
Union scale—musicians' fees for the band—$350 per player per day (two players)	$14,000	$28,000
Side players/guest soloists	$3,000	$10,000
Engineer ($400–$1,100 per day)	$8,000	$30,800
Mixing		
Mix studio—$2,500 per day (15–36 days)	$37,500	$90,000
Tape—½-inch mixdown tape, 10 reels @ $60 per reel	$600	$600
DATs for digital backup	$200	$500
Mix engineer ($1,000–$1,500 per day)	$15,000	$54,000
Producer's fee	$25,000	$110,000
Miscellaneous		
Cartage	$2,000	$10,000
Lodging	$3,000	$30,000
Strings/sticks/skins, etc.	$500	$1,000
Mastering	$4,000	$10,000
Total.	**$188,600**	**$523,000**

Note: These figures are the average as of press time.

As you can see, the cost of doing business more than doubles once a plateau of success is established, mainly for two reasons: (1) Vendors are less likely to discount their rates, and (2) the artists pay themselves more and treat themselves to better accommodations.

[8] Studios have three sets of rates: (1) the "card rate," which is their advertised rate; (2) the "professional rate," which is what they will actually settle on, usually about half the card rate; and (3) the "favor rate," which is the very least amount for which they will book time. Favor-rate time is usually bumpable, meaning that if a higher-paying client calls for time, the favor-rate client will be bumped from the session. Favor rate is usually between 50% and 70% below card rate. Add to this the fact that many studios will do six-day weeks and 20-day months if you pay in cash or have a good rapport with them. Ironically, larger studios are in a better position to offer discounts than smaller ones, so you can get a better value there even though you pay more.

[9] Members of a band and even the artist need to be paid union scale to perform on their own records on major labels. As the artist climbs the ladder of success, they will charge themselves double or triple scale for their time. If they ask a friend in another successful band to be a soloist on their record, the friend will get a higher fee as well.

⊘ Non-All-In Deals

Most all-in deals described above are found in R&B and rap projects, where you have what I call "producer-driven acts," meaning that the producer often writes the songs and does the arrangements and basically *is* the artist. The producer's own fee in the recording budget is usually the only money that will have to be recouped before the producer will see royalties. For this reason, the producer will want to keep that fee as low as possible, especially if he can get kickbacks from vendors.[10]

However, in rock and other types of music where the band is more the focus of the record, not the producer, you tend to have *non-all-in deals*. In this setup, the producer still prepares the budget, but his or her production fee is paid directly from the label on behalf of the artist. The producer is relieved of administering the budget and will have no opportunity to scam.

[10] See "Kickbacks," page 82.

A veteran producer will get about $150,000 as a fee to produce the record. Depending on his or her clout, this either will or will not be recoupable out of future royalties. If it's not recoupable, that means the producer starts to earn royalties from the sale of the first record, while the artist has to wait until the entire recording fund is paid back to the label before he or she sees any more money from record sales. It's easy to see why artists have love/hate relationships with producers.

As artists get more successful, they usually try to exercise their muscle by taking more control over the production of their record. Most of the time, self-producing is a formula for disaster. It tends to have the same effect as a person giving themselves a haircut without a mirror. Sometimes it works well; there are some artists who have excelled at producing themselves, like the artist now once again known as Prince. But most artists, even many who've been making hit records for years, like Paul Simon and Billy Joel, hire people to at least coproduce their albums.

In the typical rock production, the producer acts as a sounding board for the varied and sometimes conflicting ideas that the artist has for the songs. Often, the producer will help arrange the material, and sometimes he or she writes bridges for songs that are missing that "certain something." The problem with rewrites is that the artist can get a bit touchy about sharing the copyright of the songs with the producer (even though a good producer is improving the song; see "When the Producer Wants Publishing," page 84).

⊘ The Spec Deal

Speaking of the producer being taken advantage of, the "spec deal" seems like a good place to talk about his or her vulnerabilities.

Unknown acts often seek producers—either by themselves or through their managers—to produce the magic demo that will get them the big deal. If it's a manager coming to the producer, it's usually because he has a very talented group on his hands that seems unable to record anything. Maybe they're too disorganized or don't know their way around the studio. The group tends to have an expectation that the producer, if he likes them, will finance a recording and shop it to a label.

Producers are generally reluctant to take on these type of spec (short for speculation) deals unless the band is both very good and very willing to make the back end of the deal attractive for the producer. Attractive, in this case, usually means:

1. A 15% finder's fee taken off the top of the advance to the artist.
2. The right to produce the record for a fee of no less than $25,000 plus a 3% or 4% royalty.
3. A large participation in publishing—50% if it's rap, hip-hop or R&B, 25% if it's rock.
4. A demo fee of upwards of $5,000 per track (song).

All in exchange for producing a recording and getting the band a deal.

Let's see how those numbers play out in a typical scenario. If the producer gets the artist the deal and they get a $200,000 advance to make the record, they must first pay off the producer. Fifteen percent off the top leaves $170,000. Then there's the demo fee. If the producer did four songs (typical), he will take $20,000 for that work, leaving $150,000 for the artist. Now comes the producer's album fee of $25,000, leaving $125,000 to make the record and for the artist to live on until the royalties start coming in.

This will seem, to the artist, as if the producer is raping and pillaging, but consider three things:

1. The producer has an enormous risk in doing the project at all. He is not a multinational corporation like a record company, and although he has had some success (or you wouldn't be talking to him), that doesn't mean that he has the 20 or 30 grand lying around to develop the act.
2. The producer's reputation. The artist, at this point in his or her career, has nothing to lose. The producer, on the other hand, can damage his reputation and waste his time by getting involved with a loser act.
3. No one says the artist must hire the producer. If the artist thinks the

producer wants too much, then the artist is free to produce the record and get the deal himself

The artist will quickly see that large labels, as a policy, will not deal directly with them but rather prefer to go through a party they are familiar with.

❯ Kickbacks

Here we get to a dark subject and one that is the source of the most industry quibbles—kickbacks. In the secret code of the industry it's called many things: good business, greasing the wheels, doing the right thing. Others just call it thievery. Consider the following examples:

Kickbacks to the Artist and Manager

Often when the producer gets complete control of the recording fund, as in an all-in deal, the artist's manager may want a little piece of it. He will say the money is for his client, but we know better. If the money ever actually reaches the artist, the manager will likely commission it. But not to worry: It rarely does. The manager will try to convince the artist to let him keep it to recover the costs that he has incurred managing the artist for the past year or two before the record company signed the artist. The artist will often agree, out of guilt or loyalty.

Should the producer elect to pay the manager, it will be somehow camouflaged as some other expense in the recording budget, which means it will be recouped out of the artist's royalties. In other words, the artist pays for this kickback twice—once when they give up the money to the manager and again when it's recouped from their royalties.

The record companies know this goes on; no one is being fooled. There is, however, an accepted level of theft the industry has sustained over the years, a nebulous threshold known only to those who are in on the deal. This is why it can be hard to understand all the ins and outs of the record deal from the outside. Relationships are the foundation of the deals, and therefore everybody is scratching everybody else's back.

Kickbacks from Vendors

The producer also has relationships with studios and engineers. He will in turn sometimes ask for a kickback from each of them to help put more money in his pocket. (See the sidebar "Kickback or Commission?", page 83) His agenda is that only the producer's fee as listed in the recording budget is recoupable. Therefore, whatever other sources of income the producer can create will be his to keep, free of recoupment.

KICKBACK OR COMMISSION?

I was once hired to engineer a big-budget R&B record on a major label. The producer and I had a good relationship that went back two or three years. He had used me on several recordings, which helped build both of our reputations. This deal was his big shot. The budget for the album was over $300,000 "all-in" just for the recording. This was going to mean a lot of money for the producer, if he could be clever about it.

During the production he would frequently show up hours late for the session, leaving me, the artist, and the studio assistant sitting there twiddling our thumbs at a collective billing rate of about $300 per hour. I couldn't figure out why. I knew he had a lot of cash to make this record with, but why waste it? Then it hit me.

When he asked me to work on the recording he said he would pay me $60 per hour. I was delighted, not only to work on what seemed to be an important record but also at twice my usual rate of $30. But there was a catch: I would have to give him back $15 per hour in the form of a commission check. I did it. But what I began to figure out during the course of the production was that every vendor involved, including the studios, was giving him commissions. So while the record company was paying hundreds of dollars per hour in fees and charging them to the artist's account, the producer was making about $100 per hour under the table in addition to his fee. If I were him, I would take my time as well. Yes, this really was an all-in deal. It was "all in" the producer's pocket.

The artist sued the producer when he found out about the kickbacks, even though the record was a hit. The record company held the artist's royalties in escrow until the two parties worked it out. (How nice of them to keep an eye on the several million dollars collecting interest in their bank while the lawyers quarreled.)

I said nothing. Eventually the record company paid off the producer, and he and the artist went their separate ways. When the artist made his second record, he decided to produce it himself. It was a bomb. He has since been dropped from the label's roster. The producer, on the other hand, is still making records for that label. In fact, he called me recently to work on his next one. Get the picture?

Kickbacks to A&R

Corruption can go on at higher levels as well. I've heard of an A&R person who had an under-the-table deal in which the producer agreed to give them a kickback if the A&R person convinced his VP to get the recording budget up past $300,000. Once again, the artist pays for this greasing of the wheels.

There is no question in anybody's mind that this *is* stealing. But record companies have been known to look the other way on one condition—if the record is a hit. If it is, all will be forgotten. If not, the producer may find himself at the wrong end of a lawsuit.

Kickbacks from Musicians

There are more subtle ways that a producer can scam money off the budget and stay in that gray area between right and wrong. For instance, he may ask the sideperson (a musician who is not part of the band but is used as a soloist or fill-in player—formerly known as a "sideman" before the days of political correctness) to give him a commission or "finder's fee" for the gig. These fees can run from 10% to 25%. Usually they will be paid from the sideperson to the producer directly and will therefore bypass the album's accounting.

Whatever the producer's angle, this must be done carefully, because at the major label level, everything in the budget goes through the business affairs office—the office that writes the checks that pay the producer's bills. If the producer is not careful and the budget is audited, he might have some explaining to do. On the indie level, the accounting is often less precise, so the producer has more latitude for his creative budgeting.[11]

❷ When the Producer Wants Publishing

Paranoid ideas have been instilled in artists and writers that their publishing is something that they should never give up—that if a producer or manager asks for part of their publishing, they should run the other way. These concerns are good ones, but they don't tell the whole story. Here's why:

When a song plays on the radio, the law provides that the writer of the song earns a royalty. But what about the record company that put up the money, the producer who contributed scores of arrangement ideas (or who may even have rewritten portions of the song), the musicians who played on the record, and even the engineer who "played" the mixing console, determining the sound of the record? These are all "authors" of the sound recording, yet they receive nothing.

[11] For complete budgets and how to steal money, see "The Virtual Budget," page 133.

More recently the use of samples has created an even stronger argument for producers to receive a share of publishing. For example, snippets of James Brown records have appeared on literally thousands of records in the form of samples, yet the original producers haven't seen a nickel for the sample rights on these recordings.[12]

One could argue that the label and producer are not as important as the songwriter, without whom there would be no song to record, but a producer's contributions to the "sound of the record" should be worth some form of authorship royalty, don't you think? Well, the truth is more complex than a simple yes or no.

The Copyright Act of 1976 provided for a clause that could, at some future date, be amended to include a special royalty for the "authors of the sound recording," but to date it has not been initiated due to tremendous opposition. The resistance comes largely from TV networks and rights organizations like BMI and ASCAP, all of whom have used their influence to prevent the establishing of a statutory rate for sound recordings. TV companies are fed up with the license fees they already pay (discussed previously). The rights organizations also feel that a new royalty would take money out of their client's, the songwriter's, pocket by splitting the royalty pie even thinner.

Advocates of the sound recording author's rate point out that if record companies and producers had their own publishing money to collect, then they wouldn't have such a strong argument for going after the artist's publishing. (Record companies would try to go after it anyway, but that's another matter.) Regardless, both sides will have a chance to prove their cases soon. New amendments to the Copyright Act of 1976 have established the creation of a royalty for digital transmissions of sound recordings. The Copyright Office has not yet set a rate, but it will soon.

From the ASCAP/BMI/SESAC perspective, the whole battle is a bit hypocritical. On the one hand, these organizations will argue that they defend the rights of authors. On the other hand, they don't assist the producer or record company in collecting their royalty as authors of the sound recording.[13]

There is an equitable solution to the "producer wants publishing" argument that I've known some artists to agree to. In many cases it may be agreed that the producer will get a 10% to 15% interest in the writer's share of the publishing but will not share in any publishing advances or have the right to administer (control) the copyright.

This means that if the artist has a 50/50 publishing deal as described earlier, then the writer is retaining 75% of the pie, and the producer will get 15% of the 75%, or 11.25%.

In real dollars this is hard to translate, but figure if the record sells a million copies, the publishing rate payable to the artist, assuming the artist wrote all ten songs on

12 See "Sample Rights," page 72.

13 In my opinion, PROs (performing rights organizations) like ASCAP and BMI and SESAC are motivated not by principle but by fear. They're only as powerful as the share of dollars they can control. If their income goes down, they lose power. Don't misunderstand me: This would ultimately be a horrible thing. These companies have made outstanding strides toward reform in the record industry, and I'd hate to see a world where PROs don't have the clout to collect for their writers. This controversy is just another example of having to take the good with the bad.

the record, is $600,000 (at the ¾ rate), of which the producer would get $67,500. However, this does not include the radio and TV royalties, which are based on the number of times the song is played.[14]

[14] If you are confused by the formulas and don't know what a 50/50 publishing deal is, then please go to "Publishing Deals," page 69.

THE RADIO HIT ARGUMENT

It is difficult for some people to justify that if a record is a hit on the radio, only the writer of the song should get a piece of the royalty pie. If it were not for the record company, there would be no money for the recording, and if it were not for the engineer, there would be no quality recording, and if it were not for the producer, there would probably be a *big mess*. That's why producers feel justified in asking for publishing on songs that they contribute to.

Think about it this way: Long after record sales stop, a hit song is still played on the radio—whether it's for a review of the Top 100 of that year, or a "Where Are They Now?" show, or just because it has become part of our culture (like the song "Wild Thing," which is still played hundreds of times a year and is used in film after film). This airplay rarely leads to any substantial new record sales, so does it seem fair that while the record companies, producers, and musicians get zilch, the writer collects on airplay? Denying a producer publishing is the same thing as saying, "You don't have a right to make a royalty if the song is a radio hit," meaning that it gets lots of airplay but the airplay doesn't translate into record sales. Yet despite this inescapable logic, a producer asking for a piece of publishing is still met with criticism.

CHAPTER EIGHT

❧The Major Label Deal
from the Record Company's Point of View

At last, we get to hear from Father Christmas. I needed to save him for last because, as you can see, these deals can be complex. Let's examine the game from the perspective of the raping and pillaging record company and find out just why they're so mean. I suggest that if you are not familiar with the differences between a label and a distributor that you read "Understanding Distribution," page 47; "Record Companies," page 32; and "Distribution Companies," page 39.

❧ The Distribution Vig

The word "vig" is short for vigorish—the difference in percentage between the cost of business and the net reward. It's often used to describe the commission paid to a bookmaker in sports betting.

The crux of why anybody is stingy usually boils down to one thing—how much money is it costing them to do business, or what is their vig? Why, when a CD costs $18, does the artist only get 83 cents and the producer 27 cents? Where does the rest of the money go? In this chapter we will answer that question.

The first cut in the pie is the distributor. The distributor sells new releases of mainstream artists to the large record chains for about $12 per CD. The record store marks it up to $16.95 or $17.95 and eventually, if the record is not selling, will mark it back down to $13.95 or $10.95 to get it out the door.

If distributors sell the record to retail stores for $12, what are *they* paying for it?

It depends. If the label that created the record is distributing itself (like Warner Bros. Records being distributed by WEA), they don't pay anything per se. But if it comes from one of their "indie" labels, like Rhino, then they will pay Rhino about $9.60 per record on bona fide sales.[1]

The distributor marks up the record $2.40, about 20% of their wholesale price of $12.

Why would a small label let a Big Five distribute them and let them make that extra $2.40 if they could just take the records to the store themselves? The answer is because the smaller label stands a better chance of getting paid by the retail store if they are affiliated with a Big Five distributor.[2] However, the sacrifice can be costly, because it brings the profit margin down.

Regardless of who produces the record, $12 is about the going rate for what a retail store will pay. The point being made here is if a parent label like Warner sells records produced by one of the labels it wholly owns (like Atlantic Records or Elektra), they make all $12; if they distribute records on behalf of one of their one-deep labels (like WEA Latina), they keep only the difference between what they agree to pay the label (about $9.60) and the $12 they sell it for, or a net of about $2.40. This is the vig: what the middleman tacks on to make a profit. Every time you put another middleman between the label and the store, you can count on an additional vig of about 5%. So if you're a two-deep label, the vig is a bit higher (25%), and if you're a three-deep label, a bit higher still (30%). The farther away from the trunk of the tree you move, the wider the spread between what you make as a label and what the record sells for in the store.

❧ Deductions

Once the distributor passes the $9.60 on to the label, the label will try to keep its overhead down in order to increase its profit margin. But there are some deductions that it has no control over.

To the Writers

In the previous publishing chapter, we looked at mechanical licenses and the

[1] Note: They do not pay on records shipped, only sold. The distributor will then apply the same reserve and return clauses to the labels it distributes that those labels apply to their artists. See "Returns, Reserves, and Cutouts," page 61.

[2] Retail stores can be just as sleazy as anyone else. Sometimes they don't pay their bills. However, they dare not screw with a Big Five distributor, lest they not receive the big artists that sell millions of units. See "The P&D Deal," page 111.

compulsory rate of 8 cents per song that's paid to the writers. Here is where it comes back to haunt the record company.

The law requires you, the label, to pay this fee to the owners of the copyrights you're reproducing. But what if the artist you sign turns in a master with 20 songs that are all 30 seconds long? Will you then be required to pay .08 x 20 songs, or $1.60 in licensing fees per record? Well, fortunately, although the law says you have to pay this fee, it doesn't say exactly when or that the author can't give up the right to receive the fee.

Usually the record company will ask the writer/artist to do a ¾ rate of the 8 cents, or 6 cents, and also to keep the royalty applicable to only ten songs.[3]

If the artist on the record is not the writer of the songs, then the record company will have no leverage in asking for a ¾ rate and will have to pay the full rate of 8 cents per song. This would increase their deduction from 60 cents to 80 cents—a 20 cent difference. This may seem trivial, but it adds up to a lot when you have a record that sold several million copies. Based on this, it's easy to see why labels prefer artists who write their own material.[4]

And what about the artist who samples other people's records? Should you, the label, be asked to pay those licensing fees as well? If you agreed to this, then an artist could just turn in a record with no original material and the label would have to pick up the bill. To act as a deterrent to this, labels of late have been adding up any additional licensing fees that need to be paid to copyright owners other than the artist and deducting them from their all-in licensing fee.[5]

The ¾ rate for a package of ten songs brings the total deduction to 60 cents, leaving $9.00.

To the Artist

Eventually, the label will have to pay the artist his or her 83 cents and the producer his or her 27 cents,[6] but only on 90% of sales,[7] which brings us down to $7.90.

To the Musicians

There is a fund established by the Musicians' Union, the AFM. (American Federation of Musicians), on behalf of all musicians who play on records. They take 5% of retail,[8] or about 8.5 cents, bringing the record company's share down to $7.81. This fund is important for two reasons: (1) It supposedly gets distributed to the musicians who perform on the sessions.[9] (2) If they don't pay into this fund, then as per their agreement with the union, the record company is not supposed to be able to register the title with the RIAA for gold and platinum certification.[10]

[3] This means that even if there are 11 songs on the record, the writer/artist will only be paid for ten.

[4] See "Publishing Deals," page 69.

[5] See "Sample Rights," page 72.

[6] See "Recoupable Financing," page 55, for a complete breakdown of this.

[7] Unless it's a two-deep indie, in which case the current industry norm is 100% of sales.

[8] This calculation is very rounded. The real calculation is rather complex and based on the amount of units sold and at what price. It also doesn't kick in until at least 33,000 units are sold, making most indie releases exempt.

[9] See "The Musicians' Union," page 36.

10 (From previous page.) Although there are ways around this, too; see "How To Get Even," page 230. And since the RIAA is far more interested in pleasing the record company than the union (since the record companies are the ones keeping the RIAA's lights on), this becomes an unenforced provision.

11 Writer/artists and producers used to be able to look forward to getting paid full rate and given larger percentages of sales on smaller "indie" label deals. However, this trend is lessening due to the consolidation of labels and the "new economy." A full description is given in "Publishing and Royalties," page 116.

12 However, since the direct distribution label is wholly owned by the Big Five distributor, it keeps the $2.40 for which it sells the record to the store, so its profit is really $7.32. The $2.40 vig is recorded as profit for the distribution branch, however, not the label branch.

Giveaways, Returns, and Special Programs

Without freebies and giveaways, the new artist doesn't stand a chance. Even though the record company takes this into account when they only pay on 90% of bona fide sales, it still comes out to more than that for them. About 18% of all new-artist records sold will be deducted as giveaways; this amounts to about $1.80 per record, bringing the bottom line down to $6.01. In reality the record company makes money on only about 50% of the records they manufacture, even on the artists that *sell well*.

Packaging and Manufacturing

Finally, remember the cost that the record company charges the artist, at about $4.50 per unit, called the *container charge*? Well, if you have a friend that has ever put out an album out of their garage, they can tell you that the real unit cost of manufacturing the CD is about $2.50, and that's without pressing tens of thousands of units. At the level that Big Five distributors reproduce CDs and tapes, the real cost

EGGHEAD BOX #4

Where does all the money go? A breakdown of costs to the label.

	Direct distribution	One-deep distribution	Two-deep distribution
Distributor's price to retail	$12	$12	$12
AFM's piece of the action	$ .085	$ .085	*Exempt* usually due to low volume (under 33,000 units sold)
Wholesale (distribution) vig	$2.40	$3.00	$3.60
Mechanical license (to songwriters)	$0.60 (¾ rate)	$0.60	$0.70[11]
Artist's royalty	$0.83	$0.83	$0.83
Producer's royalty	$0.27	$0.27	$0.27
Giveaways (free goods)	$1.80	$1.80	$1.80
Duplication/packaging cost	$1.10	$1.10	$1.20
Gross profit to labels before overhead	$4.92[12]	$4.32	$3.60
Gross profit to labels since 1998[13]	$4.37	$3.92	$3.20

is somewhere between 80 cents and $1.10. Using the high number of $1.10, our total distribution vig is $7.08 and the balance averages out to a grand total net of $4.92. Please refer to Egghead Box #4.

Now let's re-examine the record deal from the label's point of view. From the profit displayed in the chart above, the record company will have to pay its salaries and rent. A biggie like Warner Bros. Records, which carries overhead in the hundreds of millions of dollars per year, must sell tens of millions of records just to break even.[14] However, the label pays the artist/writer a royalty of 83 cents based on the *full retail price* of the record and another 60 cents for the songs. That's a total of $1.16 going to the artist (provided that he writes his own songs). The artist nets almost 25% of what the label nets, yet the artist puts up zero dollars for the production and promotion, and their overhead is infinitesimally small compared to that of the record company. From the label's point of view, this must seem outrageously generous of them. Think about it. I go into business with you. I start a corporation, hire hundreds of people, put up 100% of the capital, incur 100% of the risk (and records are plenty risky), and you get 25% of the profit for playing in night clubs and hanging out in recording studios. Not a bad deal. Add to this the fact that 90% of what I, as the label, invest in will fail to sell enough records to float my boat. So, one successful artist has to compensate for all the losers on the roster. This reality forces labels to adopt a rationale that dictates many of their decisions:

It's more profitable to have one artist that sells millions of records than to have several that sell hundreds of thousands.

The reason for this should be fairly clear. Once you have a proven formula, it's easy to repeat. Each new band comes with new idiosyncrasies, new risks, and new marketing decisions. With that in mind, we turn our attention next to the marketing department and its point of view.

❷ Image Molding

Did you ever notice that a band that you know from the club scene looks drastically different after they have signed with a major label? This is due to the marketing department and its recommendations for the band's image. The marketing department will assign an *image consultant* to turn the five kids who look like they might mug you into five kids that look like they could mug you but can afford not

[13] (From previous page.) These figures are taken from the previous edition of *Confessions* and demonstrate that despite all the new economy hoopla, record companies have not increased their profits substantially in the last five years, while other industries have seen higher gains percentage-wise.

[14] As a generalization, major labels' payrolls tend to run into the millions per month. Smaller major labels are in the ballpark of $750,000 per year, and the two-deep baby labels are typically about $200,000 to $500,000 per year.

to. All this is done in the name of trying to sell more records by making the band look more hip, cool, or whatever to the public. What the producer is to the band's music, the image consultant is to the band's look.

It has been my experience that record company philosophy leans toward the opinion that music purchases are largely impulse/tactile buying decisions where people see a record in the store, and if they like the packaging, they grab it. (An impulse buy, in other words.) This feeling is substantiated by the rise in sales following the release of promotional material such as videos. The visual imagery of the band and its logo or images that are in the video touch a nerve, the buyer reaches for the record, and a sale is made.

Nobody can argue that the band's looks will not play a role in a buying decision. Unfortunately, the band, left to their own devices, will rarely have the marketing savvy to design their own wardrobe. In fact, they usually reject such ideas as a sellout.

A Bit of History

This practice of "dressing up the act" is nothing new. In fact it goes back to the dawn of the pop/rock music industry in the early 1950s, when record companies wanted to sell rhythm and blues, a form of African-American ghetto music, to the

---

POP QUIZ

On the left are some names of pop singers you've probably heard of. On the right are their real names. See if you can match them up.

Bo Diddley	Gordon Sumner
Sting	McKinley Morganfield
Taylor Dayne	Ellas Bates
Muddy Waters	Declan Patrick McManus
Elvis Costello	Leslie Wonderman
Lou Reed	Louis Firbank

Answers to Pop Quiz: Bo Diddley = Ellas Bates, Sting = Gordon Sumner, Taylor Dayne = Leslie Wonderman, Muddy Waters = McKinley Morganfield, Elvis Costello = Declan Patrick McManus, Lou Reed = Louis Firbank.

IS IT A TAPAS OR AN APPETIZER?

Latin rocker Richie Valens's most famous hit, "La Bamba," was the first song recorded in Spanish to enter the Top Ten. Interestingly enough, Richie's real name was changed by the record company from Richard Stephen Valenzuela, and he didn't speak a word of Spanish.

record-buying masses, which were largely white suburban kids between the ages of 15 and 21.

The institutional racism of that time was unfavorable to African-Americans, and record company executives knew that parents would never let their sons and daughters have LPs in the house with pictures of black people on the cover. So they went about trying to market rhythm and blues to the white market. The result was artists

AGE BEFORE DUTY

Youth plays an important role in the artist's commercial viability, so many artists misrepresent their ages in order to keep their youthful appeal. Perpetually 30-something Madonna is the classic example. Another example is LaToya Jackson, whose press releases still claim that she is in her thirties. She's hoping we'll all forget that she is Michael's *older* sister (born in 1955).

In researching this section I sent my assistant to the library to confirm some facts. She scanned through *The Unauthorized Autobiography of Michael Jackson* looking for some info on LaToya. To her surprise the several pages that mention LaToya's name were torn out.

Trips and phone calls to other libraries yielded the same results. In several public libraries across America, the same set of pages had been torn out.

Could Michael be trying to hide something? Certainly he has the resources to have someone go around and do this. Or perhaps it's just a jealous fan.

like Elvis Presley and Jerry Lee Lewis, some of whose tunes were written by black artists; these were sped up a bit and called "rock 'n' roll."

Over time, rhythm and blues separated itself from rock 'n' roll and became known as R&B (industry slang for "black music"). Jazz and bebop, originally called "jungle music" by many a white parent in the 1950s, has not only found acceptance in the mainstream market but is now considered a national treasure.

Almost all American pop music started out as "black music" (a more polite term than some that were used in the early days) and was supported by black audiences before becoming economically viable for big record companies to invest in. Once they did, singers changed color, as did the backup bands. Another example of this is disco, which was funk gentrified for the mass market, and hip-hop, which is rap combined with R&B for the masses.

Rap and hip-hop, the most recent example of the above, needed to be marketed with a crossover audience in mind before the genre could gain widespread acceptance. Producers of the megastars New Kids on the Block must have been in tune with this reality. Groups like Color Me Badd were directly influenced by black groups like Guy, and many critics called the Beastie Boys a white version of Run DMC, among others.[15]

Anyone who has been listening carefully and critically to music for more than

[15] This not to imply that the race of the band made the music of any less quality. (I'm a big Beastie Boys fan.) The point I'm making is that the music was *no different*, only the packaging, and that the repackaging radically affected sales.

WHERE'S MY FLANNEL?

The term "alternative rock" started in the late 1980s, when rap, R&B, and country completely dominated the market. Rock bands were becoming too expensive to promote, and trade magazines ran articles about how rock had finally died. The only radio stations that were playing "band-oriented rock" were the college stations and the smaller underground stations, usually referred to as "alternative stations."

Little by little these stations started to gain a larger listenership, proving that rock was alive and well but was now part of the counterculture again instead of being in the mainstream as it had been in its heyday in the 1960s.

Today there is nothing alternative about alternative rock. It's just as mainstream and just as heavily marketed as all other forms of pop music. But the terminology has stuck.

ten years can easily see how the pattern of recycling and reusing old formats of music works. What makes the recycling process possible is how the music is marketed each time around. This, more than anything, is probably why the over-35 generation tends to think that the new music sucks. It's because they've heard it before in a purer form, ten or 15 years ago.

Don't think that bands are not in touch with this process as well. Super-groups could not continue to make smash records without understanding the formula for why their music works. Those who understand the realities of how the public perceives the artist usually profit greatly. Those who refuse to accept this reality rarely profit at all.

❷ Sponsors

Speaking of reality, you may have noticed that lately superstar artists have become synonymous with certain brand names of soda, liquor and long-distance telephone services. Wow—we've come a long way since artists refused to allow their

---

TECH ME TO THE RIVER

One example of image molding that I was witness to occurred when I was working on a rave album.

Techno was just starting to fly in 1991, and this fellow, whom I'll call Barfly, approached me to do a demo with him. We recorded it in my home studio, and Barfly got some money from a label with a one-deep distribution deal with MCA, selling them with the story that the record was produced by a Czech DJ in his basement studio in Prague. They bit.

When the record came out, my recording studio was not credited, nor was I listed as a cowriter or producer. Instead, the studio and all other credits reflected a production that originated in Prague.

Barfly said to me, "Kids don't buy techno records made by two over-30 guys who live in Queens." I was a bit ticked off at first. Then the next year I witnessed a fistfight that had broken out at the New Music Seminar about whether "true" rave music had come from Cleveland or Europe.

Barfly, if you're out there, you were right.

---

music to be associated with something as benign as a shoe company for fear that they used third world labor to make their product.

These days it seems that unless you can find a corporate sugar daddy to slip a few million in your liner notes, marketing your record on network TV is a pipe dream. This is probably a serious legal antitrust riddle, but it does go on. Companies like Proctor & Gamble, Seagrams, Johnson & Johnson, Coke, Pepsi, and phone giants AT&T, Sprint, and MCI basically own the airwaves when it comes to network TV advertising—which is still, even after 35 years of cable TV penetration, the most effective form of marketing.

A 30-second spot on network prime time is so costly even major labels, who spend millions on radio spots, don't go near the little screen. Instead, they look to slip in the back door by partnering up with some of these corporate giants and get the artists to do endorsement deals. The labels do not get the sponsorship money, but they enjoy a benefit, because every time a grungy rock tune by your favorite alternative band underscores a quirky AT&T commercial, it translates into record sales. Many, many of them. So to the label, it's free advertising. The artist gets millions from this type of exposure with no down side (except for the possibility that in the next life they might come back as an ad executive).

In the near future you can count on more co-op sponsorship deals, especially now that the Big Five are doing everything they can to recapture the perceived value of their product—the $18 CD. Soon CDs will be bundled and "given away" as part of promotions for things like BMWs. When this becomes an important consideration, not only will an artist's image play a significant role in their signability, but so will their willingness to play a direct, proactive role in selling products with their music.

CHAPTER NINE

>The Single

T he use of the word "single" has changed dramatically over the years. Throughout the '60s, records were sold in two forms: the 12-inch 33⅓ rpm LP[1] (usually containing eight or ten songs) and the 7-inch 45 rpm single (which had only one song on each side). A record company would introduce a new artist by releasing a single. If this did well, a second single would follow, then an LP that contained both singles and several other new songs put together on one disc.

Today, the 7-inch record is almost defunct. Record companies tried to adapt the concept to CD singles, but they were too pricey and defeated the concept of a random-access medium. Cassette singles were the prevailing source of single sales, but they have started to taper off lately as well. Only some college stations still consider 7-inch records *cool*—and even this diehard trend will have its limits. So what is a single today?

Even though A&R still uses the phrase "put out a single," this rarely refers to a separate CD or 7-inch that has one song on it. "Single," in today's A&R parlance, means the one song that will be used to promote/launch the record. It is the one song that they will push to radio and, in most cases, the one that will be made into a video for MTV and the other video networks. This is usually done by creating a promotional EP ("extended play") record, a CD

[1] rpm: revolutions per minute. LP: long-playing record. An LP plays for a total of 40 minutes. This may seem silly now that CDs can hold over an hour, but this was a marked improvement over the 78 rpm record, which only played for about 10 minutes.

[2] Another outmoded term: a "side" was once a song that occupied one side of a single—or before that, one side of a 10-inch 78 rpm record.

containing about four "sides,"[2] all edited to no more than four minutes in length and sent only to radio stations and promoters.

When industry people say, "I don't hear a single," they are saying that not one song in the artist's repertoire will be usable as a marketing tool. This is not said lightly, and it's a bad sign for the new artist.

❯ Who Picks the Single

Wars have been fought over the crucial decision of what song from an album will be the single. Artists often feel that they are best qualified to choose how the public will first perceive them. Record companies usually disagree. Marketing a song is the most expensive part of promoting an artist for a record company.

I've seen both sides of this argument struggle to the bitter end. If the artist wins, the label will oblige them and promote the artist's choice, but rarely with the same enthusiasm that they would have if they were promoting their own choice. If the label wins, they end up with a less-than-enthusiastic artist playing an encore that they will in time grow to hate. Perhaps this is because the label's choice for the single is the song that the artist feels least represents what they are about.[3]

[3] For a frightening account of how this can end up, see the sidebar "Extreme Measures," page 182.

As a decision-maker at a record company, you should try to never let an artist dictate how you market your catalogue. This sounds a bit callous, but consider the alternative: How would it be if actors decided on their own hair, makeup, and wardrobe in a film (some do . . .), or if news reporters got to decide what the front page would look like? Perhaps you are the sort of individual who thinks artists should make these decisions. You are certainly entitled to your opinion, but I wouldn't recommend advertising this belief if you intend to raise money to start a record label.[4]

[4] Somebody, please prove me wrong!

❯ The Hit Parade Charts and the "Hit Single"

To the average person, a "hit single" usually means that the record is on the *Billboard* Hot 100 chart in one of the top ten positions. Most people assume that the chart is compiled by tallying up the record sales for that week or is based on the amount of airplay that the song has received. I think it would shock the average person to learn that until 1991 the *Billboard* chart had nothing to do with actual record sales or even airplay! Behold . . . .

Billboard or Bullboard?

"The charts," as they are called, are another form of advertising for the artist (and thus for the label). The prevailing industry attitude has been, if the song is on the charts, it might persuade people to buy the record. To the layperson I know that this must seem like the tail is wagging the dog, but if you've been following this book, you'd know that things tend to work a bit cockeyed in this industry.

Now, *Billboard* has always professed to be about album sales, and, in its defense, the magazine has reported the charts as accurately *as it can.* The inaccuracy comes from two weak links in the "chain of truth." First, until recently *Billboard* had no way of tracking actual record sales at the retail end. It used to rely on the shipping invoices of record companies and retail stores to determine which records were selling the most. As we have seen in other chapters, many records are returned from the retail stores, so shipping receipts are a very misleading yardstick to use.

The second problem with *Billboard* is who reports the sales information to them. Knowing that shipping is an unreliable yardstick, *Billboard* will call various record stores and speak directly to a shipping clerk or manager about what's selling that week. Unfortunately, these clerks can be easily corrupted. Rumors are rampant in the industry of how record company promotion departments offered concert tickets, promotional gifts, and outright bribes to stock personnel for "exaggerating" a bit to *Billboard*'s researchers.

If all this sounds like a big joke, it's no joke to artists whose careers depend on the perception of their record. Record companies use these charts to make important decisions about trends, which artists to keep, and which ones to drop.[5]

[5] Something that never ceased to amaze me was that even though most record executives in the 1980s would admit that the charts were manipulated, they would still use them to make "informed decisions."

LOOSE AS A BRUCE

The most blatant example of how misleading *Billboard* charts can be was the 1986 triple live *Bruce Springsteen* album, which opened up, in its first week of release, at No. 1 on the *Billboard* 200 chart of top albums. The retail stores reported an initial order of over two million units—instant double-platinum status right out of the gate. You can imagine the publicity that Bruce gathered because of this rare occurrence.

Unfortunately, many of those records shipped back several months later, unsold. *Billboard* has no chart that gives you that information.

SoundScan

In 1991 a small company called SoundScan perfected software that can read and tabulate the bar coding on the backs of CDs and keep fairly accurate records as to how many records are selling. *Billboard* charts now use the SoundScan system for determining which records are No. 1, No. 2, and so on. SoundScan also issues reports on a weekly basis with (somewhat) exact numbers as to the sales of each record on the top 200 selling records of that week. This report is available to anyone who subscribes to it. It is not a perfect system, in that it does not get complete information from small mom-and-pop stores (which can make up over a third of the sales on a major and half the sales on an indie release), but it's vastly better than the old system, which was vulnerable to graft.

In time, every store in the free world will be on SoundScan or a similar system, and then real sales figures will be available to anyone (including the IRS, which loves to audit the record industry). As these systems gain more popularity, record companies will have to find other methods of manipulating sales figures.[6]

Other Types of Charts

Billboard is not the only authority in the music industry, although it is the most prominent. Since the college alternative stations and mom-and-pop retail stores have become more prevalent, other magazines with their own charts have cropped up. The most innovative of these is the *College Music Journal* (CMJ) chart. This follows the college radio stations and uses SoundScan's figures to determine its chart placement. Because it is more of a grassroots publication, it services mainly the indie labels. But many A&R people at the majors consider it a more accurate source for what's selling on the street level. When an act rises into the Top 40 on the CMJ chart, you can be sure that a major label will take some interest in that artist.

Other charts are more exclusive, like the *R&R* chart, published only in *R&R* (*Radio & Records*) magazine. *R&R* is the No. 1 "insider's" information source, generally subscribed to only by VPs and higher A&R staff at major labels. If you've got a hit on the radio already and want to keep track of your record's progress on stations across the country, this is for you. It's very expensive and, unlike *Billboard*, is not likely to be available at your local newsstand. *Gavin* allegedly has the most trustworthy reporting regarding what's getting spun. Record execs love it, because unlike other charts, *Gavin* tracks "crossover" hits.[7] *Hits* includes an interesting chart not featured in the ones above: "Requests," a chart based on calls from radio listeners. *Hits* also features charts that are crossbred between radio airplay and retail sales.

[6] Actually, they already have. I have heard of one process, which I call sound-*scam,* that has cashiers being paid to run CDs over the scanner two or three times for each legitimate sale. The computer doesn't catch the error until the sales reports are already published in *Billboard.* SoundScan claims this is not possible, and I have not been able as yet to verify the accuracy of this report, but if this method doesn't work, trust me, someone, somewhere will figure out something else that will.

[7] "Crossover hit" refers to a song that has been entered into the regular play list on more than one type of radio station (or market), like an R&B song that "crosses over" to pop. Example: Run DMC's rap tune "Walk This Way" (which featured its original authors, Aerosmith) made a dent in both rap and rock charts.

⊗ Airplay & Webcasting

When you watch a video on MTV, it probably doesn't occur to you that you are watching a *commercial for a record*. Likewise, when you listen to the radio you believe that this has been designed for *your* enjoyment. Record companies, however, see it as for *their* enjoyment. The airwaves are the most effective way to advertise their product—the artist.

When a radio station or television station plays a song or a video, they are required by law to pay the songwriter a royalty of several cents per play. Isn't it curious then that the media has to pay an artist for helping them sell their song? How do they stay in business? Well, the answer is that, aside from charging advertisers to put their commercials on the air, they also charge the record company large fees to put their songs on the air. The pay-for-play fees can be much higher than the performance fees they are required to pay by law.

Isn't that illegal or unethical or something like that? The only fair answer is "yes

---

RADIO: THE SUPERMARKET OF THE MUSIC WORLD

The selling of any item where there is limited shelf space usually involves graft. My friend Shlomo managed a supermarket and told me that product manufacturers pay the supermarket a fee to have them put their brand at eye level on a shelf. They know that the average person will see their product first, and that the placement substantially increases the odds of outselling their competitors. Think this is dumb? Maybe this will sober you up: the fee for a major product in a major chain can run as high as $200,000 per month!

The shelf space in the record biz is *airplay*, which gives the public their "free sample" of the goods. The eye-level shelf space is pop radio, the format with the largest listenership. The only difference is that to pay a program director a private fee to put a song on the air is illegal. This doesn't seem consistent when you consider the supermarket example. Supermarkets are not required to inform the public that Proctor & Gamble paid $200,000 to be at eye level on the shelf.

---

and no." Accepting a covert fee in direct exchange for playing a song is considered bribery. The under-the-table money given to the radio station's program director is called *payola*.

A little history on the subject will explain a lot about what you hear when you listen to your favorite station.

Promoters and Payola

Since the dawn of rock 'n' roll in the '50s, record companies have known that radio is what breaks the record to the public. In the '60s, many stations consolidated, thereby creating a situation where there were fewer stations and thus less airtime. As with all supply-and-demand situations, competition (in this case the fight to get a song on the air) became intense, and the battle was fought with the major players' sharpest wits.

To outgun their competition, record companies hire independent promoters to "push" certain artists to the radio stations for a good position in the station's rotation (i.e., the list of songs currently being played). Why a station would cooperate with this system is simple to understand. It makes most of its money off advertising—selling products between the songs. In order to charge a lot of money for advertising, a station must have a large listenership. In order to have a large listenership, it has to play *the most popular songs*. But how can a radio station know that a new artist is going to be popular? It can't, but it can figure out how much exposure a new artist will get by the amount the record label is willing to spend on the artist's promotion.

"THIS RECORD HAS SUCH A SOUND, IT'S THE SOUND OF MONEY"

There is an old story from the days of 12-inch vinyl records that tells of an exchange between a promoter and a station manager (SM). The promoter would give the SM a recent release and ask him to play it next week in a prime slot. The SM would hold the record up to his ear and move it back and forth. If he heard an envelope sliding around inside the sleeve of the album, he would reply, "This sounds like a great record!"

Hiring an independent promoter used to cost as much as $250,000 per song for the label. For this fee the record label was assured that the song would be played on several top stations in a given territory. This guarantee was a lock because the promoter would bribe the station manager to put the song in the rotation for a week, or a month, or whatever he thought he could negotiate. If the label wanted national airplay, they would have to pay the same fee to a promoter in each region of the United States. This got very expensive. But that was all right with the labels; keeping the service expensive made it inaccessible to their main competition—the small indie labels.

The practice of using independent promoters is hard for artists to accept. They work for years to develop their sound and songs, and whether they become famous or have to go back to working in a warehouse all depends on some wise guy in loud clothing, chomping on a huge cigar, greasing a program director with a bribe. No wonder so many artists take drugs!

The irony of the whole thing is that after the labels have spent this ungodly amount of money, they don't even receive any royalty for the airplay. The only people who receive a performance royalty from airplay are the writer and publisher of the song.[8]

While the record company is spending hundreds of thousands to get the song on the radio to sell the record, the artist/writer gets about a hundred thousand dollars in performance royalties *per song*.

The indie promoter scam has died out a bit of late. The major indie promoters (not to be confused with indie record labels) were, for the most part, tied to the Mob. As the Mob's interest in the record business thinned out in the late '80s (due to government shakedowns and sales to multinational conglomerates) and as competition from new, more legitimate promotion companies sprang up, these grifters of radio promotion found new marks.[9]

Labels were slapped with large fines for racketeering and now, as a result, let the artists hire the independent promoters themselves. Even though it means more work for the artist, it also means that the artist has a bit more control over his or her career and expenses. In lieu of spending the big bucks on promoters, record companies are now free to come up with clever legal ways to promote records.[10]

What has been happening in the past few years is this: A promotion company would seduce station managers with concert tickets and prizes. These are charged back to the artist's recoupment fund as promotional expenses. It has to be done in the form of a rebate on merchandising, but make no mistake—it's a bribe. I remember one campaign for the 80s group EFM where the record company sent a promo tape around to every program director for their consideration. The tape came present-

[8] See "When the Producer Wants Publishing," page 84.

[9] The book *Hit Men* by Fredric Dannen tells some of the most intriguing stories in print about this corrupt era in the music industry, as does *Stiffed*, by William Knoedelseder.

[10] The new concept in artist promotion is for record companies to buy blocks of airtime to promote a new release. This would function just like an infomercial. This is not only legal, but it takes the guesswork out of radio promotion, and it's much cheaper. This was the technique used to launch the band Limp Bizkit in 2000. It worked quite well.

ed in a top-of-the-line Sony Walkman worth about $150, with the cassette inside the machine cued up to the single called "Unbelievable." The Walkman was considered packaging for a promotional demo. Uh-huh.

The reason for all this nastiness in getting songs on the radio is the hope that by pure repetition on the air, people will "learn to like the record," generating a sale.

IS THE INTERNET REALLY "FREE"?

How is it that at a time when media companies keep such close guard of their copyrights, a company called Napster, started by a teenager, managed to hold every major record company at bay and let millions of people make legal copies of popular songs for free? Napster allows two parties to share each other's files by streaming them through the Internet. But isn't that just a high-tech version of making pirated tapes in your basement?

The answers come from a glitch in the Copyright Act of 1976, which defines a "copy" as a duplication on a "fixed" medium. Radio stations do not pay fees for the use of a copyright, because causing a song to wisp though the air is not considered "making a copy."[11] Similarly, neither is "streaming" —moving data though the Internet pipeline. Streaming is not considered "making a copy" as defined in the 1976 Act. The person at the other end might be "making a copy" by storing it on his computer, but even this is arguable. And even if storing a song on your hard drive were considered "making a copy," the file-sharing service is not doing the actual copy-making—it's only providing the means for two parties to communicate.

As of this writing, file-sharing remains active, although Napster was required by a Federal judge to do everything in their power to try to prevent people from pirating music via their service. There has been some success in this area. Napster downloads have diminished now that the service is harder to use, but there are many other similar services that will be harder to discourage. New legislation will plug the hole in the old copyright Act, but this, too, will not be without challenge. Until all of this is hashed out, file-sharing sites—despite their obviously unethical behavior—are operating within the boundaries of the law.

[11] Radio stations pay performance fees to performing rights organizations, like ASCAP, BMI, and SESAC. These are not copyright fees. See: "Performing Rights Organizations," page 34.

There is plenty of marketing data to confirm that this can work, but here is a bit of solace for you purists out there. Although record companies tend to be very secretive about which promotion scams work and which ones don't, I believe in the Abe Lincoln philosophy, which goes, and I'm paraphrasing, "You can make most of the people buy a crappy record some of the time, and you can make some of the people buy a crappy record most of the time, but you can't make most of the people buy a crappy record most of the time." (SoundScan seems to back me up.)

Basically, you can't make enough people buy a record they hate no matter how much money you throw at it. Although it seems that major labels sure do try.

For those of you who have ever wondered why the radio doesn't play your favorite underground or indie band, you should now understand: It's because their label doesn't allocate the money to bribe the right people to play it. So the next time one of your relatives tells you that you should be a singer because your voice is so much better than "the junk on the radio," you can now explain to Aunt Sophie that it isn't *that* simple.

Net-Hype

Now that the Internet seems like the hip way to promote singles, record companies have become very clever; they are hiring scores of college students to "assist with promotion" by entering chat rooms and hyping up a new artist. They're not the only one doing this. Unsigned artists commonly bulk e-mail incentives to people to go to an online record company and "vote" or click on their single in hopes of inflating their apparent appeal. They know that A&R people watch these statistics to see who is getting attention. It seems to work. In the past two years, several large deals were "discovered" this way by major labels.

CHAPTER TEN

>The Independent Record Deal

The Birth of the New Indie

U p through the 1970s, record companies were entities that exploited their product largely through the leverage of their relationships with labor unions and radio conglomerates. Without a multinational company behind them, smaller companies were squeezed out of the pop music game. As we've seen in other chapters, the cost of promotion would escalate beyond a small company's ability to turn a profit, and the distribution channels that a small record company would use were owned by their primary competition—the major labels. In addition to this, the main source of advertising for a new record—radio airplay—was locked up by major label marketing scams, which included expensive promotional gifts to station directors.

Ultimately, an indie's catalogue would be bought out by a major label, if they were lucky. If they weren't lucky, the label, its groups, and its catalogue would disappear into obscurity.

But things have changed in the last ten years. The information age has caught up with the notorious informality of the music industry and has made it far more difficult for major labels to hide a mediocre product behind a tidal wave of publicity and payola.

1 Although labels claim that this 5% number is real, it is not. Even if not every artist turns out to be a super-star, the economics of major label deals are such that the label recoups their initial invest-ment in far more than 5% of their acts. So while they may not make a bundle on each gamble they don't loose too much ei-ther. You can't fly the CEO around the world in a Lear jet on 5% success ratios.

2 This doesn't include the so-called "bedroom labels," obviously. And, in addition, these labels sales are not tracked by the RIAA. See "The RIAA" on page 42.

3 This became abun-dantly evident when, in late 2000, labels almost lost control of the In-ternet as a distri-bution system. See the sidebar "Is the Internet Really 'Free'?" on page 104.

For the first time, any person who desires can have actual sales figures by sub-scribing to SoundScan. Lo and behold, the revelation of this has shown the indus-try that the major genre of music selling today is adult contemporary, of which coun-try music makes up a large part. (And all this time they wanted us to think that peo-ple over 30 didn't buy records.) Pulling in at a close second for the record buyers' attention is rap. In fact, one in three people in the United States who bought a new release in the late '80s and early to mid-'90s bought a rap record, proving its abil-ity to cross over into several markets. Rock and what's now called alternative rock are third place in the national market for the time being. This is up substantially from the mid-'80s, when you were hard-pressed to find even two rock songs on the pop charts at the same time.

According to *Pollstar* (an industry trade mag), there are about 4,500–6,500 ac-tive artists each year being distributed and promoted by major labels and/or their one-deep and two-deep labels. A standard formula for success in the record busi-ness is 5%, meaning that less than 5% of these acts make money for their compa-nies.[1] This means that the record sales industry, an eight-billion-dollar-a-year in-dustry in the United States, is being floated by 225 acts! But if 225 acts are splitting $8 billion, each of these is yielding an average of $35,555,555 a year, to their respective labels. This is highly unlikely.

A more likely figure is about two thirds of this, or about $23.5 million. Assum-ing for the moment that this is true, it means that almost $2.7 billion is going into the hands of *non*-major label affiliates, which I consider true indie labels. That's $2.7 billion going into less than a couple of thousand hands, which crunches out to approximately $1.3 million per year per label *on record sales alone*.[2]

In terms of catching the crumbs that fall off the plates of the big players, this is real money. As hundreds of acts get dropped from major label rosters because they're not cost-effective, indies are cleaning up, not only by keeping their over-head down but by homing in on the local market that made the band worth sign-ing in the first place.

Like a large ocean liner turning in the sea, major labels have been slow to re-spond to the iceberg visible on the horizon. Although they have tried to control the so-called indie market by employing the same "promotional" techniques with the college stations, they have been unsuccessful. The indie market refuses to subscribe to the pay-for-play attitude, and because of this the major labels have had a tougher time controlling this market the way they have pop radio for so many years.[3]

The main reason is that the parameters of each market change from city to city, and the radio personnel and website editors change with each new college semester. These uncertainties have forced major labels to all but get out of the artist development end of the business, leaving it to the indies, much the way the smaller independent production companies have produced nonunion films for half the money of a big studio.

Naturally, there are many exceptions to this. Major record labels still take enormous risks on new artists, but by and large they look to the indies the same way that the NFL and NBA look to the colleges for new talent. Today, more than 75% of the deals done with major labels are simple P&D (pressing and distribution) deals, in which the major takes a substantially smaller percentage than they would on artist development (P&D deals are covered in the next chapter).

This is the best service that their clout and power has left to offer the modern rock 'n' roll act, most of whom are looking for a bit more than a large advance from a label that eventually will drop them from the roster when they don't sell half a million records right out of the box.

CHAPTER ELEVEN

❯ The Independent Record Deal
from the Point of View of the Record Company

❯ The P&D Deal

Most smaller, true independent labels are actually production companies that have what is called a *P&D deal* with one of the independent distributors. P&D means "pressing and distribution." The distributing label actually presses and ships the records to the stores and charges the indie label a 25% commission. Unfortunately, the contracts for these arrangements are somewhat precarious. Indie labels often change distributors every couple of years. Sometimes it's for positive reasons: maybe the label has grown and is seeking wider placement. Other times it's because the relationship between the label and the distributor has collapsed in a sea of audits and accusations.

Even the stability of the distribution contract doesn't change the frightening costs that face the label taking risks on new talent. Considering the amount of money and person power it takes to sell a record, the indie label had better be very sure that it moves at least 25,000 units of a new title, or it will quickly become cost-*in*effective to keep its doors open. In this respect, indie labels function very much like artists: when dealing with their distributors, they have to compete with the other labels that are being shipped by that distributor.

That's why it's important for the band and their manager to be aware of what is called the "hot sheet."[1]

[1] Although we are discussing independent labels, this same competitive dynamic exists for one-deep and two-deep labels on Big Five distributors.

⊘ How Records Get to the Store: The Hot Sheets

While browsing through a record store, did you ever wonder how Tower Records, or HMV or any record store, knows what records to buy and put on their shelves?

One would think it's done in a logical manner—the store has a buyer for each department, and he or she is in touch with record labels. The label sends them all their new releases, and the store puts them on the shelf. When a title sells out, the buyer orders more.

If only it were that simple.

You see, record stores don't want to buy and stock thousands of records that don't sell quickly and abundantly. Their worst nightmare is having to ship back boxes of records from some new dog artist that nobody wants. The way to make money is to stock only records that *sell*. Well, this fairly obvious statement leads to the not-so-obvious query, "How do they know which records are going to sell?" Of course, artists like Mariah Carey and the Rolling Stones come with a certain guarantee, but what about new artists? How does the record store buyer know which new artists to pick up on and which to ignore? I'm glad you asked.

[2] See "Airplay & Webcasting," page 101.

Record stores follow the same logic as radio program directors.[2] They know that launching a new artist is very expensive. If the label wants the artist to reach a certain number of record sales, then they're going to have to spend a good amount of promotion money on the act. So a buyer for a record store, like the radio program director, will sit back and wait to see how much publicity and resources the label will allocate to a new artist. Using that as a yardstick, they judge what the label *really* thinks of the act. If they're putting a lot of money into them, the buyer will take a shot. After all, if it flops, he won't look bad in front of the boss.

The buyers for record stores receive things called *one sheets*. These are one-page posters that are ads for new records. The ads are not cheap. So if an indie label has taken the time to do one in, say, full color, it sends a clear message to buyers and program directors that they'd better get their orders in early or be embarrassed when it's a hit and they're out of the loop.

But it doesn't stop there. The promotion department of the label and the distributor will also call up the buyers and sell them on the act. They might offer them premiums and kickbacks to take a shot on a new artist (see "Marketing Mishigas," page 219). This is why the artist only gets paid on 75–85% of sales: The distributor will give away a lot of records to make the deal smooth with the retailer. The giveaways will register as sales on the books, but the label will not get any money for them because they were freebies. Even though the label doesn't get money for giveaways, many indie contracts require the label to pay the artist on 100% of sales. This is clearly unfair to the label, but you'll be hard-pressed to find people with a sympathetic ear for record labels' problems. The perception is that labels make fishnets full of money from unreported sales, so whatever the artist can get away with is okay.[3]

An indie distributor will handle anywhere from 30 labels to well over 100 at a time. Clearly they do not have the hours in a given week or the personnel to individually promote the five or six acts on *each* label they distribute. So each week they pick several acts that they will concentrate on. The sheet that has the names of these chosen acts is called the *hot sheet*. And, as an artist, you want to be on the hot sheet frequently.

How does an act get on the hot sheet? This is where the manager earns his 20%. The manager calls the label and the distributor every day and bugs the shit out of them until they include his act on it. Often it's as simple as that.

Buzz is the name of the game in the record biz. The strong buzz, the word on the street, is what sells the act. Generating a mystery and aura around the artist and their music is the yeast that raises the dough. With that in mind, here is yet another bit of record industry Talmud:

The best label for the band is the one that will be the most excited about putting out their record.

Here is where an indie can really excel over a major label. In a major label deal, the promotion department is responsible for pushing the record to the stores. A&R people are virtually useless for this part of the game. The promotion department of a label quite often does not want to deal with the A&R department's dogma about which act they should be pushing that week. It's a twist on the cliché, "Don't let the right hand know what the left hand is doing." Here the right hand knows, it just doesn't care. Meaning: it does a band no good if the A&R department of a major label signs the act and then the promotion department decides that it isn't cost-effective to push them. Or if the marketing department doesn't see how to get the act off the ground so they recommend dropping the act (see "Speed Trends," page 117).

In an indie deal, the promotion department and the marketing department and

[3] See "Clears, Cleans, and Fake Masters," page 177, and "Getting 'Cutout' of Royalties," page 62. Also, the reality of this has changed somewhat in the past few years. The unstable "new economy" has forced smaller labels in the food chain to form alliances with the bigger fish (safety in numbers). These deals come with a major caveat: They must accept the "structure" of the Big Five's contract, which almost never pays on 100% of sales for a new artist.

even the A&R department all have intermingled personnel, because people at indies usually wear several hats at a time. This knocks out a lot of red tape and makes the machinery work more efficiently. Remember, if a record on a major label sells 60,000, it's a flop. If a record sells 30,000 on an indie, it's a smash!

Majors can afford to sign an act, spend $500,000, and then drop it like a bad habit. Indies have to be more choosy. Because they need to be more selective about their investments, they tend to have more loyalty to them. As you'll see in the next chapter, an artist on an indie can oftentimes have the opportunity to make more money than on a major.

CHAPTER TWELVE

⊘ The Independent Record Deal

from the Point of View of the Artist

T he indie deal contract will read more or less exactly the same as the major label contract, except there will be less up-front money. This, however, can be a good thing. Most indie advances are between $5,000 on the low end and $75,000 on the high end. Taking the high end into our recoupment equation, we see that the artist is completely recouped after only 100,401 units.

EGGHEAD BOX #5

Artist break-even equation

Artist & Producer's share		Aggregate sum		Producer's share
$1.10x	=	$75,000	+	.27x
$ .83x	=	$75,000		

x = 90,361 divided by .9 [90% of sales] = 100,401

If the band is a hardworking act and plays out several times a month, they can actually see some royalty money before they are eligible for social security. I have known many situations where the indie band starts to see money long before the major label band because of this exact situation.

Also, the indie labels and two-deep labels tend to let the artist have more artistic control over the recording.[1] Despite the financial constraints, an indie is often the best place for a new act with a strong regional following.

> Publishing and Royalties

If you refer to the breakdown chart on page 90, you'll notice that the Mechanical Royalties paid to the artist/writer are somewhat higher on two-deep labels. On the surface this seems like a good thing for the talent, but there are a few pitfalls that you should be aware of.

A lot of indies entice artists to sign publishing agreements along with recording agreements by offering to pay "full rate" on the compulsory license (8 cents per song or 80 cents for the full album). In exchange for the full rate, the smaller label may pressure the artist to cross-collateralize the mechanical license with the album royalties. This is a bad move, but artists' lawyers allow their clients to do it every day.[2]

This means the writer(s) of the songs on the albums (almost always the artist on an indie record deal) will potentially make about 20 cents more per record. There is just one problem with this: Even though indie labels may agree to it contractually, they often don't pay artists mechanical royalties, and since they are rarely affiliated with the Harry Fox Agency, they are not ever going to come under audit, unless the artist him/herself initiates the audit.[3]

How can they get away with this? Simple. Follow this logic: An indie gives you, the artist, $5,000. You spend it on making a record. It sells about 25,000 units (a big number for an indie). This means you're entitled to receive, after deducting the $5,000 advance, $15,000 for your mechanical royalties. You ask them for it, and they say, "Be patient, we're having some cash flow problems." Instead, they offer you $10,000 for your next record. What do you do? They're offering to let you make another record and giving you $5,000 less than they owe you. Can you take the $10,000 for your next record and still insist they pay for the $15,000? Sure, but you won't be making any more records with that label. You could sue, but the cost of suing will eat up half of what they owe you. Most artists, in my experience, take the $10,000 and count their blessings.[4]

The above also holds true for record royalties. If they don't pay your royalties,

<hr/>

[1] Often this is because the label can't force the artist to hire a high-priced producer on the pittance of the advance they give them.

[2] See "Cross-Collateralization," page 63, and "Publishing Deals," page 69.

[3] I'm not suggesting that this happens frequently, but it does often enough. An important note is that so-called "online" record companies that offer cheap distribution often make the artist waive any mechanical royalty payments. See "The Harry Fox Agency," page 41.

there is little you can do about it. What's agreed to in the recording contract seems to be more a list of suggestions or an indication of good intentions than a set of hard-and-fast rules. Only if the artist gets tough or gets huge will the label hold up their end of the bargain.

However, this is a worst-case scenario. Reputable indie labels pay their royalties eventually, even if it's not every six months as the contract requires. They do this, if for no other reason, because most have hopes of someday attaining the prestige of being distributed by one of the Big Five.[5]

In order to achieve this, the indie label can't have acts on their roster suing them. Granted, this is not foolproof protection, but it does create some balance of power for the artist.

❷ Speed Trends

Probably the best reason for doing the indie label thing, if you're an artist in search of a contract, is the speed at which the machinery works. Consider the following fictitious example: Band A, Pavlov's Dogs, is signing with an indie on January 1st. Their friends are in band B, the Impulsives. They held out for a major label deal and got one. They too are signing on January 1st. Both bands have strong local followings.

February: Pavlov's Dogs are in the studio cutting the tracks for the record. By March it's finished, and by April it's on the shelves in a record store. Meanwhile, the Impulsives have just gotten the approval of their budget from the business affairs department and are finalizing the contract with their producer. They're scheduled to go into the studio at the end of April.

July: Pavlov's Dogs have sold several thousand records, have paid back most of their advance, and are planning a second record in December. They're packing the local clubs due to the notoriety of the record and its play on local college stations. The Impulsives are trying to find a remixer to finish the record. By the end of July, the record is finished and delivered to the A&R department for approval. A&R approves and the marketing department begins making its assessments.

Now it's December. The Dogs are starting their second record and planning a tour down the East Coast. The Impulsives' record hasn't hit the shelves—the marketing department has decided that they shouldn't try to break a new band during their fourth-quarter Christmas season, when most people are buying releases by the more established artists. The release date will not be decided upon until after the holidays.

4 (From previous page.) Some artists have sued their record/ publishing companies; you read about it from time to time. Sometimes it's to their benefit, but most often it's not. It's damn near impossible to get a deal on another label once you've sued the label that took a shot on you. This is not legal advice; it's just an opinion. Each case is different, and you as an individual must decide which battles are in the best interest of your career.

5 Not only do Big Five labels tend to have higher (usually about 5% higher) distribution fees and wider distribution, they also pay sooner and with more consistency. In addition to this, presidents of labels distributed by one of the Big Five make a shitload more on salary than they do running the label out of their bedroom.

6 See "The Hot Sheet," page 112.

By February of the next year, the Impulsives have made the hot sheet[6] and are being released. The label has started the radio promotion, and the stores are starting to stock the record in the front of the store. But the Impulsives have discovered that their pull in the local clubs will need to be rebuilt, because they haven't been around for a while. Meanwhile, Pavlov's Dogs have their second record out and it's selling about 2,000 units per month.

June rolls around. The Impulsives have sold only about 40,000 records and are trying to get on a national tour to help promote the record. The radio play has tapered off, and the record company is thinking about dropping them from the roster. Meanwhile the Dogs have sold about the same number of records between both of their albums, and their record company is enthusiastic. Their single has hit No. 35 on the CMJ chart, and the label has shopped their contract to one of the Big Five and has gotten some nibbles.

By December, the Dogs' contract is about to expire with their indie and they are speaking to a major about having their next record distributed by the major. The Impulsives have been dropped from the roster but are free to take any unreleased masters with them. They shop a deal to another major and even a few indies for a second release. Of course, they have realized no royalties because they didn't recoup their recording fund.

In January, two years after the initial signing, the Dogs re-sign their contract with the one-deep "indie" with the proviso that the record will be distributed by the parent/Big Five label. A major label has been noticing them climb the CMJ chart, and they're getting massive hits on MP3.com. They want to distribute the record. The band is in preproduction on a third album with a producer who believes in them and is working on a small or deferred fee. They now have a manager as well. The Impulsives are thinking about personnel changes within the band and are also looking for new management, because their manager doesn't want to work with little indies.

There you have two years in the lives of two typical bands. Of course, I've manipulated the story to make a point, but the situation here is more common than you might think. While the major label is stewing in red tape and procedure, the indie has gotten two records out on the street while the band is fresh, and created a strong buzz. This is no small point. This is the difference between a band that grows and one that comes out with a campaign that is too big for their market. In the Impulsives' case, they sold 40,000 records but flopped. The Dogs sold about the same and came out winners.

*Good sales are relative to the point of view
of the observer.*

**—Albert Einstein
(I changed it a little bit.)**

⊘ Super-Duper Cross-Collateralization

If you're considering signing with a two-deep or three-deep label, there is one major pitfall to watch out for. It's when one label is collateralized "inside" another—for example, the two-deep (or imprint label) collateralized inside the one-deep. To see how this works, let's return to the blackjack tables in the casino that I spoke of at the beginning of the book.

You're watching the table from the sidelines and you start to notice something strange. Big Charlie, who never leaves the table, is the house favorite. He knows everybody and everybody loves him. He has a huge stack of chips, and even though he's playing at the $2 table, he plays $50 at a time. Next to him is his little brother, Little Pete. Little Pete has borrowed $600 from Big Charlie in order to play, but he has a funny angle on the game as well. Instead of playing the one hand that he's dealt, he has found five friends and given each of them $100 to play five different positions at the table and kept $100 for himself to play. He figures that this gives him six chances to win. He's also made a deal with his five friends: they have to give any profit they make back to him. Once they have collectively given Little Pete enough money to pay back Big Charlie the $600 he borrowed, then they can start to take some profit for themselves.

So if player one gives Little Pete back $400 (a 400% return on his money) but the other players lose everything, Little Pete will be unable to pay back his total loan of $600 from Big Charlie. Therefore, player one gets none of his 400% profit, nor do any of the other players get any profit they made. Only if they collectively make enough to pay back Big Charlie do they keep whatever profit they individually earned.

This may, on the surface, sound unfair: borrow $100 and have to be responsible for how much money the other players pay back before you get anything? But for the players it's not a bad offer: If they lose it all, they won't have to pay back a dime to Little Pete or Big Charlie. It's risk-free money.

What a deal. There's a greater incentive to lose than to win. Where do I sign? The answer is, sign a two-deep or three-deep record deal.

Up until recently, many of these deals were cross-collateralized against the advance from the parent label that was financing the so-called "indie." If the small label didn't pay back its full advance, the parent label would take over all of the contracts and ownership. Like all takeovers, this was usually accompanied by cuts to the roster.

Let's say the fictitious major label used in this book, Pacific Records, has a smaller imprint label that specializes in dance music. This label is called Slam Records. Slam does big business, 50 releases per year. Suddenly they find themselves unable to adequately service their techno/rave market. So they set up a new label, XTC, and the head of A&R for techno/rave music will now become the head of XTC Records. The records put out by this label will carry all three logos: Pacific/Slam/XTC (see "Understanding Distribution," page 47, if you're confused).

The new president is going to get an initial advance of $700,000 to start XTC. This money will be divided up as follows: $200,000 for overhead and salaries, and the remaining $500,000 for the development of ten new acts. That leaves him $50,000 for each act. Remember that this budget has to include promotion for these records.

The first thing the new president will do is hire as many of his friends as he can get away with. The second thing he'll do is go out and find acts desperate enough to sign a deal with a cross-collateralized label. Since most of the acts that he will be talking to are young, inexperienced acts, they will usually accept any terms to get a first record out.

Most artists that have been around the block know and accept that they're going to have to work hard just to get a shot at a second record, but in the deal outlined above they're not getting what they're bargaining for. Study the casino example carefully and apply it to this very real-life scenario. They could work hard and sell thousands of records, but if the other bands on their label don't pull their weight, they could still end up with zilch.

In the event of this occurrence, which I call "indie label implosion," the parent company/major label would step in, trim the fat, and renew the profitable contracts. But what happens if the deal is not just two-deep but three- or even four-deep away from the distributor? If you're the artist on a four-deep deal, you might have to wait a long time before you see any royalties, even if you are selling many records. If you're a vendor for this kind of label, like a side musician or an engineer, you may have to wait months to get paid, if you ever do.

The good news is that most of this type of stuff went on in the '80s. In my experience, these days it only rears its head periodically in oddball indie deals, usually in the R&B, rap, and dance markets, and also on producer/production deals, which we will examine shortly (see "The Artist/Producer Production Deal," page 124).

One other question you might want to ask: What if the two-deep label loses their distribution contract after you are signed to them? It happens—often. If I were an artist signing with an indie label that was distributed by a major, I would want to know intimate details about their distribution contract and its stability. If I were the label, I would want to keep it confidential.

The point in each of these cases is that as an artist you should know who you're in bed with and what kind of protection they use. If you are considering doing business with a so-called "major label affiliate," you should understand that anything more removed from the main distribution arm than a two-deep label is, for all intents and purposes, a "production company or a vanity label."[7] And that's the subject of the next chapter.

[7] In some states, like New York, a company cannot file for a business license using words like "Associates" and "Partners" in its name unless there are actual associates or partners in the company. Unfortunately, there is no similar requirement in the record business. So, for example, a company called Magnum Records may never have produced or released a record. They could be anything from an accounting firm to a recording studio. Don't be lulled into a sense of security because a company has a prestigious-sounding name.

CHAPTER THIRTEEN

⊜The Baby Record Deal

S ince it is my guess that most of you reading this book are either up-and-coming artists or producers, or a new pro cutting their teeth on such a client, the "baby deal" is the most likely type of deal that you are currently looking at to get your career off the ground. For this reason I've devoted a good deal of space to the ins and outs of such a deal.

No matter what the size of the company, if an artist or group is being asked to sign over rights to their sound recordings or songs, it *is* a record deal. The only difference between a baby deal and a major label deal is the ability of the contractor to distribute the recordings. The two most common types of baby deals are:

1. The vanity label: a deal where the label is really a production company with one or two acts on it. They have no direct distribution and little money.
2. The artist/producer production deal: one where an artist contracts with a producer, without a record label as the intermediary. We have mentioned this type of deal a lot throughout this book, and now we'll look at it close up.

An important note: Rather than break up this chapter into distinct points of view, as I have with the other deals, I've argued both artist and producer/label points of view together on an issue-by-issue basis.

❯ The Artist/Producer Production Deal

There are three types of production deals between artists and producers. All of them have one thing in common—the artist is not signed to a distributing label. Some artists are savvy to the information in this book and have asked themselves, "Why should I give 88% of my profit to a label when I can make and distribute my own record?" For some of these artists, this is a very realistic question to ask. In fact, many recording artists make a good living distributing their own records off the side of the stage at their performances. These artists form vanity labels and sometimes contract a producer to act as a consultant in the production of their record. (We'll look at the pros and cons of this in the next chapter, "The Vanity Label.")

In this situation, there are three ways that the artist/producer relationship can be structured: (1) the mini-record deal, (2) the joint venture, and (3) as work for hire.

The Mini-Record Deal

The mini-deal is just what it sounds like. Here the producer signs the artist to his or her production company the same way a label signs an artist to their roster. The artist, at this point, is under contract to work *for* the producer. They show up when and where the producer asks them and do as many takes as the producer requests. The producer pays for everything. In exchange for the artist's services, the producer usually gets the same thing that a record company gets, roughly 85% of the record and a publishing deal with the artist for 50% of the artist's publishing, if the artist is a writer on the album. When the tapes are finished, the producer will shop the master to a major or indie label in hopes of getting distribution for the finished master recording. This can take on three forms:

1. Master buyout: This is where the record label buys the completed master recording and pays a fee about equal to the cost if they had signed and developed the artist themselves (about $25,000 per song). There is also a royalty to the artist and producer—usually 12–14% of the SRLP (suggested retail list price)—the same as if the record label had signed the artist initially.

The advantage here to the record company is that they don't take a blind risk on whether a new artist will deliver a good master (a "deaf risk," actually). They can hear a finished product before they buy. However, it's important to note that even though the label has bought the master, the artist is not signed to the label. They are signed to the producer's production company. The label signs the producer to a deal that is exactly like the one the artist would sign if he were signing directly with the label. The producer is called a "furnisher" in these contracts, because he is "furnishing" (or providing) the artist to the label. To ensure that the artist cooperates with this deal, the artist signs what's called a *side chain letter*. This letter states that the artist will perform exclusively for the label that the producer now has a deal with, even though they are contracted only to the producer. It's a bit confusing, but it makes sense when you get used to it. Perhaps the diagram below will make it clearer.

2. Master licensing deal: Same as above except that the record label doesn't own the master, they just own the license to distribute the master for a period of time. It's sort of like a trial basis or a lease with an option to buy. The money for these deals is substantially lower, usually a licensing fee paid to the producer/production company of $5,000-25,000 per song and 12% of SRLP.

Side Chain Letters
Flow of Performance Commitments

3. P&D deal: As discussed earlier. Here the producer is trying to take his production company up a peg into the realm of record company and will have a major or indie label just distribute the master.

The Joint Venture

The joint venture goes by several different names. I have seen cases where it is simply called a "production deal" or a "producer/artist deal," but this is too easily confused with what's described above, so for the sake of clarity I'm calling a joint venture any agreement where the artist and producer are on *equal footing*. In this scenario, the producer and the artist agree to share the finances and the responsibilities equally until the partnership is dissolved.[1]

A typical joint venture is one where the artist puts up the money to do the recording and pays the producer a minuscule amount (usually $300 or $400 per song as an arranging fee or producing/engineering fee) and 5% on the back end. The producer brings his or her expertise in producing records and industry connections to finish a master and get a record deal once the master is finished. A typical budget for something like this is about the same as an indie record deal—anywhere from $5,000 to $40,000.

Joint ventures are my favorite type of deals of the three mentioned here. The artist and producer have more clearly defined roles and are working together, not as adversaries, as in the artist/producer production deal and the work for hire deal, below.

The Work-for-Hire Deal

For the control freaks out there, this takes the opposite approach from the mini-record deal. Here the artist hires the producer, usually for a solid fee of $2,000 to $3,000 per song, to produce the recordings that the artist writes. Everything the producer does is at the artist's request and is owned by the artist. When the production is finished, the producer walks away with his or her money and has no claim on the master recordings other than perhaps a small percentage (3% to 5%) on the back end. Here the artist has the upper hand in paying the royalties to the producer. In my experience they will claim endless amounts of expenses before recoupment, just like the labels do to them.[2]

[1] The dissolving of the partnership is usually done at the insistence of a major record company wanting to sign the artist and not retain the producer for the record. See "Buyouts," page 138; and "Overrides," page 137.

[2] For the intimate details of the mechanics of this deal, see "The Vanity Label," page 131.

WATCH OUT!

It is not that uncommon that an artist who is signed to a production deal with a producer and has signed a side chain letter with a major label *and* has a good-selling record *makes little to no money*.

The label isn't required, under their contract, to give the artist anything—they pay only the "furnisher," who is the producer. The producer's company collects the entire artist/producer royalty (usually 12%–15%) and pays the artist their 9%. The record company also makes the producer pay a flat annual fee (usually about $12,000) to the artist. If the contract is a standard one, the producer will only have to pay out anything above the $12,000 to the artist *after* the producer has recouped his out-of-pocket expenses incurred in recording and promoting the recording. The producer could continue to claim *forever* that he hasn't yet recouped for producing the master, and so can't give the artist *any additional money*. This is how you hear about top artists who sell millions of records but get only a few grand for their efforts.

The artist's only recourse is to audit the production company. Not only will this destroy the relationship that exists between the artist and the producer, but just try and do it. Producers are not like record companies. They don't occupy huge offices. They are very small and mobile, and their money is easily converted into other entities. If you get my meaning.

By telling you this, I'm not suggesting that the mini-deal isn't a legitimate way to get a foot in the door—it is. If you're the artist, have your lawyer mention a *letter of direction* in the contract. This letter will instruct the record company to pay the artist their 9% royalty directly, bypassing the producer. If you are the artist, you should bring this point up to the producer when negotiating your production deal with him or her. If you're the producer, don't mention it at all. If it comes up, hope it goes away. If it doesn't go away, decide how badly you want this artist. Here's why: Some labels won't accept letters of direction. They hate it because it makes them liable for payments to both parties. (See "Letters of Direction," page 144. This is important; don't skip it!)

⊘ End-Zoning—
Cutting Out the Producer

It may seem from everything above that the producer has the lion's share of power when the artist signs a mini-record deal, but in fact the producer has several Achilles' heels. The act of cutting someone out of your deal involves a strategy called "end-zoning," named from the play in football where the fullback runs around the end to score a touchdown, bypassing the other players. Once the producer's work is finished, their contribution is the hardest to protect.[3] In many cases artists try to eliminate the producer after they get a deal on a major label. The customary way to handle this is with "go-away money," a fee paid to the producer to take a walk, after which the artist will record their major label debut with a new producer.

[3] See "Screwing the Producer," page 141.

This power play is rarely met with enthusiasm by the producer. Producers often develop attachments to the artists they discover. They didn't develop the act and incur financial risk just to take a walk before getting the chance to produce a major label recording. Producers may start to rationalize that their replacement is not right for "their" act. Or that the label itself is not the right label. They may even be correct. But right or wrong, if the producer is stubborn and doesn't want the go-away money, they will often kill the deal. Hopefully they will be successful in getting a better one, because the artist will have *no say in this decision*. In a production deal the artist is under the thumb of the producer for the life of the contract.

Informal Agreements

Sometimes artists can be very suspicious of producers who try to pin them down with exclusive agreements. If the producer believes strongly in the act, to ease their paranoia he or she may agree to produce and shop them without a formal agreement—sort of a handshake deal. I have seen many cases where once the label takes an interest in the artist, the artist then decides to dump the producer for a more prominent one. In this way artists are also capable of deception.

It is almost impossible for the producer to protect himself from this (see "Contraceptive Contracts," page 129). However, it should be noted that if the A&R man really wants the original producer, he will try all his powers of persuasion to make the band see that they should stick with what they've got. If he is unsuccessful at that, he will then turn to plan B, which consists of giving the band a list of producers that the label is comfortable working with. They will be allowed to interview and choose one of these or go back to the original producer. This seems fair, except that the A&R man has usually stacked the deck with inappropriate choices or ones he knows the band will hate for one reason or another.

This bit of skullduggery will usually result in the band doing one of two things: sticking with what they've got, or picking one of the stragglers from the list. Neither will make the band happy, and the net result is usually an album that lacks a certain luster. When the band is not happy, they don't perform well—it's that simple.

Contraceptive Contracts

Producers over the years have tried to write clauses into their contracts that protect them from the above effect.

Things like "finder's fees" have been tried in contracts to insure that the producer at least gets something out of the introduction he makes for the band. Unfortunately, in the states of New York and California there is a little snag in the law that makes it easy for lawyers to throw this clause out. The acquiring of a recording contract is considered the gaining of employment. The only people who are allowed to collect a commission from someone else's gaining employment are licensed employment agencies and business managers. Producers are neither.

To be an employment agency, many states require a person to incorporate and put up a bond of $50,000 to get a license. This is somewhat impractical for the start-up producer. This is why many attorneys of producers sometimes try to persuade their clients to have the band sign to a *management contract* with their client. In New York and Los Angeles, you need no license to be a business manager, therefore *anyone* is eligible.

But crafty lawyers try to protect their artist/clients by putting a small clause in the agreement that points out the producer/manager's limitations under the law. If you look closely at many management agreements and production agreements, you'll find a line that reads something like, "The manager is not a licensed employment agency, and the artist will not look to the manager for the purposes of employment."

This one line is the legal trap door that cancels out any finder's fees that the producer/manager might try to enforce.

Because the lawyers have gotten too clever on this issue, producers have tried other things to somehow marry themselves to the deal. Most of them have been unsuccessful. State laws are too mellow to deal with the standards and practices of the music business. Therefore, the best defense the producer has against being cut out is to maintain a good relationship with the artist. Or they could just hold onto the masters.[4]

4 See "Holding the Masters," page 139.

CHAPTER FOURTEEN

⊘ The Vanity Label

Until the mid-'80s, the vanity label was a bit of a joke. Usually it was associated with a trust fund kid living a rock 'n' roll fantasy or a bad pop act desperate to put out their own record. Today the vanity label has evolved into a serious force in the new music industry.

In the late '70s, vanities first showed their power by putting out the punk records that the majors thought were trash. While majors search for the "perfect" recording star, the little indies, with their ear to the street, are making cheap records and selling them through the mom-and-pop stores. Rap, in the mid-'80s, proved to be the next genre that had a life outside of the mainstream. Rap producers would make super-cheap records and distribute hundreds of thousands of them literally out of the back of cars all over urban areas.

In many cases these start-ups are run out of people's bedrooms until they gain some recognition. But don't let that fool you. Rick Ruben ran Def Jam out of his college dorm room. Below are a few rinky-dink vanity labels that have become contenders in the industry, and the releases that put them on the map.

Artist	Label
Mike Oldfield	Virgin
Run-D.M.C.	Def Jam (now Island Def Jam Music Group)
Superchunk	Merge
Discord	Minor Threat
Enigma	Charisma (now absorbed into Virgin America)
Heavy D and the Boyz	Downtown
Tsunami	Simple Machine
Veruca Salt	Minty Fresh (debatable)
various artists	SpinART

The up-and-coming producer is the type likely to be attracted to this sort of label. Perhaps they have several good credits either in the songwriting or the engineering department. Or perhaps they were the "good ears" of a known act. Sometimes they are studio owners or house engineers with a flair for producing.

The budgets in deals like this are so small that there is usually little or no producer's fee. Instead, the producer's compensation is derived *exclusively on the back end* and contingent on the hope of attracting a Big Five label to the act. The producer will be working hard, calling in favors and using all of his or her ingenuity to pull off the small miracle of getting a record completed for the measly $5,000 or $15,000 that they will have to work with.

As you will see, after pulling off this magic act, their reward is that they are the first person to be sacrificed if a big label *does* come knocking at the door.

Without a doubt the most common type of deal that the new producer or artist is likely to come in contact with these days is the vanity label deal. Earlier we saw how the artist, the producer, and the record company make up a triad of chicanery, each with their own agenda. (See chapters five, seven, and eight.) But in vanity deals, the artist and the record company are usually *one and the same*, thus creating only a two-sided conflict. This being the case, I am going to focus mostly on the producer's perspective here because it is the producer who is the most vulnerable.

⊘ The Virtual Budget and the Virtual Producer's Fee

Generally the producer will be asked by the artist, the artist's manager, or the production company/vanity label to prepare the budget for the recording. The artist rarely wants to bother with these details, plus the producer can probably get better deals on tape and studio time because he or she has ongoing relationships with the vendors. Still, there are many artists who insist on doing these administrative matters themselves. Some are afraid of kickbacks, and rightfully so.[1]

[1] See "Kickbacks," page 82.

Because the producer is putting his reputation on the line, if he's smart, he will want all the money for the project up front to make sure that the vendors (recording studios, rental companies, sideplayers, etc.) get paid. If they don't, he can kiss them good-bye as business connections.

There is one other reason why producers like to keep things "all-in" on these small production deals: their so-called fee is contingent on what they *don't spend*. If anything is left over, they get to keep it, much as with the all-in deal on a major label.

There is an interesting psychology that kicks in when the artist is negotiating with the producer. It usually goes down like this.

The producer will ask for a $3,000 fee and $7,000 for the recording budget (a typical example), making a total of $10,000 for the cost of making the record. The artist, thinking he or she is a savvy negotiator, will say, "Can't you come down on your fee?" Sometimes the artist will offer a bigger back end royalty in exchange. Here is where the producer's business head comes into play more than his musical head. The crafty producer will offer a compromise: "Okay I'll do it for $2,000, and we'll put $8,000 into the recording."

The artist will usually agree to this, thinking that he or she is getting more for their money. But, as you might quickly figure out, all that's happening is that the producer has found a way to scam $1,000 off the budget into his pocket and get his fee of $3,000 anyway. The artist, even if they are looking for this, will probably not be able to catch the experienced producer. Try as they may, the producer's receipts will always balance out at the end of the day.

Study the breakdowns of the two album budgets in the sidebar on the next page "Indie Recording Budget."

On the surface it seems that the artist is getting ripped off by the funny numbers in these two budgets, but consider these three rationalizations on the part of the producer:

INDIE RECORDING BUDGET

Below are two sets of numbers for the same project. One is the budget the producer submitted to the production company/artist. The other is the real budget that the producer kept to himself. The budget is for a $10,000 album. The rhythm section is to be recorded in a large studio live onto a small-format digital 8-track. Overdubs are to be recorded in a smaller studio and then mixed back at the big studio. Note: There is no stated producer's fee. (Special thanks to Dave "Bee Boy" for this contribution.)

SUBMITTED BUDGET

Basic tracks
Large studio at $1,000 per day
   for 3 days of basic tracks $3,000.00
Engineer at $300 per day
   for 3 days $900.00
Rentals, outboard gear
   for 3 days $1,000.00

Overdubbing
Studio—smaller overdub room
   at $500 per day for 3 days ..$1,500.00
Engineer for 12 hours per day
   for 3 days at $20 per hour $720.00

Mixing
2 days at large studio
   at $1,000 per day $2,000.00

Materials/tape...........................$180.00

Miscellaneous
Food, cabs, cartage, etc.............$800.00

Total $10,100.00

PRODUCER'S PRIVATE BUDGET

Basic tracks
Large studio for 3 days $2,750.00
Rentals, outboard gear $555.00

Overdubbing
Studio + engineer,
   home studio 8-track $700.00
Rentals, outboard gear $880.00

Mixing
Studio + engineer.......................$930.00

Mastering $750.00

Miscellaneous
Food $232.00
Transportation, etc. $95.00

Supplies
Drum heads, strings,
   pens, sharpies, etc. $50.00
Tape $360.00

Total $7,302.00

This leaves the producer with a surplus of $2,798. Here, the secret to the virtual producer's fee is in the kickback given to him from the engineer of the overdub studio and the owner of the larger basic tracks studio. Both have long-standing relationships with the producer and agree to do whatever was necessary to make the deal look good on paper.

BUDGET #2

Traditional 24-track recording with an "all-in" budget of $25,000; two-deep indie; small producer's fee. (Special thanks to R.C. for this one.)

SUBMITTED BUDGET

Basic tracks
Rehearsals for 1 week
in rehearsal room $600.00
Lockout for studio, 7 days $4,000.00
Tape (10 reels of 2-inch at
$150 per reel) $1,500.00
1 day in smaller studio...............$700.00

Overdubs
1 week in smaller
owner/operator studio.............$2,500.00

Mix
11 days at mix studio $10,000.00
Tape (5 reels 996, $50 per reel) ..$250.00
Rentals $1,000.00
DATs $60.00

Postproduction mastering
Digital editing, 32 hours $1,200.00
Sequence premastering,
4 hours at $40 per hour $200.00
Mastering,
4 hours at $175 per hour $700.00

Engineer/producer fee $3,000.00

Total $25,710.00

PRODUCER'S ACTUAL BUDGET

Basic tracks
Rehearsal in studio....................$560.00
1-week lockout in large studio $4,000.00
Tape.......................................$1,720.00
Tips..$50.00
Assistant...................................$140.00

Overdubs
2 weeks at smaller studio $2,600.00
Assistant $1,400.00
Maintenance fee...........................$40.00

Mix
11 days at studio $5,000.00
8 reels of ½" tape at $50 + shipping....$400.00
Rentals $450.00
DATs $88.00
Travel $200.00
Miscellaneous.............................$200.00
Mix engineer $1,000.00
Phone $100.00

Postproduction
Digital editing, 32 hours
at $40 per hour $1,280.00
Sequencing/premastering
at $40 per hour......................$200.00
Mastering, 4 hours
at $175 per hour....................$700.00

Engineering/producing fee....$4,000.00

Total $24,128.00

Rebate from tape return........$1,112.00

Adjusted total $23,016.00

Here the producer has managed to skim an additional $2,694 by doing two things. The first is the standard kickback arrangement we saw in the previous budget. The second is quite clever: The tape rebate is this producer's way of hiding additional profit. This is tape that was unused and was returned to the supplier for a credit. This credit will never be reported or passed back to the label as it should be. Artists and small companies rarely keep track of how much tape is used on a project. In the next budget to the next client, this producer will overcharge them tape costs as well, and again return the unused reels. Over time, the producer can build up quite a hefty reserve at the tape supplier. This reserve is eventually converted to equipment or cash.

1. The artist has no clue how much work the producer will have to put into the project in terms of his or her time or how much it costs to actually get things done. Therefore it is arrogant for the artist to assume that the producer is asking too high a fee in the first place. And although it might seem that a healthy chunk of money goes in the producer's pocket, when divided by the time it takes to produce something of quality, it still averages out to very little.
2. The producer promised to deliver a master for $10,000. So what difference does it make how much of that ends up in his or her pocket? The bottom line is, does the producer deliver a good master on budget?
3. The producer will probably never get the back end royalty promised by the artist/production company. Why? A diligent production company is supposed to remit accounting statements and receipts showing how many copies of the master were run off and sold. But they often "forget" or misplace the paperwork. And because the artist has no intention of hiring a business manager to keep track of the producer's royalty, who is really ripping off whom?

In addition to the above reasoning, the producer has expenses that the artist or production company will never want to hear about, such as their attorney (who will eat into much of the surplus profit), their general daily overhead, phone, stationery, equipment, and other things that he or she will be asked to "throw in" to make the deal viable.

⊘ Producer's Compensation Package

Since there is little or no up-front money on a vanity project, the incentive for a producer taking on a new artist on spec is the hope that he or she will be retained to produce the second album on the major label for a much higher fee. Artists generally agree to this in the beginning, but often wish they hadn't after the record is successful. Money-making masters are rare, and now that they have one, they don't want to be beholden to a particular person. Since the producer is aware that they are likely to be ditched like a dress on prom night, they tend to ask for a slightly overreaching compensation package. Let's check it out.

5% Royalty

The indie producer shouldn't be afraid to ask for a little more than the usual 3% of the SRLP. Five percent of the SRLP has always seemed fair to me, the logic being that in a standard record deal the artist is getting 9% and the producer 3%, or one third of what the artist gets. Since the artist/label will be selling the record themselves and keeping over 60% of the net profit, 5% seems *more* than fair. And since the producer is not getting an advance of any real size, I also feel that it is fair to ask for payment of this royalty to start from the sale of record one (instead of waiting for the artist to recoup their expenses, as in a major label deal).

Overrides

In the initial agreement with the artist, the producer should ask for an overriding percentage of the artist's second record (hopefully being produced on a major label) and sometimes the third as well, even if he or she doesn't get to produce it. The override is usually 1% (1 point).

From the artist's point of view, this is burdensome. Once the artist is on a major label, the all-in royalty package will be 12 points, with 3 going to the next producer. Now, the artist will have to find a producer who will take 1 point less; otherwise the artist will have to dig into their 9 points to give the next producer the 3 points that he or she will want. This will cut down their money substantially.[2]

Why does the producer feel justified in inconveniencing the artist in this way? Is it just because he feels he can bully them into it? No. Here's why.

In many such start-up cases, the producer is bringing more credibility to the project than the artist, especially if it is a production deal or if the producer has several platinum albums to their credit. But no matter how good the record comes out, the fact is that it probably won't sell more than 100,000 even if the band is extremely lucky. New artists on major labels rarely sell more than 60,000 units on their first record. That means it will lose money from the artist's and producer's point of view.[3]

However, even with low sales, the major label is likely to give the artist a second shot with a new record and probably a new producer. This record will have more of everything: more money for production and more money to promote the record. Simply by the law of averages it will probably do better than the first record. The second producer will make more than the first simply because of their position in the game. The producer of the third record will make even more, and so on until the popularity of the band starts to diminish.

But what of the first producer? They tend to feel that the first record is the launch

[2] Sometimes the record label will give up the point from their side if they feel the situation warrants it. But they don't have to.

[3] See "The Major Label Deal from the Artist's Point of View," page 53.

point usually forgotten about by the third album (where most pop acts start to break the Top 40 barrier). This is why the first producer will feel justified in asking for the override on the second album if they do not get to produce it themselves.

Buyouts, or the "Screw You" Clause

Sitting right next to the override clause in most contracts is the "buyout" clause. This comes into play when the artist doesn't want to continue working with the producer under *any* circumstances. Instead the producer is given an amount of money to take a walk. This is often called "screw you money" or "go-away money." Despite the harsh terminology, it is a welcome friend to both sides.

"Go-Away" in a Production Deal

A production deal, however, has a different dynamic. Here the producer is bringing the act to the record company and is contractually tied to the artist for the life of the deal. But sometimes the label may want to sign the artist with the intention of bringing in another producer with a better track record. The "go-away" fee in these deals takes the form of the producer/production company selling off the artist's contract.

❯ The Producer as a Virtual Partner

After all the above, the artist will undoubtedly think of the producer as a thief—asking for 5%, or a nonrecoupable advance, or a record one payment, or an override on the second album whether they produce it or not, or a percentage of publishing. But remember, the odds of the producer collecting *anything* on the back end are *slim to none*—and as you will see in the chapter Who Earned What, of the three parties we're examining here, the producer makes the least off a successful record.

Artists love to bitch about how the producer drove a hard bargain and asked for more than he should have. What they are forgetting is that a producer is not a partner in the act's profits, even though the artist's manager might try to imply otherwise. The producer doing *work for hire* is an employee of the artist. In trying to get the producer to "be reasonable," the artist usually makes him feel he is part of a team with lines like, "If it hits, we'll *all* be rich."

If that were true, then the producer would receive an equal share in *everything*—

as in a joint venture. "Everything" means publishing, any and all advances, merchandising, and so on. But just try to actually ask for this as the producer, and you will soon find yourself looking for a new client. It's a double standard that seems impossible to shake.

The fact is that if the artist's record hits, the producer makes the least money, because he won't share in any money made from personal appearances, publishing, or any subsequent records (unless he has an override). So if you are a new producer and unless you need the practice producing an act, get a good deal *up front*. Don't let vanity labels or artists guilt you with sob stories and bullshit about "industry standards." I'll bet most vanity labels learned about industry standards by skimming through a 1992 edition of *This Business of Music* that they forgot to return to the public library for the past decade or so.

❷ Where's My Contract?

It's not uncommon for small recording projects to start and sometimes even be finished *before* a contract is signed. This is bad for all parties, but it happens a lot. The reason it happens is because contracts are expensive and neither side wants to pay for one until they hear some positive results. One could spend $1,000 negotiating a production agreement only to find out that the producer and the artist can't work together. In major label deals, these things tend not to be issues, because producers have track records and the artist is usually happy to get someone with good credentials to work with them. But in the indie world and particularly the vanity label world, the norm is for *all* parties to be new at this stuff.

The net result is that everyone works on good faith with a handshake or a memo agreement binding the deal. When the project is halfway done and it is proving to be fruitful, then the investment in a contract is justified. Vanity labels have been known to wait until after there's an offer from a label before finalizing the deal between themselves, the artist, and the producer. This leaves the artist and the producer floating out in "legal limbo" until the lawyers sort it all out.

❷ Holding the Masters

Invariably it's the producer who stands to lose from the informality described above. In order to keep the deal rolling along smoothly, he has "gone along with the good faith vibe." Especially if everyone involved is a drinking buddy. Rarely do people set out to con anyone, but somehow when the dust settles, the producer, who's the most vulnerable, is usually left out in the cold. There is one sure way for the producer to protect him- or herself: *holding the master recordings*. It's my advice to new producers to retain the master recordings and all the finished mixed master tapes until a formal and final contract is signed between the producer, the artist, and the vanity. Whoever has the masters controls the destiny of the project.

The vanity and the artist will bitch and moan about this and once again turn to dogma about "industry standards." The producer should articulate that it's a good and ethical business standard to have a written and signed contract *before you start work*. Therefore, it is not an unreasonable request to hold on to the masters as collateral; this is the only bargaining chip that the producer will have in ensuring that the vanity keeps their word.

◈ What You Don't Know *Will* Hurt You

One bit of power that the smart producer has in his arsenal is the fact that most artists and small vanities are not very familiar with the copyright law and how it protects authors. While everyone is busy arguing about publishing and points, they are completely ignoring a common legal opinion—that the producer is also an author, an author of the *sound recording*. This is accepted as true whether he's given up the masters or not.[4]

This is no small point. I have seen many deals where the vanity or the artist tried to cut out the producer by never forwarding his contract to him. They believe that by not formalizing the agreement they could leave the producer stuck in a "he said, she said" kind of argument. What they are not understanding is that without the producer's signature on a release, no one is free to exploit the master in any way—including making copies for shopping a deal.

The Copyright Act of 1976 implies that three people control the authorship rights of a master recording: (1) the artist, (2) the party that puts up the money (record label), and (3) the producer of the recording, unless the producer has signed a work-for-hire agreement with the entity that paid for the recording.

In any standard licensing agreement or master buyout, there is an *indemnification clause*. This means that the person who is selling the master to the label is warranting that the master is free of any claim of rights by any third parties. If the scamming artist in our example tries to cut out the producer and license the master to a label, the producer can prohibit its use unless they get him to "sign off" on his portion of the rights. If the producer has not given up his rights expressly, then

[4] Authorship of the recording should not be confused with the authorship of the songs themselves. See "Sound-Alikes" and "Sample-Alikes," pages 171 and 173.

any artist licensing the master behind the producer's back is committing fraud.

This doesn't stop them from trying. I know of numerous deals that have gone south because the vanity label sold the master and then a producer came forward demanding compensation in exchange for his or her signature. This is why it is best for both sides to get a finished contract with all the signatures on it before the deal starts to get too big and people get too greedy. As much sense as this makes, many vanities and artists just don't think about it or don't care. They figure they'll find a way to end-zone the producer later.

THEY STOLE MY ARRANGEMENT

Sorry, they didn't—because you can't protect your arrangement. An arrangement is not considered protectable by most lawyers unless it is so unusual and unique and/or you notated every lick and groove of it on music manuscript paper and registered the full score with the Library of Congress.

Here's how Section 102 of the Copyright Act reads (subject matter of Copyright: subparagraph B):

> "In no case does copyright protection for an original work of authorship extend to any idea, procedure, process, system, method of operation, concept, principle, or discovery, regardless of the form in which it is described, explained, illustrated, or embodied in such work."

In other words, the informal pop or band style performance is considered by most courts an "explanation" or "interpretation" of the actual copyright — the song itself. Boo.

❯ Screwing the Producer, or the Re-Record

The most common type of end-zone tactic used to remove a producer who has control of the masters is the re-record.

A standard contract states that if the producer's tapes are used on the record,

HAVING "BIG FUN"

Several years ago I was asked by a vanity label to produce, on spec, an unknown band we'll call Big Fun. Big Fun's manager was putting up the money and started this thumbnail-sized vanity label to front the whole project. He couldn't pay me anything and so promised me 5% on the back end in exchange for an investment of over 100 hours of my time. There was no contract; we just shook hands on the deal with the understanding that I would keep all the masters as collateral on our agreement until he sent me a contract.

I produced the record. After it was completed, the vanity label shopped Big Fun to every major label in the industry. Everyone passed.

One afternoon, about a year later, I got a phone call from a new two-deep label. They were interested in buying Big Fun. They wanted me now to turn over the master tapes for pressing. I told them that I would love to, except that I had never been given a contract (even though I had asked the vanity label for it time and again).

Well, now it was time for the vanity label to settle up and put into writing my 5%.

What I did not know (and later found out) was that the vanity, desperate to make a sale and wash their hands of Big Fun (and pay back the seed money borrowed from the Irish mob), settled with the two-deep label for only 15 points. Nine were contractually to the band, and Five were previously promised to me, leaving the vanity label only *one point*.

They informed me that I was to settle for 3% so they would have more for themselves. If I refused, they threatened to have the band re-record the album, which would leave me completely out of the deal.

I called their bluff. I knew re-recording the record would not guarantee that the new master would pass muster with the label. They had a sale, why blow it?

The vanity finally settled with me, but I was cast as the bad guy, damaging my relationship with the band. To this day I'm not sure the trade-off was worth my principles.

then he must be paid. If the artist or production company wants to get around this, all they have to do is simply re-record the songs with the exact arrangements that they did with the producer. They could even hire the same engineer and the same recording studio. The producer will be powerless. Since the arrangement of a song is an idea (and therefore not copyrightable), the artist is not violating the copyright law. The producer is not an author of the new master and is completely removed from the loop.

However, there are attorneys who will argue otherwise. Some producers have tried to sue on the basis of a "sound recording copyright infringement" but it doesn't seem to stand up in court. Nor does the sometimes-tried "derivative work lawsuit," wherein the producer will contend that the new master is a derivative work of the old one and therefore a royalty must be paid. The problem here is that since Congress, at present, hasn't established a statutory rate for sound recording authors, all the producer wins is a royalty of $0.[5] (See the sidebar "Who Is the Songwriter in Rap Music?" on page 19.)

Situations like my experience with Big Fun (see the sidebar) are quite sad and, more often than not, are brought on by both sides being too stubborn about a settlement. The bad karma of the litigation usually destroys the vibe and the buzz of the project, the record flops, and both sides lose. I can't help but put some of the blame on the pros. Lawyers tend to polarize the sides and make a settlement harder, boiling the entire experience down to one of mutual exploitation between the artist and the producer.

Because of this, the savvy producer should want to deal with the vanity label as little as necessary. If this is how they behave when there is no money on the table, imagine how they get when it comes time to pay the royalties! Indeed, the only way a producer can hope to get paid in these situations is to get a major or indie label to distribute and promote the master. Then theoretically the producer won't have to deal with the small vanity label. Or will he?

As we saw in the section on the artist/producer agreement, the major label signs not the artist but the vanity label/production company. This means all producer royalty money travels through the production company. So how can the producer make sure that the production company/artist pays him if they get a distribution deal with a major? The answer is with a *letter of direction.*

Pay attention—this is no small point.

[5] But this is about to change. Within the next few years the copyright office plans to introduce an SR (sound recording) royalty that will be implemented for downloading off the Internet. This new royalty will probably find its way into several lawsuits by producers who can now claim damages for the theft of their arrangements.

⊘ Letters of Direction (LODs)

This may be the most important section in this book. Here you will learn to ask for what most people don't even know exists: the only paper trail you can create to insure that you, the producer or the artist, get paid—the letter of direction.

In this chapter I use a lot of terminology from the sections on vanity labels (page 131), artist/producer production deals (page 124), and the major label deal from the artist's and producer's points of view (pages 53 and 75). You may want to scan those before going on.

We're going to learn about LODs by way of the example we've been constructing in this chapter. A producer is being hired by a vanity label/production company to produce an artist signed to the vanity label. It's a spec deal with a back end percentage of 5% for the producer. Since the producer isn't getting any advance money, he argues reasonably that he shouldn't have to wait to recoup *anything*, but should get paid from the first record sold (typically called a "payment from record one"). Sounds fair, right?

The producer is taking a big risk in terms of an investment of time here. A vanity label is a production company or record company that has no specific deal to distribute its records. Once the project is finished, the vanity label shops and gets a deal with a bigger, more established major label that will market and distribute the artist. The major gives the vanity label an "all-in" royalty of 20% (20 points) for furnishing the talent, meaning that the vanity label pays out all the vendors (the artist and producer are vendors here) from their 20%. The agreement that the vanity label has with the artist typically requires them to give the artist 9 of those 20 points. The producer gets 5 points, leaving the vanity label with 6 of the 20 points.

It can take as much as a year and a half for the vanity label to collect the first money from the distributor. What happens if, during that period, the vanity label goes out of business or files for Chapter 11 bankruptcy? How do the artist and producer collect their money? The answer is—they don't.

This entire dilemma can be solved with a letter of direction. This is a letter attached to the producer's contract with the vanity label stating that if the vanity label is successful in placing the artist with a major label, the producer's royalty is to be paid from the major label *directly* to the producer, bypassing the vanity label (see diagram on the next page). The logic here is that the major label is likely to be a more stable and rooted company than the vanity label, so the producer won't have to chase anyone down the street for his or her 5%. The major label, or one-deep label, signing the artist will do all the accounting and write the checks.

This seems fair to all concerned, doesn't it? The vanity label doesn't have to worry about paying the producer, which means less accounting for them to do, and furthermore they are not liable for any errors in the royalty payments. Everyone is happy, right? Wrong.

Production company/vanity labels that have been around the block know that most labels will raise objections to letters of direction regarding the producer (or the artist, for that matter), for two reasons:

1. For the very same reason that it excuses the vanity label from doing the accounting, it is a liability to the major label.

2. It means more money has to come out of the major label's pocket sooner. Since the producer's agreement stipulates that they are to be paid from record one *before recoupment*, they must pay him or her *first*.

For both of these reasons, the major label will usually reject the artist who presents an LOD as part of the contract, unless they want the act real bad.

If the vanity label didn't realize that this would be a problem when they made the agreement with the producer, they will now be between a rock and a hard place

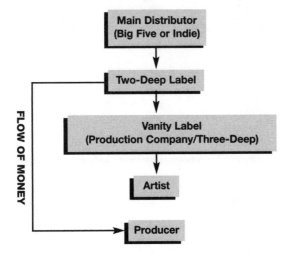

Letter of Direction Money Flow

NOTICE THAT THE PRODUCER IS PAID BEFORE THE ARTIST

since the LOD *must be part of the deal*, and therefore the vanity label will be bound to find a major label who will honor such a condition.

For this reason, artist's managers and vanity labels fight not to give in to the producer on this point. If you're the producer, my advice is to hold out; without an LOD you're not likely to ever get paid, and if they want you bad enough, the vanity label will cave on this.

However, the producer must be prepared to compromise come the day that a major label wants the act. When this happens, all parties will be asked to give up a little of what they were promised to make the deal work. For this reason the producer might want to ask for more points than is customary on a standard deal; he or she will probably have to give one of them back as an act of good faith.

❯ Artist's LOD

An interesting point that is often overlooked is that an artist rarely knows to ask for a letter of direction instructing the label to pay the artist's royalties directly to them and not through the vanity label. As we saw above, the producer will not hesitate to ask for this, but artists usually don't. Not having this letter means that they stand the risk of never seeing their money should the vanity label/production company get into financial trouble. Without the letter of direction, the artist cannot go to the distributor and ask them for money or advances of any kind.

Lately, however, indie labels are more accepting of LODs from artists. It's my guess that within the next few years, as many producers and artists become more aware of the mechanics of the business, almost every artist/producer production agreement and vanity label deal will have at least one LOD attached.[6]

[6] For more goop on this subject, see "Letters of Misdirection," page 189.

CHAPTER FIFTEEN

⊘ Wrap Up— Who Earned What?

U sing all the information from the previous chapters, let's see how each party—the artist/writer, the producer, and the record label—fares in a typical successful record deal. This is designed as an exercise only. All of the numbers below are approximate, and don't take into account an individual's tax bracket, deductions, and other minor variables.

Let's assume we have a four-member band where all the members share writing credit, and that they have written all the songs on all their records. They've signed a four-album deal where all of the records are cross-collateralized but no publishing is cross-collateralized. The first record sells 100,000 copies, the second record sells 250,000, the third record sells 1,000,000, and the fourth record sells 2,000,000. The combined recoupable recording advances and promotion costs for each record amount to $500,000 for the first record, $500,000 for the second record, $750,000 for the third, and $2,000,000 for the fourth (which includes a $1,000,000 bonus for being profitable enough to deserve a fourth record). Here's the breakdown:

> Artist

When examining the numbers below, keep in mind that these are the dollars earned for a very successful artist during what will probably be the five most successful years of his recording-artist career. Much like athletes, artists have a shelf life. In the recording business that shelf life is about five years.

Artist/Writer Record Royalties

1st record	$.83 x 100,000 units = $83,000.00	
	subtracted from $500,000.00 = ... –$417,000.00	
2nd record	$.83 x 350,000 units = $290,500.00	
	subtracted from $1,000,000.00 = ... –$709,500.00	
3rd record	$.83 x 1,350,000 units = $1,120,500.00	
	subtracted from $1,750,000.00 = ... –$629,500.00	
4th record	$.83 x 3,350,000 units = $2,780,500	
	subtracted from $3,750,000.00 = ... –$969,500.00	

That's right—after selling more than 3.75 million records, the band is still almost a million dollars in debt to the label. It's a good thing they have other income from the sources below.

Recording Advances

This chart shows an estimated surplus in the recording budget, which is kept by the artists. This is the only money they will see off of record sales, since they are still in debt to the label. It is based on normal costs for record production.

1st record	$250,000.00	surplus $50,000.00
2nd record.........................	$250,000.00	surplus $50,000.00
3rd record	$375,000.00	surplus $125,000.00
4th record	$650,000.00	surplus $1,200,000.00

Total	**$1,425,000.00**

Publishing 1: Mechanical Royalties

This is money earned by the songwriter (whom we are assuming is also the artist in this example) for the licensing of material on a record. The formula for calculating this on a typical major label deal is as follows: (10 x the statutory rate of $.08) x (75%) = $0.60 per record sold.

1st record .... 100,000 units	$60,000.00
2nd record .... 250,000 units	$150,000.00
3rd record .... 1,000,000 units...........................	$600,000.00
4th record .... 2,000,000 units	$1,200,000.00

Total mechanical license revenue for artist	$2,010,000.00
Harry Fox auditing adjustment of about 5%	-$100,500.00
Adjusted total	$1,909,500.00

Publishing 2: Radio Play

An average royalty for a hit single for one year is about $150,000 when collected and passed on to publishers by ASCAP, BMI, or SESAC.[1] We'll assume the band will have one hit on each of their first four albums (they should only be so lucky). Here the artist/writer has a typical 50/50 publishing deal in which the publisher gets 50% of the publisher's share (25 cents on every dollar earned, for those who skipped chapter six).

$150,000.00 x 4 albums = $600,000.00

Publishing total:	
Mechanicals	$1,909,500.00
Radio	$600,000.00

Total	$2,509,500.00

Minus 10% administration for publisher	-$250,950.00
Subtotal	$2,258,550.00
Minus publisher's cut (25%/75% split)	-$564,637.50

Total	$1,693,912.50

[1] The formulas are mind-bogglingly complicated, but basically boil down to this: about 450,000 plays at a mean average of 3 cents a play.

Touring

If the artist is a superstar they can multiply these numbers by ten, but suffice it to say that a band with moderate endorsements and a song on rotation at several stations could expect to net about $15,000 per show for the second two album tours.

$15,000.00 x 4 shows per week =.. $60,000.00

$60,000.00 x 15 weeks (average tour)=.............................. $900,000.00

$900,000.00 x 2 album tours =.. $1,800,000.00

Sponsors

Any successful band generally has a sycophantic sneaker company or Jägermeister wannabe hanging around wanting them to sell their soul for an extra few bucks. So let's tack on another $500,000 in sponsors and endorsements for the last two tours. Total income from this: **$1,000,000.**

Which Adds Up To…

Here's how the band's financial picture looks over this four-album period:

Record royalties of –$969,500.00 (forgiven debt)........................... $0.00

Surplus from recording advances................................. $1,425,000.00

Publishing... $1,693,912.50

Touring... $1,800,000.00

Sponsors.. $1,000,000.00

Total... $5,918,912.50

Minus 15% manager's commission................................ –$887,836.87

Minus business manager's/professional fees of 5%....... –$295,945.62

Adjusted gross $4,735,130.10

Minus 40% for income taxes (including Social Security).... –$1,894,052.00

Total... $2,841,078.10

Divided by five years [2]... $568,215.62
per year

—————————————————————————————

Divided by four group members (if equal split) $142,053.90
per year

[2] It is divided by five years and not four years, because four albums on a major label generally take about five years to be realized.

❯ Producer

In all likelihood the same producer would not work on all four of a single artist's records, so I've broken it down by four records of comparable success. Also, keep in mind that a producer works on several records of different budgets each year. So the calculations below are difficult to apply to the same structure as the artist above.

1st record	$0.27 x 100,000 units	$27,000.00
2nd record	$0.27 x 250,000 units	$67,500.00
3rd record	$0.27 x 1,000,000 units	$270,000.00
4th record	$0.27 x 2,000,000 units	$540,000.00
Total gross earnings		$904,500.00
Minus 40% tax		-$361,800.00
Adjusted gross		$542,700.00
Divided by four albums		$135,675.00

From this, the producer must pay his overhead. But as you can see, the construct does not hold up, because any producer selling this many records is probably netting far more than $135,675 a year. A fairer guess would put a producer of this caliber closer to $500,000 a year, after expenses.

❯Record Company

Album	Units Sold	One-deep $4.32	Major Label $7.32
1st record	100,000	$432,000.00	$732,000.00
2nd record	250,000	$1,080,000.00	$1,830,000.00
3rd record	1,000,000	$4,320,000.00	$7,320,000.00
4th record	2,000,000	$8,640,000.00	$14,640,000.00
Total record company earnings		$14,472,000.00	$24,522,000.00

Advances & non-recoupable
promotion costs
(all four records) ....$0.00 ....$6,000,000.00
(flowed through to major)

Adjusted gross ....$14,472,000.00 ....$18,522,000.00
40% taxes ....$5,788,800.00 ....$7,408,800.00

Gross earnings before overhead... $8,683,200.00 ....$11,113,200.00
Compared to 1998 edition............. $6,432,000.00 ....$8,802,000.00
Percentage increase...............................35.00%.....................26.26%

There are as many variables to the above conclusions as there are artists, producers, and labels, but this will give you a good starting template. Also, you have to keep in mind that the above is based on a band that sells almost 4,000,000 records. Less than 5% of all artists signed by major labels go to this level. Actual circumstances may vary; record companies may make more on the publishing if they have a publishing division, and artists may make substantially less if they don't write their own songs.

The final score is artist $2,841,078.10,[3] producer $542,700.00, the major label roughly $11,000,000, and the indie or two-deep label roughly $8.7 million. This has increased by about 26% since the late 1990s for Big Fives and about 35% for one-deep labels (during which time labels have justified massive layoffs by saying they can't make enough to pay their employees). Labels are pretty good at adding up numbers. And the numbers above show that it's more cost effective to keep labels small and boutique-like, rather than the old style of label with big offices and glamorous boardrooms. It would not surprise me if this conclusion forces Big Fives to consolidate further and push all artist development onto the smaller one-deep and two-deep labels—in other words, imprints and vanity labels.

Artists have seen a significantly better increase of about 50%—but this number can be misleading, as it applies only to major stars. Also, it should be noted that artists are earning more not because they have succeeded in getting a larger piece of the record-sales pie, but rather because of alliances with advertisers, like Pepsi and Britney Spears. Count on seeing more of this in the future as well. For the average recording artist and producer, the increase has been about 12%. Unfortunately, this has barely kept pace with inflation brought on by the "new economy," so it is not a well-realized gain. To add to this, artists and producers with less clout don't always get their record sales money, for various reasons that we'll explore later, so

[3] Approximately 29% of that ($813,078, after taxes and commissions) is just from songwriting.

their actual earnings need to be adjusted further. But the record company always gets paid. *Always.*[4]

So now you know how you earn your money and how much you have the potential to make. You are in a unique position. Most people entering this business have no idea how to gauge their success.

Now that you know how much you *should* make, in the next part of this book we are going to explore all the ways that folks will try to cheat you out of it.

[4] For an in-depth look at the mechanics of this, see the follow-up book to *Confessions: Secrets of Negotiating a Record Contract.*

PART TWO

Scams and Shams

Successful and fortunate crime is called virtue.

—Seneca

⊜Watching
Your Back

D id you ever notice that as you gain more experience in things, you find out that nothing is exactly the way it first seemed or the way you were taught it should be? It appears that nothing in nature looks the same when you examine it closely. In fact, the record industry has a direct parallel in nature: it's the observable comparison between the physical or Newtonian world and the subatomic world.

Huh?

Quantum physics teaches us that when you look really, really closely at the molecules and particles that make up the world we live in, you notice that nothing acts the way it seems to work to the naked eye. For example: Gravity is something we all experience and can observe. Isaac Newton wrote laws of gravity that work well as long as you only apply them to the macroscopic (directly observable) world. But when Albert Einstein wrote the theory of relativity, he suggested that gravity is not a force that pulls everything down, but merely an illusion, that things only appear to "fall down" because that's the perspective from which we observe them moving. Quantum mechanics later proved that subatomic particles, when observed closely, appear to "fall" in all directions and even move backward in time.

What the hell am I talking about? Well, the above example may sound a bit confusing, but it's worth taking the time to understand it. Quantum physics can teach us an important lesson about business in general—namely, that nothing moves in the direction or at the speed that we think it does. This is doubly true in the record industry.

This section talks about the devious things I've either been witness to or heard about through the grapevine. Let's take a look.

CHAPTER SIXTEEN

⊗The Myth of Copyright Protection,

or "Hey, They Stole My Song!"

I f you've ever asked a lawyer about how you can protect your song, he or she will probably give the stock answer—register it on a PA (Performing Art) or SR (Sound Recording) form with the Library of Congress. Others might say that all you have to do is mail it to yourself and never open the envelope that it is in—the postmark will document the date of your copyright. Others will tell you simply to notarize the lyric sheets—the notary stamp always has a date on it. The best yet is the poor man's copyright, which is a manipulation and loose interpretation of the Copyright Act of 1976; that is, you don't have to do anything, because the minute a piece of music is recorded, it is automatically copyrighted.[1]

But in practical terms, all of the foregoing are equally useless. The plain truth is that there is only one way to protect yourself from having another writer steal your song, and that's to make the song famous before anyone else does.

Right now there are about a thousand lawyers out there squirming as they read this, about to write me a nasty letter. But they know it's true. Here's the scoop.

Let's say that you wrote a song and did all the necessary procedures to register the copyright. Let's say you even wrote out the lead sheet (something most

[1] Whether the postmark or the notary stamp would stand up in court is debatable. It's true that you own the copyright of a piece of music that you record even if you do nothing to *register* the copyright, but if you ever find yourself facing a legal challenge, your lawyer will tell you that before you can go to federal court you must have registered the work with the Library of Congress.

2 You should by
now understand
the difference. If
not, review "Pub-
lishing Deals,"
page 69; and
"When the Pro-
ducer Wants Pub-
lishing," page 84.

songwriters never do) and registered that with the Library of Congress as well. So now you've copyrighted the song, the arrangement, and the sound recording of the song.[2] You've covered your ass, and so you confidently go about shopping your demo to record companies or publishing companies.

One day you're sitting in a restaurant on a hot date. You're warming up to each other, thinking about later in the evening back at your place, when suddenly over the restaurant sound system you hear something that's distracting you. It sounds awfully familiar. It's your song!

Your date is befuddled as you start to explain in a panicked voice, "That's my song we're listening to. I wrote it about a year ago. The same lyrics and melody—everything." There are a couple of arrangement changes, but it's still yours. They've stolen your tune. "Those sons-of-bitches!" you scream. Now you're gonna make them

WHAT EXACTLY IS A COPYRIGHT?

We've all heard of the word, seen it in print. Maybe you have a friend who is an author and you've heard them talk about protecting their copyrights. But how many of us really know what the word really means?

As obvious as it might seem, the meaning of the word "copyright" is literally the "right to make a copy." Just as with the right to freedom of speech, the laws of this country protect the right of an author to decide when, where, and how to have his or her creations copied—that is, duplicated. Whether it's a story or a song, the minute you write it on a piece of paper or record it on tape you become that work's author, and the law says that, *at that very moment,* you have rights. Your main right is the decision to have that work copied or *not* copied. It's your choice as the author; no one else's. This is how authors make money: by controlling that right. If you then assign the right to make commercial copies to another party, like a book publishing house or a record company, you're giving them the right to make copies for sales to book or record stores. In all cases you must be paid money for this right, just as if real property were changing hands. It's the law. It's called "giving consideration." If you give someone your copy-pay! Well, we'll see. Maybe yes, maybe no. In this chapter we're going to examine the ins and outs of suing stars and several cases of those who tried.

❯ Suing Stars

You're hopping mad that someone has stolen your precious hit song. The first thing you do is go back to your lawyer friend, the one who told you to fill out a PA form and you'd be fine. You ask him to sue the bastard. (We'll call the culprit Johnny Rock Star.) But your lawyer doesn't sue people, he just does contracts. You need a *litigator*. So he refers you to someone else. The someone else he refers you to is not a slick wheeler-dealer type of attorney like yours was. This guy is a bit starchy, very down-to-earth, and serious. He's not going to tell you fairy tales, because un-

right and they don't pay you for it, then there has been "no consideration" and a court of law *could* find that the contract is not valid. Just as when you're selling a house or a car, you must be paid, even if it's only a dollar.

Have you ever seen a funny cartoon and made a Xerox for your refrigerator? Or how many times have you seen an article on something that may be of interest to a friend and made a copy? Most of us have. I copied an Al Capp cartoon for my seven-year-old niece once. She laughed for ten minutes and kept repeating the joke all weekend. I'll bet you didn't know that when you made that copy, you were breaking the law. It's true. Every time you make a copy of something without the permission of the copyright owner (often, but not always, the author) and pass the copy on to a friend, you're breaking the law.[3] When I made the copy of the Al Capp cartoon and gave it to my niece, by strict interpretation, I broke the law.

Now don't worry; no one's going to court over this. If they did, you'd be protected by a legal doctrine that goes by the fancy Latin name *De minimis non curat lex*, which translates to: "The law does not concern itself with trifles." Another legal principle that you're more likely to have heard about is the "fair use" doctrine (see the following sidebar in this section). The Copyright Act includes certain exceptions that are considered fair use: Teachers in a public school can make copies and pass them out to their students, for example.

[3] If you buy a CD and make a tape of it to listen to in your car, the Supreme Court has said that you're not violating the rights of the copyright owner. But if you give the cassette to a friend, you've broken the law. It's called piracy.

like your music attorney, this guy generally works on commission. That means he doesn't take a case unless he thinks he can win and win big.

You start to tell him about the PA form and how you wrote to the Library of Congress and requested Johnny Rock Star's PA form. Johnny's form was dated later than yours. That means you have proof that your song came first. You've got him!

Well, not exactly. That only proves that the two of you wrote the same or similar song and that you filed your form first.

AVAST THERE, MATEY. PUT UP YER HANDS AN' THROW THE CDS TO THE DECK.

Are you a pirate? Use this excerpt from the Copyright Act as a guideline.

§107. Limitations on exclusive rights: Fair Use

Notwithstanding the provisions of sections 106 and 106A, the fair use of a copyrighted work, including such use by reproduction in copies or phonorecords or by any other means specified by that section, for purposes such as criticism, comment, news reporting, teaching (including multiple copies for classroom use), scholarship, or research, is not an infringement of copyright. In determining whether the use made of a work in any particular case is a fair use the factors to be considered shall include —

1. the purpose and character of the use, including whether such use is of a commercial nature or is for nonprofit educational purposes; 2. the nature of the copyrighted work; 3. the amount and substantiality of the portion used in relation to the copyrighted work as a whole; and 4. the effect of the use upon the potential market for or value of the copyrighted work.

In plain English, this says that if you're selling (or giving away) copies of a copyrighted work, which will have the effect of reducing the potential money the copyright owner could make, it's not "fair use" and you're a thief. Sometimes fair use is easy to determine, but other times it requires a day in court, as in the case of file-sharing companies that allow people to distribute songs digitally via the Internet. Witness the 2 Live Crew case in the main text of this chapter.

When you accuse someone of breaking a federal law (such as copyright infringement), you must go to a federal prosecutor and file a complaint. Federal prosecutors tend to be career-oriented attorneys who would rather enhance their track record by going after mobsters and inside-trading honchos, not rock stars who rip off a song from some unknown writer. You would be hard-pressed to find a prosecutor who considers the case a good use of taxpayers' money. And that's the good news.

Even if you found a crusading prosecutor willing to pull Johnny Rock Star into court, and even if Johnny *were* found guilty, intellectual property fraud is punishable by a simple fine and/or one year in jail. (The latter wouldn't happen—the jails are full enough.) In addition to this slap in the face, you would be required to appear in court several times, exposing you to many top industry professionals who would hate you for dragging them into this. And you would receive not one penny for your effort. The fine goes to the state—you've done your civic duty by acting as a witness.

So what about all those big settlements we hear about in the papers about so-and-so being sued for stealing samples and lyrics and so forth?

Those are not criminal suits. They are *civil suits*—a lawsuit done in civil court, where the plaintiff (that's you in our example) is seeking a money damage award for the theft of their property (in this case, the theft of a copyright of a song).

Since *you* will claim that *you* have been robbed of money from the copyright from a song that *you* wrote, it will not be enough to prove that Johnny Rock Star stole the song. You have to prove that he stole the song from *you personally!*

In legal terms, this is called "proving access." You have to prove that Johnny had the *opportunity* to steal your song by being in proximity to you or to a copy of your song. If you *can't* show access, then the court will in all likelihood be forced to conclude that it is a mere coincidence that you and Johnny wrote the same song around the same time. In this case Johnny may walk away *with* the copyright and the cash.

Think this is easy? Let's look at several actual cases.

Mick Jagger and "She's the Boss"

This was a case in 1985 involving Mick Jagger of the Rolling Stones and a Jamaican reggae artist, Grand View Alley, who had several small successes in the Virgin Islands. He sued Jagger for stealing a song of his and putting it on Jagger's first 1984 solo record, *She's the Boss*. It was big news at the time, and radio stations played both the reggae version and Jagger's rock version side by side on the air during the trial. To the average listener, they did seem to be the same song with different arrangements.

Before the trial began, lawyers from both sides took statements from all the witnesses that would be brought before the jury. (The statements that witnesses give are called "depositions.") During the taking of the depositions in this case, it was learned by both parties that Jagger's current drummer had played on the original demo of the reggae version of the song. Grand View Alley seemed assured of a favorable outcome at the trial. But when the drummer was called to the witness stand during the trial, he testified he couldn't remember if he had played on that exact demo. This was all the jury needed to find in Jagger's favor.

Michael Bolton and "How Am I Supposed to Live Without You"

This case has similar overtones. Here songwriters Michael Bolton and Doug James and singer Laura Branigan were being sued for stealing the song "How Am I Supposed to Live Without You."

Bolton and James had originally written the song for Laura Branigan's second album in 1983. When the record came out and "How Am I Supposed to Live Without You" was on the radio, it came to the attention of a New Jersey composer named Gary William Friedman.

Friedman was no amateur—he had written several important scores and songs, including the critically acclaimed off-Broadway musical *The Me Nobody Knows*. He noticed that "How Am I" bore a striking resemblance to a song that he had written some years earlier called "Promise Me." But unlike the situation in the Grand View Alley case, Friedman would have no problem proving access. He had had a previous relationship with Laura Branigan.

Like most singers, before she got her major label record deal, Laura Branigan sang on numerous demos to make a meager living. Friedman had employed her many times to record rough versions of his songs before sending them to his publisher.

When Friedman first heard "How Am I" on the radio, the similarity was so close that he thought Branigan had actually honored him by recording the song. Upon closer examination he realized a grim truth. The melody was all too familiar to him, and some of the lyrics were altered.

He looked on the record and found that the writer credit had gone to Michael Bolton (who at the time was not a household name) and Doug James, the very person who had played piano on Friedman's original demo of "Promise Me."

Armed with a stream of witnesses and a paper trail, Friedman sought justice in a New York federal court. But even after Friedman presented the court with the canceled checks that he had paid Branigan and James for their services, under oath both claimed that they simply couldn't remember if they had performed "Promise Me."

Friedman lost the case, was stuck with massive legal bills, and did not receive one penny in royalties or recognition for the song. In the end a jury seemed more impressed with the lineup of celebrities testifying on behalf of the defendants than with the paper trail, the similarities between the two songs, and Friedman's indisputable associations with Branigan and James.

Bolton and James' attorneys offered Friedman a measly few thousand dollars to waive his right to appeal. Devastated by the crushing verdict, he took the five g's.

"How Am I Supposed to Live Without You" has grossed over $2 million for Michael Bolton and Doug James.

New Kids on the Block and "I'll Be Your Everything"

Even if your song is a hit, you may not be protected.

In 1992, teen heartthrobs New Kids on the Block were sued by George Soule for stealing the hit song "I'll Be Your Everything." New Kid Tommy Page penned a song with the same title, a similar opening lyric, and an almost identical opening melody.

The original "I'll Be Your Everything" was made famous by legendary R&B singer Percy Sledge and reached No. 15 on the *Billboard* R&B charts in 1975, about the same time Tommy Page was born.

Can two people write the same or a similar song, with the same title, and yet have no knowledge of each other even when one version is an American classic still played on hundreds of radio stations? A jury thought so. They found in favor of the New Kids. The defense went so far as to have Page up on the witness stand with a synthesizer to demonstrate how he came up with the melody. When his attorney asked him what the inspiration for the song was, he replied, "God."

2 Live Crew and "Pretty Woman"

In the above cases, the writers who filed the lawsuits probably felt that the jury was biased toward the stars. Certainly many attorneys have argued in recent years that juries are just ordinary people who often get bedazzled by faces that they've seen 40 feet high on the sides of buildings. In hindsight many songwriters who've sued have felt that they should have opted to have their case heard by a judge. Well, that's no guarantee either.

Enter the 2 Live Crew case. Here the rap group took the song "Oh Pretty Woman" by Roy Orbison and turned it into a rap tune with a much peppier title, "Pretty Woman." The lyrics of the song were almost identical as well. They even took the famous guitar riff, and yet they got clean off the hook. (Pardon the pun.)

They argued that since a part of the Copyright Act contains a section called "fair

"PRETTY WOMAN"
AS RECORDED BY 2 LIVE CREW

Pretty Woman, walking down the street,
Pretty Woman, girl you look so sweet,
Pretty Woman, you bring me down to that knee,
Pretty Woman, you make me wanna beg please,
Oh, Pretty Woman

Big hairy woman, you need to shave that stuff,
Big hairy woman, you know I bet it's tough
Big hairy woman, all that hair ain't legit,
'Cause you look like Cousin It
Big hairy woman

Bald headed woman, girl your hair won't grow,
Bald headed woman, you got a teeny weeny afro
Bald headed woman, you know your hair could look nice,
Bald headed woman, first you got to roll it with rice
Bald headed woman here, let me get this hunk of biz for ya,
Ya know what I'm saying,
you look better than Rice-a-Roni
Oh, bald headed woman

Big hairy woman, come on in,
And don't forget your bald headed friend
Hey Pretty Woman, let the boys jump in
Two timin' woman, girl you know it ain't right,
Two timin' woman, you's out with my boy last night
Two timin' woman, that takes a load off my mind,
Two timin' woman, now I know the baby ain't mine
Oh, two timin' woman
Oh, Pretty Woman.

use" and that this provision opens up the possibility for "spoofs" that parody the original to be exploited royalty-free, 2 Live Crew did not owe Orbison's estate a dime because their version was commenting on the original. (WARNING: See the footnote.)[4]

The "parody defense" is intended to apply to comedy versions of things, like what you might find on *Saturday Night Live,* and has roots going back to when popular songs were rewritten with new lyrics to be used for political campaigns. Many argue that it was never intended to be used to create completely independent master recordings that would become commercial hits.

To prevail under the "parody defense," 2 Live Crew would have to prove that their song "pays homage" to the Orbison hit, and was not used simply because 2 Live Crew wanted to create a rip-off version.

In a decision that stunned many attorneys, 2 Live Crew persuaded a judge that indeed this was the case. To make matters more interesting the ruling was handed down in a court in Nashville, known to many as the city of songwriters. The plaintiffs appealed and the decision was overturned. 2 Live Crew appealed the appeal, taking the case all the way up the ladder to the Supreme Court, who remanded the case with a ruling that was tantamount to a favorable decision to 2 Live Crew. In the final settlement, 2 Live Crew did not have to pay anything for infringement, but they agreed to pay a royalty to Roy Orbison's publisher going forward.

The original judge (who, I can promise you, was not star-stuck by these brash young men) decided in their favor because he felt that the 2 Live Crew version lived up to the fair use standard because it had contained "social criticism of the original."

The law works in mysterious ways, so please see the previous sidebar for your daily dose of social criticism.

George Harrison and "He's So Fine"

Once in a while, the writer does prevail. One significant case was a suit against ex-Beatle George Harrison. Harrison was sued by the author of the 1963 hit "He's So Fine." He claimed that Harrison's 1970 song "My Sweet Lord" was a direct clone with different lyrics. A court agreed. When asked to comment on what had happened, Harrison was quoted by reporters as saying, "Well, sometimes a tune gets caught in your head and you can't remember where it comes from."

The court held that Harrison did not consciously copy the earlier song, but it was still an infringement to copy it unconsciously. Harrison was not alone in his caper. Veteran record producer Phil Spector produced the hit that got Harrison in Dutch. Which only proves that a selective memory is contagious when working on potential heavyweight hits.

[4] Don't try this at home, kids. Creating parodies and claiming that they are fair use is the stuff that major lawsuits are made of. To prevail your parody must contain social commentary or criticism of the original. Only a court can determine if a parody is fair use. It is very risky so consult a qualified entertainment attorney before distributing any spoof recordings.

⊘More Problems with Suing Stars

The worst part of getting yourself embroiled in a case like those above is that the litigator, the lawyer whom you are trying to convince to sue Johnny Rock Star, has more reasons to *not* help you than to help you, even if he or she thinks that you have a good case. If the attorney is trying to attract the very type of client that the disgruntled songwriter wants to sue, they may be fearful of industry blackballing. For this reason many copyright theft cases never get to the courtroom.

If you hear your song on the radio and you yourself have no clout, you will find it almost impossible to collect anything unless the star you plan to sue has a policy that favors paying off "chasers" (people who try to sue stars for copyright theft).

Some stars get sued so often that they find it cheaper to settle with the plaintiffs than go through the process of litigation. This is not necessarily an admission of guilt but simply more economical. Many times a settlement of $100,000 will pacify a suing songwriter. The lawyer for the plaintiff will explain that they should take the settlement because if they go to court they will probably lose, as such cases are notoriously hard to prove. The plaintiff usually gives in and takes the cash, the song remains the property of the star, and the negative publicity is zip. The only exception to this scenario would be if the star felt that they had a particularly strong case and chose to fight. Or if, for some reason, a lot of publicity came to surround the case. In these cases the star will fight tooth and nail to win the case. They usually do.

Other stars feel that they have a reputation to protect and have a policy of not giving in to anyone no matter what. Either they have the money to enforce their policy or they are up-and-coming stars who don't want the negative publicity while they're still gaining the trust of the public. The lawyers who specialize in copyright suits know which stars are less prone to pay and try to avoid confrontations with them. They fear that a frivolous chaser suit will be met with a "we dare you to sue us" memo. The artists that have these policies tend to be the biggest of the big stars. They are the hardest to sue. They never go down without a fight, and they usually win because they can financially outdraw the chaser.

⊘ Collecting Your Money

Sometimes the stars do lose, and when they lose they lose big. You might think that once that has happened, they simply cut a check to the winning party and that's that. Sorry. Winning a lawsuit doesn't guarantee that you will collect the money. How you collect is up to you to figure out. The court will try to enforce the judgment, but in many cases their hands are tied. If the star is good at hiding his or her money, they can delay payment for years.

So years later, after the star is considered a deadbeat, the songwriter can get a court order and then the performing rights agencies will stop paying the star's account. I am told the average collection on cases of this type is around four to six years. Oh yeah, remember, a third of any money collected goes to your lawyer.

The bottom line on this subject is to beware when lawyers and people in general speak of your rights and suing for them. Most people haven't been through a lawsuit and don't know what they're talking about. Suing, in all phases of business, is a long and expensive process, and your rights are only worth what you're willing to invest in protecting them. Stars have more money and resources than most people and can afford to have an attorney on retainer to handle these things while they go about their business. You probably can't.

From the above information, we can now understand the meaning of this next piece of Record Industry Talmud:

> ### When people talk about "your rights,"
> ### they are suggesting that you spend thousands
> ### of dollars suing someone.

So if the law won't protect you, what can you do? Here are a few "unofficial" suggestions a lawyer will never make.

❧ Blockage

In 1986 I worked on an R&B album paid for by a major label. I was only an engineer, but I was doing a lot of producing on the project as well. When the project was finished, I submitted the last of my invoices, totaling about $3,500 that the production company owed me. They told me that they were expecting the last installment from the record company soon and that I should please be patient. I was patient for about six months, after which time I decided to do something covert to get my money. A friend who worked in the publishing department at EMI told me a little trick that she knew worked for a writer friend. It went like this.

Knowing that the record was due out in another four months gave me a little time to put the plan she called *blockage* into action. First, I found out if the artist was on BMI or ASCAP. This is not hard; I just called the record company and got the information from a secretary. In this case it was BMI, which I was already a member of.

Next I filled out a PA form for all the songs on the record that I worked on as an engineer and sent it in to Washington with my name and the name of the artist listed as the two authors of the songs. This was sent return receipt requested, which means that when the Library of Congress receives the PA forms, they must sign a receipt for it. Even though it will take several weeks for the PA forms to go through their computer, the receipt will act as a sort of "patent pending" for the songs. That means that until anyone says otherwise, this artist and I cowrote the songs.

Then I registered all the songs with BMI, listing myself and the artist as the cowriters. Now, one would think that BMI would do a computer check to see if the same songs were registered once before with different writers. They didn't, and last I checked (about three months before this book's first edition was written), they still hadn't. If, in fact, the song never earns any money, both conflicting forms will remain on the BMI computer forever. But the minute a royalty has to be paid out, the computer will recognize the conflict and freeze the account until all parties can settle on who the actual authors are.

Almost a year later, that's what happened. The song charted and the artist was anxious to collect his money. If you've read the previous chapters, you know how badly he needed it at this time. BMI, however, would not pay the artist a dime until they settled with me. BMI does not discriminate. They simply say, "You guys work it out and call us when you do."

When the artist's lawyer called me to settle, I told him that I had patiently waited over a year to be paid on my invoice and was not going to wait any longer. They immediately paid me the $3,500 plus interest, and I relinquished my copyright claim.

Both BMI and ASCAP frown on this sort of activity. They claim that they will excommunicate those who make false claims, but they probably would never kick out a member who has a hit. Besides, they don't seem to mind holding onto the money at 4 or 5% interest while the two parties resolve the problem.

> Name Blockage

Once a manager friend of mine was dumped by his artist right after they got a deal with a major label. Because he had only a handshake agreement, it was not hard for the band to dismiss him once he had gotten them in the door of the label. As you can imagine, he was fuming from the betrayal.

Over a drink I suggested to him that he plan a little legal revenge. I told my friend to check with the county clerk to see if the band had incorporated their name and logo or had a trademark license established for them. The odds were that they did not, and sure enough, that was the case. All my friend had to do was file a DBA (Doing Business As) with the state county clerk's office and sit back. The damage was done.

He waited patiently for almost a year. During that time the label issued advances to the band that he never got a commission for. They began recording an album, and the label started doing press for the upcoming release. Just when the record was about to come out, the label did the same name search that my friend had done a year earlier. You can imagine what they found.

Outraged, the band now had little choice but to make an offer to buy the name from my friend. (Their only other option was to change their name, but few bands want to do that after going through the trouble of gaining a reputation.) My friend was merciless and unforgiving, selling the name to them at a price more than double what his commission would have been.

Revenge is a dish best served cold.

❷ Sound-Alikes

You'd think that after you go through all the B.S. it takes to get a hit record that you can sit pretty. Well, maybe. Now that you have an important copyright, it's up to you to protect it. If you can, that is. Enter the *sound-alike*. This is another form of copyright abuse.

When a movie or TV show wants to use a popular song in their production, they must obtain the permission of several sources before they can do it. Each source will charge a fee.

The first of these fees is the synchronization license for the song. That's a license to take the song and synchronize it to a moving picture like a movie or a TV show. This license usually sells for about $2,000 and is obtainable through the song's publisher.

Next is the Musicians' Union, who will require the show's producer to pay a *performance reuse* fee to the authors of the sound recording (i.e., the performer or artist who recorded the song). Tack on another $1,000 for that.

Last but not least is the record company that owns the sound recording of the song. For a typical use of the master in a film or TV show, the money will usually add up to about $30,000, but it can be much steeper or lower depending on the flexibility of the label. I have heard of situations where masters were licensed for up to $100,000 for a single use in a film, millions if it is used in a commercial. (By the way, *none of this money necessarily goes to the artist* — it's strictly a record company fee. But recently the companies have been sharing this cash with the artist by reducing the recoupment fund.)

Several years ago I was approached by a sleazy TV producer who wanted to use a popular Rolling Stones song in one of his shows. He asked me what I thought it would cost and I described the above payments to him. He melted into his seat, shaking his head and saying, "There must be a better way." There was.

He obtained the sync license from the publisher, saying that it would be for *background use only*. Somehow he got them down to $1,500. Now came the hard part, how to sidestep the union and the record company. That's where I came in.

He hired me to "compose" and record an exact duplicate of the original recording. I did. I reprogrammed the original arrangement and, using a computer, made it exactly as it was on the original record. I hired a nonunion singer who by coincidence sounded a lot like Mick Jagger for $100 and mixed it with the exact same treatments of reverb and effects. It sounded identical to all but the most scrupulous listeners. Considering it was going to be in the background of a scene with dialogue on top of it and other sound effects, we were home free. No record company, union, or rights organization needed to be paid. I used myself plus one other nonunion musician and charged the producer an all-in fee of $3,000. His total cost was $4,500 instead of $25,000, and the best part was this was completely legal!

YOU BETTAH, YOU BETTAH, YOU BETTE

Several years ago, Bette Midler won a landmark case in California against an ad company for using a celebrity impersonator in a radio spot. Even though the ad specified that a Bette "sound-alike" was used, Midler's attorneys found grounds to sue because her signature sound was being misrepresented. The impersonation of her recognizable "style" implied that she herself endorsed the advertised product. A court agreed.

This might open up the door to make sound-alikes more difficult to pull off. In all likelihood it will always be legal, but through performance rights clearances it can be made so expensive that producers may as well pay for the real thing.

To add insult to injury, he proceeded to use the song anywhere and everywhere he wanted to—background and foreground. (Foreground licensing fees are substantially higher.) The TV show aired in Europe, which is not carefully monitored by American PROs like ASCAP and BMI, so he got away with paying next to nothing for a hit song in the foreground of his TV show.

This is now a common occurrence in the broadcast industry, and what makes it legally possible is a catch-22 in the interpretation of the Copyright Act: that the instrumental arrangement of the song, although considered part of the underlying copyright, cannot be protected unless it is deemed "unique." Otherwise it is seen only as an interpretation, or *an expression of an idea*. Ideas cannot be copyrighted.

But who decides what is original and what is just a ripped-off "idea"? Twelve people who sit in a box called . . . a jury. And while most artists believe that their sound is unique, the average citizen (or judge, for that matter) is generally less of a connoisseur of bass lines, drum patterns, and synth patches, making "unique" about as hard a standard to prove in a court of law as "obscene" or "pornographic."

Clearly this is a Neanderthal interpretation, and hopefully there are lawyers out there fighting to have the Copyright Act amended by making judges and juries sympathetic to the plight of producers, artists, and arrangers. But change is unlikely; the broadcast industries have powerful attorneys on their side as well, fighting to keep things just the way that they are, and for a good reason. This catch-22/loophole saves them millions a year in sound recording licenses. As digital technology makes it possible to make more and more accurate copies of things for less and less money, this loophole will become a noose tightening around the necks of record companies and artists trying to protect the originality of their sound. But there is hope. See the following sidebar.

❷ Sample-Alikes

A sample-alike is a close cousin to the sound-alike. To understand what this is you must first understand what the art of sampling is about.

"Samples" are the series of "borrowed" sounds that make up a portion of the main groove of a song (known as a "loop"). Sampling as an art form found its way into modern pop music with the Beatles cut "Revolution #9," which "borrowed" tidbits of British radio broadcasts and intermingled them with the song. In the '50s and '60s, things of this nature were commonly done without regard for the original own-

SIMON SAYS, "NO SAMPLING"

This is how as an engineer I helped one record company "steal" a sample from Paul Simon and get away without paying him a dime. What makes the story especially juicy is that the culprit was a major label, one that certainly could afford to pay for the sample.

This label had recorded, mixed, and mastered a song by a new artist not realizing that there was a sample loop used in the arrangement that had not been cleared. The producer took the sample off one of those "beats" records assuming that because it was on a CD of things designed to be sampled, it was precleared. It wasn't.[5] The two-bar loop, already used in a number of rap and R&B records, belonged to a cover of a song originally written by Paul Simon.

While most producers had gotten away with using this sample without consulting Simon, this A&R person decided to "do the right thing" and ask his permission. A fatal move. Simon, at that time, was notorious for being a hard-ass about such things. In this case he asked for 50% of the new song's publishing. Here is where the A&R man and I got smart. My reputation for making sound-alikes was well known. So after a few drinks the A&R person and I decided to make an exact duplicate of the loop. Musicians were contracted, studio time booked, and the "Paul sample" surgically removed and replaced with my bootleg.

But something wasn't quite right. The new sample very subtly changed the feel of the groove, even though it was all but identical. What to do? Go back to the studio? Spend more time and money to make it fit? Instead, the A&R man said to me, "You have everybody's invoice for this fiasco. Then who's to know we didn't actually replace it?"

Gambling that in case of a dispute the record company could give the appearance that they really did replace Simon's sample, they then elected not to. The Paul Simon sample remained. The record went to stores, and no one was the wiser.

It's a shame when big record companies break the very laws they lobby for. There is no honor among thieves, but there is karma: the record was a colossal flop.

[5] In fact, many so-called "beats" CDs do not have cleared samples. With these CDs, you're expected to use the samples for demo purposes only. Before using them on a commercial record, you'll need to get clearance through the original publishers that control the rights. If you're using CDs with newly recorded beat loops intended for sampling, read the fine print on the back cover or insert. Some CDs claim to contain only original, license-free samples. Even then, if you use the beat and it turns out to have been lifted from a copyrighted record, guess who pays.

ers of the recordings from which the sounds were taken. But today, whenever pieces of other recordings are used in a new recording, the authors of the new recording have to "clear" the sample. This process involves getting permission from both the record company that owns the sound recording and the publishing company that owns the rights to the song. It's complicated and can get very expensive, and that's assuming the artist is cooperative.[6]

Often the loop being used is so obvious that the sampled artist feels entitled to ask for up to 50% ownership in the new song's publishing. Many artists and labels have agreed and given in but not with great enthusiasm.

A sample-alike is a recreation of a sample using the same techniques and based on the same legal principles as the sound-alike discussed above. Thus, the bother of dealing with temperamental artists is avoided as well as the Gestapo tactics taken by labels when they realize that they have something someone needs. See the sidebar "Simon Says, 'No Sampling'" for an eye-opening example of this.

After the incident in the sidebar, I refused to do any more sample-alikes, but they're still quite common. It has become the newest way to screw writers and record companies out of their mechanical royalties.[7] As hip-hop and rap (the most sample-dependent form of music today) continue to prove profitable, sample-aliking has become a mini-industry, building the reputations of many engineers willing to assist producers in ripping off their fellow producers and writers. Tsk-tsk.

[6] Some artists feel that samples are corrupting the art form of modern music. By way of example, Electric Light Orchestra refused to grant permission for a rock act to use a sample from their hit "Fire on High." Ironically, ELO was widely rumored to be lip-synching at their live stadium concerts in the '70s.

[7] See "Sample Rights," page 72.

CHAPTER SEVENTEEN

⊘Master Fraud

T he next three examples show how record companies both large and small can manipulate both the public and their own artists with shaky sales techniques and crafty accounting.

⊘ Clears, Cleans, and Fake Masters

When I was working as an engineer, I mixed a couple of big-selling records with one producer who was very well-connected. We became good friends. One afternoon I entered the studio to find him yelling into the phone. He slammed the receiver down, looked at me very perturbed, and said, "They're ripping me off." The argument he was having was a dispute over the quarterly statement reflecting his royalty. His royalty is dependent on the sales of the records, so I asked him how he could know how many records the artist had actually sold.

He said to me, "Well, you can audit them, but don't expect to make any friends that way. You can check SoundScan and that will give you some idea. But the only way to know for sure is to have a friend in the Mafia. They can tell you the exact number, but it will cost you."

I had to assume he meant that you would owe them a favor. He continued, "If the record company says they sold two million records, they probably sold about two and a half million."

"But how?" I asked naively. "Don't the bar codes show up whenever a sale is made?"

"If the sale is in America. It's a big world, you know." He was talking about what have been referred to as "clears" and "cleans," both shady ways for big labels to sell records without reporting the sales.

Clears

In a clear, the record company would make a second master lath[1] and give it to a duplication factory that basically does not exist. This plant will make bootlegs of the record, called "clears." The label will supply the "distributor" with the pack-

[1] The steel plate used to press melted plastic into millions of 12- and 7-inch records, called "platters" by the pressing plant.

CLEAR A SPACE FOR ME

There is only one case that I have heard of where an artist tried to take a record company to court over clears.

Before the digital age, clears were easy to spot. They were pressed using a copy of the master lath. A trained ear could hear the deterioration in quality.

Armed with a crate full of these dirty-sounding LPs and an FBI file that told of the connection between the record company and a famous "family-run" bootlegging organization, this artist sued their record company for $321,000 in royalties they believed they were owed.

The case was dropped after the record company settled out of court, but in the pretrial questioning of a disgruntled record company employee it was alleged that clears were a regular part of this company's policy.

The artist never got their money. The record company was sold and two years later filed for bankruptcy. The artist never recorded another album and was dropped from the roster.

Since CD technology was embraced by the major labels in the late '70s, the situation has grown grimmer. These days, the glass master used to make a CD can be copied an infinite number of times without any deterioration in sound, making a modern clear virtually undetectable.

aging materials and whatever else is needed to make the record look like the genuine article. In fact, there is no difference between it and the normal record except that the duplication house making these records won't show up on any of the record company's invoices.

These "clears" will then be shipped by the private distributor to places unknown, like Third World countries that are not in the normal distribution channels. These places don't have sophisticated accounting equipment like bar coding; they just sell the records over the counter and ask no questions. In this manner many record sales fall through the cracks and avoid showing up in the event of an artist's audit. This is the record company's hedge against their enormous overhead and their slim vig.

Cleans

A close cousin to the clear is the clean. These are surplus records that are manufactured and sold to private vendors at huge discount prices with the intention that they will *never* be passed on to a retail store. The name comes from the now-famous tale of the corruption that pervaded MCA Records in the 1980s. Executives inside the company were authorizing the pressing of hundreds of thousands of ex-

THE KING OF CLEANS

The King of Cleans was a man named John LaMonte. In 1974 he purchased several million damaged records from Capitol Records that were to be brought to a vinyl recycling center. Many of these records were Beatles singles.

Instead of sending the units to the graveyard, LaMonte slipped a plain white cover over the records and resold them for 40 cents apiece to rack jobbers, middlemen who sell to smaller stores. The rack jobbers allegedly knew the records were damaged and that they could return the goods to Capitol for 90 cents each.

No one even noticed something was wrong until Capitol realized that there were more records coming back than there were going to the stores. They tried to have LaMonte arrested, but he hadn't done anything illegal. He bought the records legitimately and sold them legitimately, and there is no law against manufacturing plain white sleeves.

cess records. An invoice marked "Clean" was code to those "distributors" in the know that these units could be returned to the record company for a full refund.[2]

2 See the sidebar "The King of Cleans," page 179, and also "Getting 'Cutout' of Royalties," page 62.

An informer-assisted audit will usually expose cleans and clears. Unfortunately, the informer will get a commission of from 30% to 75% of what's recovered. Add to this the fact that the record company will be eternally antagonistic toward you in the future. This, above all, is what deters many artists and producers from challenging the record company's accounting.

❷ Soundtrack Scams and So-Called CD Samplers

If you've ever signed a registration book for a music seminar, then you ended up on a mailing list. Whether you know it or not, your name, along with those of the thousands of other people who signed with you, ended up in the computers of many companies. At least one will be one of the many sleazy record companies that claim to help you interface with "the industry" through their CD samplers.

These are compilations that take various unsigned acts and put a song from their demo on a compilation record. This record will supposedly be distributed to many radio stations and labels or used for a soundtrack of some bogus movie that has no studio distribution. The idea is to give the act exposure and hopefully get them a recording contract.

These offers sicken me. They prey on the desperation and naiveté of young bands, most of whom are out in the boondocks and think that the industry is inaccessible to them. Many new artists have started out on compilation records, but not the kind that these people offer to do. This is how it really works.

These companies send out advertising to artists through direct mail and hope for a 5% response. They know that there are thousands of acts out there, so all they need are 20 or so responses to go to work. Generally they charge an "all-in" fee for mastering and placement on the CD and on the liner notes. They say that 500 or 1,000 of these CDs will be sent out to "the industry." The fee for the act is generally about $5,000. This is steep by any stretch of the imagination. The fact that people go for it is somewhat depressing to me.

Think: If this company gets 11 responses, that translates into $55,000 in revenue. Mastering costs for the entire CD are about $2,000 tops, and CD duplication for 1,000 units about another $1,500. Add about $2 per unit for shipping (assuming they really send out all 1,000 of them) and you have a total production cost of $5,500.

Net profit—$49,500. Not bad for a couple of months' work.

To add insult to injury, they will always make the artist sign away their rights to their mechanical licenses (see "Publishing Deals," page 69) since they claim that all the CDs are being *given away.* Plus if the artist wants several copies, they will usually have to pay for any more than five of them.

There is no way to track or audit these fly-by-nights to insure that they are sending anything to anybody. They buy lists of names of unsigned artists from list brokers, who get them from the seminars mentioned above and the Internet, and they're usually located in some state in the Midwest or Florida.

There are a few companies that are performing this type of service legitimately. They have distribution contracts with reputable distribution companies. Ask about distribution contracts as a test to see if the company is on the up and up. Also ask for a bio of the people in the organization and who they're affiliated with. If this book has taught you anything, it's taught you that this a business of connections. If this company that wants your $5,000 is truly effective, they should be connected as well. But weigh the cost versus return carefully.

If they're hesitant to answer any of your questions, RUN THE OTHER WAY!

❷ 9-to-1 Publishing, or "Why Is There Only One Good Song on the Record?"

If you've ever gone out and bought a CD because you liked the song that you heard on the radio, only to find that it was the only good song on the record, you're not alone.

There are several reasons why this happens. The most typical reason relates to publishing. It is not uncommon after a mercy signing (described in "The Mercy Signing," page 213), or another signing where the label is unsatisfied with the finished record, that they call in a ringer to save the album.

This usually boils down to hiring a songwriter other than the artist to write the song that will be the single off the album. The single is what you'll hear on the radio and is understandably the best song on the album. Sometimes, however, an artist's manager will know that the label will want to use outside material to sell the artist even before the record deal is signed. He or she may know this because they have a gut feeling that their client's material is weak. If they feel this way, they will make sure that the artist's contract states that at least *a certain number of songs written by the artist must appear on the record.*

The reason for this should be obvious. Remember that the compulsory license is worth about 6 cents per song (after the record company's adjustments). So if the artist writes nine songs on the record and an outside writer writes only one song, but that song is the hit, the artist still gets 54 cents per album and the ringer gets 6 cents.[3]

Even though the ringer's song is selling the record, the artist makes the killing, because their nine loser songs are riding the coattails of the one hit. Managers work on commission, so they have a vested interest in how much mechanical licensing money their artist realizes. If you ever hear a manager talk about this "great song that my client wrote" and you think it stinks (even beyond the limits of your personal taste), you can now guess what's on that manager's mind. This example, of course, goes for producers and anyone else who stands to profit from the compulsory license paid to the writers of the songs on the record.

The way to spot the "9-to-1 syndrome" is easy. Look at the liner notes of the record. If all the songs are written by the artist *except the single*, be skeptical.

The other reason for the "only one good song" phenomenon is a bit more innocent. Even if the artist writes all the songs on the record, sometimes a record company will pick a song that is the least representative of the band's overall sound to use as the single. The best example I can think of was with the band Extreme (see the sidebar below).

[3] See "Publishing Deals," page 69.

EXTREME MEASURES

In 1994 Extreme's sound was very aggressive power pop. But there was one song on their second record, a tender, mellow love song, called "More than Words." The record company chose this song as the single, and if you were anywhere near a radio in the year 1992, you will remember that it was a huge radio hit.

But when people got the record home and realized that "More than Words" was the only song of its kind on the record, many of them promptly tried to return it to the local record stores. The situation got so out of hand that one record store in Atlanta had a sign by the cash register reading, "We don't take back Extreme records."

Although Extreme's career took a nose dive after that album, "More than Words" is still earning bucks on the radio. In the long run, a wrong hit is better than no hit.

CHAPTER EIGHTEEN

Sneaky Lawyer Stuff

The University of Colorado has published a study that surveyed various sides of the controversy surrounding the testing of animals in medical laboratories. After collating questionnaires from activists and researchers, the study reached a unanimous conclusion: Instead of rats, labs should use lawyers to perform their various tests on. The study concluded this for two reasons: (1) They discovered that the lab technicians didn't develop as much of an attachment for the attorneys as they did for the rats, and (2) there were some things that the rats wouldn't do.

We all love to lawyer-bash—even lawyers joke about how devious they can be. Well, it is not so funny if you happen to get your toes stepped on during the attorney minuet. Following are a few dance steps.

Disclaimer: Not all attorneys do these things. Only most of the ones that I've met.

The "I Forgot to Mark the Contract" Trick

Most lawyer tricks revolve around one main concept—wasting the opposing side's time and money. Every attorney works by the hour. Even if they agree to do a job for a fixed fee, they are figuring how many hours they will put into a project. Once that time threshold is crossed, their enthusiasm and the quality of their work will decline rapidly. The tricky attorney will try to exhaust the other lawyer's time in an attempt to encroach on that threshold.

When an attorney reads a contract for the first time, he or she may take several hours just to go through it and make notes for changes. The industry norm is to underline the changes with a blue or red pencil, making them obvious to the attorney on the other side of the negotiation. Some attorneys, in an attempt to confuse or exhaust the patience of their opponent, will make some of the changes that were requested but "forget to mark the contract." This makes the contract look like a first draft, and it now must be read from scratch, just as if it were a new contract.

Sometimes they will send a cover memo alleging that all the changes were made but in reality keep some of the old provisions. They will "red-pencil" only the changes that they want the other attorney to see.

The hope is that perhaps the other attorney is not as observant as they should be and will not take the time to read the entire contract over again.

Since the advent of word processing software that tracks changes to a document, lawyers have had to become more clever about this technique. "Tracking changes" works by automatically highlighting any alterations to a document. But all one has to do to override this is create a new document with the same name as the old one, and *poof*, you can effortlessly camouflage changes. High tech gives this old trick a villainous twist that exploits our ever-expanding trust of computers.

❯ Virtual Terms

Virtual terms are terms that are only offered when someone is trying to lure you into taking a job—for example, when a producer or label promises someone X, Y, and Z, but when the contract arrives those terms are nowhere to be found.

If you call them on this, the attorney will usually say that a mistake was made or the secretary sent a "standard agreement," not the special one that was for you. The conversation will usually end with the attorney saying that all the original terms of the agreement are still in place and he will forward the contract ASAP.

After some time goes by and it doesn't arrive, you start to worry. You call the attorney. He says (if he comes to the phone) that it must be in the mail and you shouldn't worry about it. He will probably encourage you to start the gig and you'll sign the contract whenever it gets there.

If you persist in wanting to see the agreement before you start working, expect to be fired, or else something will happen where the job is delayed and they will "call you as soon as we work it out." Not surprisingly, you will never hear from them again.

Believe it or not, these people are doing you a favor. They never intended to pay you anyway. Unless there is a contract or at least a signed deal memo—watch out.

❯ Internet Labels and Their "Nonexclusive" Contracts

In the past few years many artists have been attracted to online "independent" labels and their folksy offer to distribute records for little or no cost to the artist. These companies, which have cool animated introductions on their websites, are leveraging the popular theory that millions of people will have access to the record because there are just so many damn people using the Internet. They promise to distribute a record to stores as well as create links from other websites. They rarely reject anybody, so long as the artist pays the small up-front fees for bar codes and administration (usually not more than $100).

This "get signed for a hundred bucks" offer sounds like a dream for many artists who've already produced an album's worth of material and are tired of dealing with major label bullshit. Online indies, as I call them, offer a turnkey record deal. No managers or lawyers to deal with, and no obnoxious A&R comments like, "Well, I don't hear a single." Screw that. You'll show 'em all, put the damn record on the street, and keep all the profits. It's a nice dream, and these online indies attract excellent artists whose music is probably too "niche" (read: too original) for most major label marketing plans. But there is a real danger.

First, understand that some of these online indies are actually shells for larger labels. (To get an idea of who owns what, refer to the family trees on pages 241-247.) But aside from this trickery, here's the real snag: These companies know that no artist will sign over their *exclusive* rights to a virtual company that offers no advance. So, buried within their seemingly benign contract is a nasty loophole that could tie you to these people *forever*.

Most of these contracts start off with a congenial intro that says something like, "You are entering a special place where dreams are fulfilled and hopes grow. In order for it to work we must have an agreement, so here it is!" It will then con you into thinking that you are entering into a one-year contract that will pay you 70% of any money earned from selling your recordings through them and that the licensing of your record to them is "nonexclusive." Which means that you can enter into the same agreement with anyone else.

It's phrased like this: "We agree to provide You throughout the Territory and during the Sales Period with listing of your Recordings in E-Stores during the Term."

Followed by this clause, "You grant to us throughout the Territory and during the Sales Period the rights to use your name(s), professional and/or group name(s), photographs and other images and likeness of You, biographical and/or other information concerning You regarding all of our business activities."

Sounds good. 70%!!! The major labels didn't even offer you that much (more like 12%) and it's only a year contract. How much harm can that be? If you hate them, it's over in a year. Right?

Wrong.

The key lies in how this contract defines the "Sales Period" and the "Territory." At the bottom of the contract the following definitions can be found:

"'Territory' means the Universe."

"'Sales Period' means the time period beginning on the Signing Date and continuing in perpetuity for each of your Recordings in each country of the Territory."

For those new to this business, "perpetuity" is lawyer lingo meaning "forever."

So, an accurate translation of the opening paragraph would be this:

"You grant to us throughout the universe and till the end of time itself, the rights to use all your recordings, (even ones you didn't send to us) your name(s), professional and/or group name(s), photographs and other images and likeness of You, biographical and/or other information concerning You in all of our business activities."

Add to this the fact that you have to supply them with the produced CD and press materials. Their investment is about $0.00 and they get to own you completely.

Even though they say the licensing is "nonexclusive," they do this knowing that major label deals are *always* exclusive and will make you swear that you've broken ties with everyone else before they allow you to sign with them. Oops. Can't sell your vital organs to more than one hospital, can you? Well, you can try, but you'd be guilty of fraud. And you can kiss your career good-bye if you're caught playing that game.

You don't have to be a Harvard Law grad to see how this scam works. The virtual record company plays the numbers; they sign thousands of artists a year, waiting for the day when one of them gets an offer from a major label. Needless to say, getting off the old "nonexclusive" deal will be like a Hollywood divorce. Expect pain.

Still think it's worth $100 bucks?

Before you go disconnecting your computer, understand that many companies do this legitimately and want nothing more than to see you succeed. Knowing which type you're getting involved with can be tricky. Pay attention to the contract you are signing.

❯ The Little Squeeze

I love this one. Watching it in action is like watching *The Sting* with Robert Redford and Paul Newman. The Little Squeeze, as I call it, is when two or more parties conspire to "squeeze out" someone who is impeding the progress of the deal. Now the sad part is that the someone in question could be impeding the deal for legitimate reasons, or they could just be a pain in the ass. But in either case, everyone else involved wants them out of the way. What makes it hard is that the squeezee is usually placed so well in the game that the squeezers will have to use some finesse to push him aside.

Here's an example that I was party to.

In the mid-'80s I knew an up-and-coming manager who had only one act. He asked me to engineer the demo that he was producing and I did. Afterward I took it to a record company I was doing some work for at the time. They liked the artist but not the production. This was a small record company and they didn't have a lot of money to spend. They knew that I had delivered good masters for them in the past with a small budget, so they said they would put up some money if I produced it rather than the manager.

The manager felt that he should produce it, despite the fact that he could not get a deal with the tape he had made. Even if he had, no label would have let him produce, since he didn't have a track record producing *anything*. This point became a deal-breaker, and although everyone tried to talk sense into him, he wouldn't listen. He was determined to produce, and it was killing the deal; the artist would never get signed, I would lose the investment of my time in the project, and the label that was interested in signing the artist would not get a good act. Everyone was being screwed because of this manager's arrogance—especially his client, the artist, whose career would go down the toilet if he didn't get a deal real soon.

In came the lawyer—my lawyer. He suggested a partnership between the label and a group of us as *general partners*. The label would put up $25,000 and the partners would collectively put up the other $25,000 to make a record, making a total budget of $50,000. The record label and the general partners (GPs) would do a one-off master licensing deal. (See "The Artist/Producer Production Deal," page 124.)

The GPs would consist of myself, the manager/producer, and my lawyer. We would have 50% ownership of the master. The other 50% would belong to the label.

This kind of deal is not uncommon in the indie record world, where no one party has the full amount of money to put up. But here's the catch. The 50% ownership would be divided up equally among the GPs based on the percentage of their participation. So if the total partnership between myself, the manager, and my attorney was worth $25,000, then each of us would have to put up $8,333.33 for it to be an equal partnership. Sounds simple enough, right?

The label, the manager, my lawyer, and of course myself would transfer their share into my production company's account. The checks for the production would be written off my company's checking account, and I would be required to keep all receipts for the end of the project to verify that the money was spent.

Now, what the manager didn't know is that the label and I wanted him out of the production picture, but we needed his participation in order to sign the artist to the deal. The lawyer provided the means by drafting the partnership agreement. We gained the manager's confidence with the partnership concept and then used our money to leverage him out. Here's how:

He couldn't come up with $8,333.33 at the time we needed it. So we agreed that he would only have to put up what he had, and my lawyer and I would make up the rest. He only had $4,000 to invest, so we put up the balance of $21,000 to complete the partnership. This made the manager only a 12.5% owner in the partnership. Seems fair, right? He's only putting up 12.5% of the money. Here's the ballbuster:

In reality, the record company only put $10,000 in my account. My lawyer put in nothing. I put in $2,000 and the manager put in $4,000. That's only $16,000. That's what I made the record on. Except that I made arrangements with the recording studio to supply me with enough invoices (fake ones, of course) to total $50,000. Studios are used to doing shady things like this for producers if the relationship is a good one.[1]

The manager was actually entitled to a 25% interest, but with creative invoicing he became a tiny minority partner. With him in a minority position, it was easy to outvote him with decisions like who would produce, engineer, and so on.

To add insult to injury, I claimed to go *over budget*. In a partnership situation, when costs go over budget all the partners are required to make up the difference.

The manager claimed to be tapped out of money, so the record company paid off his share of—you guessed it—$4,000. This reduced the manager's percentage participation even further. Oh, well.

The moral of the story is:

Lead, follow, or get out of the way.

[1] See the recording budgets in "The Virtual Budget and the Virtual Producer's Fee," page 133.

❯ Letters of Misdirection

This is a name I've given to LODs when they are designed to undermine the deal.[2] It is not uncommon for an artist's or label's lawyer to argue for months over small points, driving the producer's legal bills through the roof, before they finally come to terms, only to draft a letter of direction that circumvents the payment terms. Here's an example:

The artist's lawyer will argue that the LOD is a sort of "permission slip" generated by the artist allowing the label to forward the producer's share directly to the producer. But what if the major label refuses to sign the LOD? If an artist has agreed that the producer will be paid via an LOD directly from the major label, then the assumption is that label will do just that. Despite that, many labels are reluctant to sign.

If this occurs, the producer may find himself without a right to audit the label and get his money. In order to make the label sign and honor the LOD, he will have to sue the artist for what's called "performance," meaning that the artist is not performing his or her part of the contract in making the label sign and pay. The only way for the artist to make the label pay is to sue the label. The artist, of course, will never do that.

The telltale sign of letters of misdirection is that they use language like, "This letter is a courtesy only; the producer is not a beneficiary of it." Meaning that just because the artist has given the label permission to give the producer money, the label doesn't have to honor it.

The best way to avoid this sort of thing is for the producer's lawyer to draft the LOD himself and have both parties sign it. The producer's lawyer will usually wait for the artist's lawyer to draft it because that's the way it should be—the contractor should generate the first draft of any agreement for the contractee. But it doesn't always work out that way, as you will see.

2 See "Letters of Direction," page 144.

❯ The First Draft Is the Coldest

Most lawyers will tell you that the person generating the first draft of an agreement is at a disadvantage. It's true. Not only is their hand being exposed first, but the cost of generating the first draft is the hard hit in one's legal bill. Revisions can get just as pricey, but if it's a simple and basic agreement, then the majority of the bill will be for customizing the first draft to the specific job.

Since many contracts happen after the deal is done, the sleazy lawyer will take advantage of this and send a "false first draft." This is a contract that has nothing to do with the deal that you made. Now bear in mind that this does not happen often on standard record deals and production deals, but many up-and-coming artists and producers sign unconventional deals with sleazy vanity labels to get their foot in the door.

Let's say, for example, that an artist and a producer want to develop some songs together. The plan is to record some demos at the producer's studio and then shop them to a label. Pretty basic, right?

There seems no point in doing an expensive contract at this time since it's not even clear if they will like working together, so they proceed on good faith, the way many artists do. After several months, some good work comes out of it, and the artist takes the tape to a lawyer, who gives it to an A&R person at a label. They bite, and the game is afoot. Now a contract must be formalized between the artist and the producer.

Whatever their original verbal agreement was, it will now be thrown out the window by the artist's sneaky lawyer. He will forward a contract that is a production deal, but not one that pertains to the producer as a cowriter or copublisher. Also, the points in the agreement will be ridiculously low compared to the industry standard.

Naturally the producer will respond with some surprise and confront the lawyer and/or the artist. This is where the relationship starts to break down. The label will usually side with the artist and tell both parties to work it out soon or the deal is off. The lawyer for the artist will then say something like, "Well, if you don't like my boilerplate, then you generate your own first draft." This is unethical and downright wrong, but it happens a lot. The producer will now have to spend the money him/herself to generate the contract that the artist should be paying for. Sometimes they will, but sometimes they will just go with the flow so as to not rock the boat and spoil the deal.

This happened to me twice. After the second time, I had two lawyers draft my own customized agreement that I use whenever I feel I'm dealing with a shyster attorney. When the artist's lawyer sees my agreement, they usually get in gear and do the right thing.

⊘ "Voted Out"—The Band as a Corporate Entity

When you see four or five members on the cover of a CD, the assumption is that these individuals make up the band. But what is a band?

This seemingly obvious question in fact is more complex than most musicians know. A band that plays in a garage or in some of the clubs around town can be anything. But once the act is signed to a major label, the time comes to decide who really will and will not make up the band as a corporate entity, meaning the band as a business.

Creating a corporation is the process of creating a new entity that will own all the things that the band or artist produces: songs, logos, the images that get printed on T-shirts, endorsements of musical equipment, and so on. Why not just let the artists own everything themselves? The answer given by many lawyers is, in order to protect the band from lawsuits it's simpler if there is only one artist in the group. If the corporation owns the copyright of the songs, then a chaser going after a copyright sues the corporation, not the artist.[3]

[3] In practice they would sue the artist as well. But the forming of a corporate entity for the purposes of protection is still commonplace.

PAYING A DRUMMER FOR NOT PLAYING

My friend Jordan was the drummer in Atom (not their real name), a mid-1980s hair band. Although he had been with the group since the beginning, he was asked to be subcontracted after the writing members of the group were offered a deal on A&M. Feeling a bit bitter, he asked for $1,000 a week. Feeling guilty, the band agreed, and the label agreed to cut a weekly check on the band's behalf to Jordan. As you can guess, the $1,000 was charged to the band's account.

Although the band was advanced about $500,000, most of this money went to the producer and the production of the record, a 48-track digital recording, which at the time was very avant-garde. Meanwhile, Jordan collected his check every week.

After a lengthy production and marketing campaign, A&M asked the band to do a tour to promote the record. They agreed. Jordan, still under contract, became the single most expensive member on the road.

The tour was unsuccessful. Record sales didn't budge. The market had been oversaturated with metal bands, and Atom decided to regroup and alter their sound a bit. They let go of every one of the subcontracted players, including Jordan. One problem: Jordan's contract was good as long as A&M didn't drop them from the label. So while a broke and busted Atom auditioned new members and wrote new songs, Jordan stayed home and collected his $1,000-a-week salary.

Think ahead when forming your corporation.

But what if there are two songwriters in the group? Traditionally it's only the writing members that will be stockholders in the corporation. The other members become subcontracted sideplayers. They draw a salary or are paid on a gig-by-gig basis even though they appear everywhere the two main players appear—on album sleeves, at personal appearances, MTV interviews, the works.

The sideplayers often feel cheated by this until they get used to it. Suddenly you are not a team anymore. There are advantages to being a sideplayer, however. You are guaranteed to be paid, usually by letter of direction from the main label. I have known several situations where subcontracted drummers ended up making more than the stockholders in a group (see the sidebar on page 191).

This is where it can get very tricky. Even if all the members of the band are part of the corporation, that is not foolproof protection against one member being ousted. Each band member holds a percentage of stock or ownership in the corporation. Sometimes the stock is divided equally. For example, if the band has four members, then

WHO BUTTERS MARILYN'S BREAD?

In June 1997, Marilyn Manson found himself the subject of a lawsuit by his cowriter Daisy Berkowitz. It seems that Marilyn neglected to pay Daisy (whose real name is Scott Putesky) his share of the royalties from those cool hit tunes they penned together. Daisy trusted Marilyn to be the executor of the copyrights by signing over the administration of his share to a company he thought was equally owned by the entire group.

In his suit, Daisy claimed that the group's attorney intentionally drafted the agreement in Marilyn's favor. He also claimed that Marilyn told him signing the agreement would guarantee that Daisy would be in the band *for life!*

After the record was certified platinum, Daisy asked for some money. Instead, he was fired from the band without a cent. His ten-count lawsuit includes malpractice against the attorney for not making him aware of the inherent conflict of interest in representing both sides.

I'm not holding my breath for a quick outcome on this. I think Daisy will eventually get something, but only after he spends gobs of cash. Word of advice: Before signing anything, always get your *own* counsel.

each member would get 25% of the stock. But sometimes the division is not equitable. Let's say that one member of the group is the clear frontman or -woman. They might get 51% of the stock and the remaining 49% would go to the sideplayers.

The difference between a corporation band and a regular band is that in a corporate environment decisions are made by majority vote. If the one member of the group with 51% chooses to fire everyone else, he or she can get away with it because he or she is the majority stockholder. He or she can fire a person even if that person is a founding member of the band (see the "Marilyn" sidebar).

◉ Legal-ease?

Legalese is the language of lawyers, and anyone who has ever looked at a contract prepared by lawyers can attest to the conundrums they create for the rest of us. Why say, "You can't do that," when you can say, "That action is contraindicated"? Well, the skeptical answer, and one I'm prone toward, is that it makes your client more dependent on you.

Revealed below are some of the basics of legalese. These are only a few of the key phrases, but they will get you started. (A complete book of translations would be as large as several dictionaries.)

For simplicity, the examples below are written from the artist's point of view, but they apply to producers, labels, and just about any situation where talent is being contracted.

After this section, go on to the next section, "Decoding of an Actual Warner Bros. Record Contract," and see how some sneaky lawyers took advantage of multitudes of recording artists during the '70s and '80s with an actual slimebag agreement.

Note: Nothing in this book or this section should construed as legal advice.

WHEN IT SAYS:	IT REALLY MEANS:
Some Easy Ones	
"Audiophile Recording(s)," "LPs," or "Phonorecords"	An antiquated term for a record, CD, or tape.
"Pursuant to the receipt of a financial instrument"	"When money is actually received," as opposed to when the contract *says* you will be paid. There is a distinct difference.

WHEN IT SAYS:	IT REALLY MEANS:
"Commercially satisfactory master"	An album that the record company feels they can easily sell without too much effort.
"In perpetuity throughout the known universe"	Anyplace you can think of and "until the end of time itself." This bit of sci-fi is designed to cover all possible territory in which any money might be made. It almost always pertains to the transfer of rights and is taken to mean that the rights granted are granted forever, just in case someday we find a way to sell the record on the planet Jupiter.

Advanced Legonics: Loophole Creators

"Notwithstanding anything herein contained to the contrary . . ."	"If anything else in the contract contradicts the next half of *this* sentence, then *this* sentence is the *prevailing rule*." This bit of jargon is one of the biggest red flags. Often it is used to construct a trapdoor or "loophole" by creating an exception to what is fundamentally promised in the agreement. The exception created will often be a brutal and costly one.
"Except as otherwise hereinafter set forth . . ."	"Except when the contract says otherwise further on down the page or later in the agreement." Upon seeing this phrase one should carefully scan through the entire contract to find exceptions to what is about to be promised in the second half of the same sentence. Example: "Except as otherwise herein set forth, artist will be paid on 100% of sales." For certain, buried somewhere within the body of the contract, there is a phrase that will contradict this. Often it will begin with one of the phrases mentioned in this section.

WHEN IT SAYS:	IT REALLY MEANS:
	Note that where the phrase above this ("Notwithstanding anything . . .") creates a loophole by making specific exceptions to general concepts, this does the opposite; it creates a loophole by making generalities out of things that appear specific.
"Notwithstanding the foregoing . . ."	"What follows is an exception to what was just said a moment ago." This is a first cousin to the two phrases right above it. You will often find that these three seemingly innocent words are being used to carve a loophole in certain obligations that the record company would prefer to dodge. Following it may also be the things they want the artist to do that will be over and above the "normal" duties listed in the agreement.
"Without limiting the generality of the foregoing, the Artist (producer, writer, etc.) hereby . . ."	The words *following* this phrase should be taken to have the *broadest possible interpretation.* This phrase is often used when discussing the transfer of copyrights and is a common strategy of an insecure attorney. Instead of listing every possible situation or grant of rights (and risk leaving something out), the attorney will insert a phrase like this one, which basically means "plus anything else I can't think of right now."

Advanced Legonics II: Confidence Instillers

" . . . shall be completed in a timely fashion"	Whenever the word "timely" appears in a contract, it's time for caution. Contracts that use this phrase are attempting to keep certain time frames nebulous and subjective, often for the benefit of the party offering the contract.

WHEN IT SAYS:	IT REALLY MEANS:
	Example: "The recording of the album shall be completed in a timely fashion." Who decides what "timely" is? Answer: The one who has the checkbook. A fair agreement will usually spell out time frames *precisely*.
"Company shall consult with Artist on . . ."	A meaningless phrase designed to instill false confidence in the artist that the record company is duty-bound to ask the artist's permission on a particular subject. A provision containing this phrase usually refers to cover art or selection of the single. In reality, if the company even says to the artist, "Hey, we already decided this, but what do you think?" they have "consulted." Artist's lawyers and managers use this one to bamboozle their clients into thinking they did a great job negotiating on their behalf. It's a joke.
"Approval from Artist will not unreasonably be withheld."	Living in the same neighborhood as the previous phrase will be this little trickster. It sounds as if the artist has been given power over something, but in fact it's the opposite. This phrase actually prevents the artist from holding out too strongly on any issue that needs to be determined after the contract is written (like cover art, tour support, and marketing decisions). Example: "Artist's approval of cover art not to be unreasonably withheld." Although this seems to protect both parties, in essence it only protects the record company, because they have more leverage in deciding what is and is not "reasonable."

WHEN IT SAYS:	IT REALLY MEANS:
"Prior to the expiration of the applicable period"	"Before time has run out" on whatever issue this phrase is connected to. This would be relatively harmless except that figuring out when the "applicable period" begins and ends in most recording contracts can be confusing. Scan carefully for any sentences using this phrase and see if the "applicable period" is really what you think it is. Lawyers have sneaky ways of extending a two-year contract so that it turns into a three- or four-year contract.
"The invalidity or unenforce-ability of any provision here-of shall not affect the validity or enforceability of any other provision hereof."	"If one item in the contract is later deemed in-valid or illegal, the rest of the contract will still be in effect." This can be a pain, because it gives the label a license to throw all kinds of junk into the contract that they know is uncon-stitutional. If a judge later determines that one clause is completely enslaving (in legal terms this is called "overreaching"—how demure), then the artist will still be bound to produce and perform for the company.
"Company shall give reason-able notice of . . ."	Usually pertains to the label's legal require-ment to send an artist relevant information about the status of their recording agreement. It often refers to royalty statements. In reality, the record company won't give a rat's ass whether they notified the artist or not. If the artist didn't get the notice, the label will as-sume it must have been lost in the mail, with the mail being "reasonable notice" in the eyes of the record company. Good contracts will in-sist on "registered mail" as reasonable notice.

➋ Decoding of an Actual Warner Bros. Record Contract

Now we're going to put the above lesson into action. We're going to examine a common fraud in the record industry: It's customary to offer new recording artists a sliding royalty scale for future albums. So if an artist is only getting 12% on album one, the record company might offer an incentive by saying, "But we'll give you 14% on album two and 15% on album three if you turn out to be really good and turn in all your records on time."

"On time" is the lynchpin here and the key to the empty promise of higher royalties, as you'll see in a minute.

Below are the first three paragraphs of a major label recording contract. First review the paragraph. Directly beside each you will find the TRANSLATION, broken down line by line in plain English. Then, below that, I restate the clause to show how it might actually be applied in reality. Remember, this is actual language from a Warner Bros. contract that was in common use throughout the '70s and '80s.

4 "Limpidity": legalese for "clearness."

Note: "COMPANY" refers to the record company, ARTIST refers to the recording artist. Key phrases mentioned in the previous chart are in bold for limpidity.[4]

EXCLUSIVE ARTIST'S RECORDING AGREEMENT

1. COMPANY hereby engages ARTIST's exclusive personal services as a recording artist in connection with the production of records and ARTIST hereby accepts such engagement and agrees to exclusively render such services for COMPANY during the term hereof and all extensions and renewals.

TRANSLATION: The artist shall make records only for this specific record company, and for no one else for as long as this contract runs.

REALITY: The killer phrase "all extensions and renewals," as you will see, allows the record company to extend this agreement for several years beyond what the artist thinks they are contracting for.

2.The term of this Agreement shall be for a period of one (1) year commencing on the date hereof ("Initial Period"). ARTIST hereby grants to COMPANY four (4) consecutive separate options to extend the term for further periods of one (1) year each ("Option Periods"), each upon the same terms and conditions applicable to the Initial Period, **except as otherwise hereinafter set forth.** The Initial Period and every Option Period for which COMPANY has exercised its option are hereinafter sometimes referred to together as the "Term." Each option shall be exercised, if at all, by notice to ARTIST at any time prior to the date the Term would otherwise expire.

TRANSLATION: The length of this contract is one year starting at the date when the artist signs the contract. This first year is called the "Initial Period." The artist gives the company the right to renew this contract four times, once each year. Each new year in which the contract is extended is called an "Option Period," and all the same conditions and hidden traps from the first year apply to each additional year **unless it specifically says so elsewhere in this contract.** The first year and every other year of this contract will sometimes be called the "Term." (Or it may be called something else.) Each time the company renews its option to keep the artist on the label, they will notify the artist before the end of the year.

REALITY: The length of the contract is five years, but the record company can terminate the agreement at the end of any year. While under contract to the company, the artist can record *for no one else,* including a song on a buddy's film score, making a silly home-recorded birthday announcement, or singing on a friend's demo, without express permission from the label.

A fair agreement would have an exact time frame as to when it would end and not base the end of the term on whenever the record company feels like ending it. However, the company is not without compassion: The last line of the paragraph says that if the artist doesn't hear from the label before the end of the year, they're free to go. Oh boy!

3.(a) During the Initial Period, ARTIST shall jointly perform for the recording of masters the equivalent in playing time of one (1) LP. At COMPANY's election, ARTIST shall jointly perform for the recording of additional masters provided that such additional masters shall not exceed the equivalent in playing time of one (1) LP during the Initial Period.

TRANSLATION: During the first year, the artist shall record a series of songs that total approximately 40 to 50 minutes in playing time. The company may ask the artist to record more songs during the first year, provided that the total running time of these songs is no more than another album's worth.

REALITY: If the label doesn't like the songs, they can insist the artist record more. In fact, even if they *do* like them, they can ask for more songs, provided that the total playing time of the album of songs doesn't exceed the normal length (40 to 50 minutes). This seems to protect the artist from giving the label more than an album's worth of material within each year, but they have ways around this as well, as you'll see shortly.

3.(b) During each Option Period, ARTIST shall jointly perform for the recording of masters the equivalent in playing time of one (1) LP. At COMPANY's election, ARTIST shall jointly perform for the recording of additional masters provided that such additional masters shall not exceed the equivalent in playing time of one (1) LP during any Option Period.

TRANSLATION: During each year in which the contract is still in force, the artist shall record songs totaling approximately 40 to 50 minutes in playing time. And again, the company may ask the artist to record more songs in that year, provided that the total running time of the new songs is about the same length (40 or 50 minutes).

REALITY: This is a repeat of 3(a), extending the same rights to the label for each "Option Period." Each year in which the record company is not happy with the work the artist submits, they have the right to ask the artist to record more and more songs until they feel they have enough "acceptable" material for a full-length album for that year. In effect, the artist must keep recording until the record company says they can stop. (Sure sounds like an employment agreement to me.)

And now for the killer clause. Pay attention:

3.(c) Provided that ARTIST shall have timely completed the recording (as hereinafter defined) of the first LP required to be recorded during the Initial Period or any Option Period in accordance with all of the material terms and conditions of this Agreement, COMPANY's election to require ARTIST to record a second LP during the Initial Pe-

TRANSLATION: Provided that the artist **quickly completes** the first album and complies with all the strings attached in this contract, the company's right to request a second album during that same year shall be made (i) within six months after the completion of the first album or (ii) three months before the end of the year, whichever comes later. But, if the artist fails riod or any Option Period shall be made, if at all, prior to the later of (i) one hundred eighty (180) days following the completion of recording of the first LP required to be recorded during the applicable Period or (ii) ninety (90) days prior to the expiration of the applicable Period. **If ARTIST shall have failed to have timely completed** the recording of the first LP required to be recorded during the applicable Period, then COMPANY's election to require ARTIST to perform for the recording of a second LP during such Period may be made, if at all, at any time prior to the date the applicable Period would otherwise expire. **Notwithstanding the foregoing,** if ARTIST shall have **failed to timely complete** the recording of any such first LP for reasons solely caused by COMPANY or solely within COMPANY's control, then COMPANY's election to require ARTIST to perform for the recording of a second LP during the applicable Period shall be made, if at all, not later than ninety (90) days prior to the expiration of the applicable period.

to deliver the album **in an amount of time that the company thinks is reasonable,** then the company's demand for a second album could be made at **any time before the end of that year.** If, however, the artist is unable to complete the first album during the year because of something the company did (or failed to do), then the time limit for the company's request for the second album must be made at least three months before the end of the year.

REALITY: Although written in a very contorted way, this basically means that the label can ask for two records within one contract year. This is the case even if the artist was not able to complete the first record due to a screw-up on the part of the label. The label also has up to six months after receiving the finished recordings to ask for this second record. This effectively extends the time of the contract, since the six-month deadline could fall after the end of the contract year. As a weird form of concession, the label agrees that if the album can't be completed because they, the label, screwed up somehow (like not giving the artist recording money or not approving of the producer and the studio, as you'll see in a minute), then they only have three months before the end of the year to request a second album. Well, that's a relief.

3.(d) ARTIST shall record masters for COMPANY hereunder in a recording studio selected or approved by COMPANY at such times and with such individual producer as COMPANY may designate or approve. COMPANY shall advise ARTIST of the financial terms of any agreement with any producer and ARTIST shall have the right to approve such financial terms, **which approval ARTIST shall not unreasonably withhold.** Moses Avalon shall be the producer of the first LP required to be recorded during the Initial Period of the Term of this Agreement.

TRANSLATION: The artist shall record the album when the company says, where the company says, and with a producer that the company will choose for the artist. The company is required to tell the artist how much they are paying the producer (and tagging onto the SSC) and how many points from their end of the deal they are giving to the producer. The artist shall have the right to object if they think it's too much, **but not too strongly or they will be in breach of this agreement.** Moses Avalon will produce the first album of the first year.

REALITY: The artist is *working* for the label, period. The label says how much it will cost (i.e., how much the artist will owe them) and who will be in charge. The artist can object, but they'd better not get pushy about it.

3.(d) (cont'd) ARTIST acknowledges that COMPANY has advised ARTIST of the financial terms of COMPANY's agreement with Moses Avalon and that ARTIST approves of same. The masters recorded by ARTIST hereunder shall consist of ARTIST's newly recorded joint studio performances of material selected or approved by COMPANY and not previously recorded by ARTIST. Each such master shall be subject to COMPANY's approval as commercially satisfactory for the manufacture and sale of records. Upon the request of COMPANY, ARTIST shall re-record any selection until a **commercially satisfactory master** shall have been obtained.

TRANSLATION: Even though in the last paragraph the artist agreed to be reasonable about objecting to how much the company would pay the producer, here the artist acknowledges in advance that the financial terms of company's agreement with Moses Avalon are A-okay. The songs recorded by the artist for this record shall consist of new material, approved by the company and not previously recorded by the artist. Each song shall be subject to **the company's standards of quality.** If the company requests it (and they will), the artist has to re-record any song until an album of songs has been completed that **the company thinks it can easily sell.**

REALITY: The label has complete control of every element of the artist's recordings.[5] But even though the label has complete control of the recording from jump street, they still insist on a massive *six-month* grace period after the delivery of the record before rejecting it and requesting a second record. Mind you, if they exercise this right, it could now be a year and a half after the artist has signed and quit their day jobs before they have to start recording this second new album. What does the label offer as a means for the artist to earn a living in the meantime? Not much.

3.(e) ARTIST shall complete the recording of the first LP required to be recorded during the Initial Period or any Option Period within six (6) months following the commencement of the applicable Period. ARTIST shall complete the recording of any additional masters required to be recorded during the Initial Period or any Option Period within sixty (60) days following COMPANY's request therefor, unless COMPANY shall otherwise advise ARTIST. **Notwithstanding anything to the contrary contained** in this Agreement, COMPANY shall have no less than one hundred and fifty (150) days following the date of ARTIST's completion of recording and COMPANY's acceptance in accordance with all of the terms and conditions of this Agreement of all the masters required to be recorded by ARTIST during any contract Period within which to exercise its immediately succeeding option to extend the Term.

TRANSLATION: The artist has to complete the first album of each year within the first six months. The artist has to complete the recording of any additional songs that the company insists they record within 60 days following company's request, unless the company specifically says they don't have to. **If anything else in the contract contradicts the next half of this sentence, then what follows is the prevailing rule:** The company has *at least* five months after the completion of each album, and their acceptance of all the additional songs and recordings that they requested, in which to decide whether or not to renew the contract for the next year and thus to extend the term.

REALITY: The artist has to complete an album within the first six months of the beginning of each contract year. The label has five months to reject it, and then the artist has 60 days to remake it (good luck). After this, the label gets another six months to exercise their option to reject the new record and dump the artist. How is this possible if the label has exercised their option from paragraph 3(c) to wait six months and then ask for the second record from the first contract year? If this happens, the artist will now be in year two of the agreement and have to record the second album for year two while re-recording the first album from year one *at the same time!* The way this is phrased, the label can keep the artist engaged in recording for several years before releasing anything to the public. And they can do this every year for a minimum of five years.

Timetable

Artist signs with label .... Jan. 1, 1999

Artist completes first album.. June 1, 1999

Label rejects first album and requests
    more recordings. Artist begins
    re-recording first album and
    starts recording second album .... Jan. 1, 2000

Artist completes re-record of first album .... April 1, 2000

Artist completes second album .... June 1, 2000

Label releases first album while requesting
    a re-record of second album,
    while artist begins recording third album .... Jan. 1, 2001

Artist finishes re-recording second album .... April 1, 2001

Artist finishes third album .... June 1, 2001

. . . and so on and so on .... till 2006

❷ Conclusion

We can now have a bit more compassion for artists who seem to have "sold out" after their first record. They have the years before they are signed to prepare for the first record, but only one year to prepare their second record, and six months to prepare their third. The absurd time constraints make it nearly impossible for the artist to achieve this production schedule at all, let alone with any degree of quality. Don't forget, a working artist or band is touring for six months out of the year, so they're doomed to be in breach of this agreement. If they don't comply with the above schedule, then they don't get their royalty increases and stay at the old rate. Thus the fraud.

Since any record label is usually required to release only *one album per year,* the label gets to keep the second recordings and can release them whenever they want to—even after the artist has flown to another label. Hence things like "previously unreleased masters" hit the market long after an artist has retired or the band has broken up.

If all this isn't bad enough, all the fancy legalese turns a five-year/five-album contract into a 7½ year/14-album contract (since the extension of the term and the "acceptance" of albums are related). Every time the label asks for a new record, they automatically extend the option period by six months (6 months x 5 albums = 2.5 years additional term time).

And this is only the first three paragraphs of a 25-paragraph agreement. Today most similar clauses are not that severe—largely due to progressive and more insistent lawyering, not record companies becoming more benign. Watch out for new and improved incarnations of the above as new areas of law like "digital transferring/transmission" and "electronic rights" start to creep into recording agreements.

But remember, many lawyers let their clients sign this exact agreement (or some version thereof) for years. Now go back, reread "Lawyers," page 6, and make sure you have a good one.

⊘Miscellaneous Myths and Untruths

Nothing so needs reforming as other people's habits.

—Mark Twain

CHAPTER NINETEEN

A & R Dogma

If you haven't thrown down this book in disgust, then you are ready for this next chapter. In the next pages we'll dissect some of the conventional wisdom that gets passed around on how to make it in this game. As we'll discover, much of what musicians receive in the way of well-meaning advice is irrelevant or just plain wrong.

A Good Promotional Kit Is the Key

Totally false. I have heard many stories to the contrary from friends who work in A&R departments. They rip open the package, listen to the tape, and *then,* if they like the music, look at the materials. If they don't like the first song on the demo, they toss the entire package without ever looking at it. If the picture doesn't match the type of music, they toss it as well.

One friend said to me, "A good early warning sign of a clunker tape: If the package looks *too well put together, neat and pristine,* it probably sucks. Bands who put together elaborate promo kits are trying to compensate for something." Conversely, it's often the tape with an illegible, torn label with no information that seems to have a more compelling allure to it—provided the music is good, of course.

Work on the music. That's what will grab the A&R person's attention. It's like the old cliché about dating (one that I hope the female readers will find cute rather than sexist): It's been said that a woman decides in the first five minutes after meeting a date whether or not she's interested. The rest of the evening, or subsequent dates, are merely for confirming her decision.

My experience has taught me that A&R people are similar. Their first impressions are the strongest. They decide in the first viewing, dare I say in the first 60 seconds of the first two songs, whether or not they are going to sign an act. The rest of the meetings, showcases, and conversations are just part of the courting game, helping the A&R person feel secure in their decision.

Take it with a grain of salt if you wish, but experience has shown me that despite all the business factors that play a role in what bands to sign, A&R people usually go with their gut.

❷ Gigging a Lot Is Good Exposure to the Industry

Many new bands think that if they get gigs in the best clubs in town, they're assured of eventually being exposed to the right people. They're right, but is this a good thing? In planning the strategy of an act, it's a good idea not to make them too visible too soon. This destroys the allure that is necessary for A&R interest. Yes, A&R wants to sign a working act, but not one that has been working too long.

The rationale is that if they have been out there for a couple of years and no one has signed them, there must be a reason. You should by now understand the insecure position of the average A&R person. This issue of a band being "too visible" and "too accessible" is all they need to tip the delicate scales of rejection. A band that seems too eager can destroy the thrill of the chase that A&R people enjoy. Remember, they want to discover something new and exciting—that's what gets them fame and bonuses. Signing an act that has been knocking around for a deal for a couple of years is about as exciting as going home with the drunk person that has been hitting on you all night at a bar.

This is especially true in the major cities, where about half of the signing for major labels is done. The lines below by two distinct, but equally quoted prophets, illustrate the logic one should apply to attracting A&R.

The prophet is without honor in his own land.
                                                    — Jesus

I'd never belong to a club that would have
me for a member.   *— Groucho Marx*

Solution: Many savvy managers try to book their up-and-coming acts in the suburban areas outside the major music cities such as New York and L.A. Not only do the venues tend to pay more, but the audiences are far more appreciative of a big-city act coming out to them than the city folk are about hearing "just another local band from the sticks." In this way the act can build up a better following. When the time comes to showcase for the record companies in the city, an artist's manager will canvas the suburban areas where the artist is popular. The hope is that their crowd will drive in to see them. This pads the audience for the A&R people and gives them a better impression of how hard the band has been working.

❷ Second Sendings

A second sending is when a band has been rejected and then follows up with a second tape several months later. Despite the party line—that A&R people are always open to hearing your latest—the truth is that they rarely change their minds.

At this point the band is better off changing their name than sending a new tape, basically for the same reason described above—they're not fresh anymore. So make sure that your first foot forward is your best. If they don't say yes within a few months, you're better off moving on to another A&R person or label. But saying yes is an elusive thing, as you'll see in the next paragraph. However, there are almost as many exceptions to this rule as there are examples of it.

❷ "We Love It, but . . ."

Show business in general and the music business in particular is an arena where yes usually means maybe and maybe usually means no. For this rule, I promise you, there are few exceptions. It is very frustrating for me to listen to artists tell me that the label they solicited loves the tape but they have "filled the roster for that month," or they think it needs a remix and then they'll reconsider it, or "the vocals aren't strong enough but the music is great," or the classic, "Can we hear more material?" All of these means *they didn't like it*.

I know this is hard for many artists to hear, and it isn't easy to say, but it's true. The fact of the matter is that if the A&R department really thought you were great they would offer to sign you—period, no matter what the circumstances. The only exception to this could be that they are considering another act with a similar sound. In this case, their request for more material could be legitimate.

In my experience, when a person in the music business is excited about what they hear, they tend to ask important buying questions, like, what does the artist look like, how did they record this tape, and are they playing out right now? When they think it's not for them, they say, "We love it, but . . ."

The real reason for this waffling doesn't cast entertainment professionals in a very good light: it's simply done out of fear. People don't tell you what they honestly feel because they never know who might be where in a year or two. The manager to whom an A&R person says, "I hate it" this year, might be the director of his label next year. There is also the possibility that the "passed over" artist gets signed and does well on another label. A&R people can't afford to be wrong. Their entire perceived value is based on their ears.

In all fairness, there are many A&R people who rise above these shortcomings, but these are things that artists and producers should be aware of. Odds dictate that if an A&R man says "no" (however he phrases it), he has a 95% chance of being right even if he thinks the tape is good. Ninety-five percent of all artists fail for one reason or another. So why take a risk unless it looks and sounds really good?

Yes means maybe. Maybe means no.
No means call back.

❯ Labels Sign Bad Acts for Tax Write-Offs

Nonsense. This myth is probably perpetuated by sour-grapes bands who hate to see their friends get signed and not them. A&R signs bad acts often enough to make a person wonder what their agenda is, but the idea that a record company, which generally operates on a small profit margin anyway, would sign an act and spend half a million dollars just to avoid paying taxes is absurd. Anyone who tells you this has no understanding of how corporate taxes work and has even less idea how the politics of labels work. If a major label wanted a tax write-off, there are much deeper wells they can go to than signing a bad act. They could just press about 500,000 CDs of one of the loser acts they already have (every label has at least one). The records would ship back from the stores, and not only would they get a tax deduction, but they would also be able to charge more return fees to that artist's recoupment account. (See "The Major Label Deal from the Artist's Point of View," page 53, for what a recoupment account is.)

I think this concept started because in the '80s there was a lot of funny accounting going on in the record industry (and there still is). A&R people would ask for kick-backs from the producers in exchange for large advances. If this was the A&R person's agenda, then it didn't matter if the band was good or not. To cover up this type of fraud, the labels themselves may have started the rumor that they signed a bad act for tax purposes. Maybe it helped them save face with their parent holding companies, whose primary concern is where all the money is going. [1]

The other possibility is that the tax write-off signing is being confused with a very real phenomenon—*the mercy signing*.

[1] See "The Big Picture," page 237.

The Mercy Signing

A&R people build up relationships with various producers and managers over time. Let's say that during the course of one deal the A&R person asks the producer to step away from the act. The producer may agree to do this if the label signs another of his other acts with no questions asked. If the relationship is strong, the A&R person will do it.

Another type of mercy signing is when a relationship between the A&R person

SHOOTING BLANKS

To give you an idea of the extent of A&R paranoia, I'm reminded of an experiment done by a trade magazine several years back. They sent a false promo kit around to several labels with a *blank demo tape* inside. Out of the 15 submissions to major labels, only one called them on it. The rest sent back a form rejection letter that basically read, "We think this shows potential but we are currently not signing any new acts this year."

and the manager is a very long one and over the years the manager has given that A&R person first look at all of his choice acts. If the signings have been profitable for the A&R person, then the manager would not hesitate to ask that the label sign a clunker and then drop them later so that the manager can get a commission and pay some bills.

Also, most managers' contracts have a clause that states that if the manager is not successful in getting the artist signed within a period of time (usually not more than two years), then the artist is free to go. It is not unknown for the manager to persuade an A&R friend to sign the act at the very end of the contract to a "development deal," thus extending the manager's hold on the artist. The deal will usually take several months to negotiate. In that time the manager will continue to collect money off the artist for their personal appearances, royalties, or any other income.

Make sure the person representing you has your best interests at heart.

A twist on this scenario is when an A&R person is being pressured to sign someone because the manager has told him that if he doesn't, then that manager or producer will never bring him *anything* in the future. If the A&R person values the relationship, he could be pressured into signing the act where before he was ambivalent about it.

Unless the label is truly convinced that the act is good, any pressure used in manipulating them to sign an act will usually mean that the artist will not receive the label's full attention and dedication. This is not always the case, and there are numerous examples where the sleeper act on a label's roster turned out to be a winner, but in general the mercy signings tend to get dropped shortly after the record comes out.

By the way, indie labels don't have the money for this sort of bullshit. They tend to sign only what they believe in, so an artist on an indie can expect a higher level of commitment.

CHAPTER TWENTY

⊘Production Boners

Next, let's take a look at some of the myths that can trip you up in the recording studio.

⊘ You Need a "Master Quality" Demo to Get a Deal

"Master quality" is perhaps the most misused bit of jargon that circulates within the industry, next to "digital." The term master quality and whether or not an artist gets signed are *unrelated*. I know of many artists who were signed on the basis of 4-track demos made in their living rooms.

In a recording contract, the term master quality will be used to describe the level of quality that the label will accept for commercial distribution of the final recording. This clause is in there to prevent the producer or artist from taking a hundred thousand dollar advance and delivering a 4-track Portastudio final mix.

In these contracts the term "master" means the final version from which all other copies will be made. It does not necessarily mean 24- or 48-track digital recordings, although those are the norm. On the contrary, record companies have been known to release the original 8-track home recordings if the sound is good enough. So the de facto definition of master quality can only mean a recording that the label deems *acceptable* for commercial distribution.

Since labels have, at one time or another, deemed all formats of recording acceptable, there can be no specific definition of master quality that relates to the number of tracks that are used or whether the recording is analog or digital. So if the label can't define what format a master recording should be recorded in, how can they only accept master quality for submissions? You see the paradox?

❯ You Must Record on 24- (or 48-) Track Tape

While we're on this subject, I want to dispel another myth concerning master quality. A federal judge once said, in his decision concerning a pornography case, that he couldn't define pornography, but he knew it when he saw it. It's the same with "master recordings." Since so many records have been done on so many different formats over the years, no one can really use a particular format to define master quality. The only thing you can do is use your ears. If it sounds like a record, it is a record—period.

Far more important than the number of tracks that are available is the quality of each track and the quality of the equipment used to deliver the audio signal. I'd rather have eight quality tracks to produce with than 24 poor ones.

To prove my point, here are a few examples of hit records that were *not* recorded on large formats:

Dark Side of the Moon—**Pink Floyd** 8-track

Abbey Road—**The Beatles** 8-track

Sgt. Pepper's Lonely Hearts Club Band—**The Beatles** 4-track

"Brown Sugar"—The Rolling Stones 4-track

"Sweet Dreams Are Made of This"—Eurythmics 8-track

"Stairway to Heaven"—Led Zeppelin 8-track

"Respect"—Aretha Franklin 4-track

Look Sharp!—**Joe Jackson** 8-track

ABC—**The Jackson 5** 4-track

Most pre-1975 Motown records 3-track

> Why the Cassettes Sound Muddy

Well, aside from the fact that CDs sound cleaner than tapes in general, there is a more tragic reason why commercially produced analog audiocassettes tend to sound awful.

CDs are digitally transferred to each copy. Since it's a pure digital transfer, that means that there is no generation loss from copy to copy. It also means that each machine will receive the information exactly the same way as the previous machine.

With tapes, however, the duplication process is quite different. The music is transferred to a large tape loop. This loop is put in a bin that winds the tape over the playback head very fast. As it spins, the music is transferred to many cassettes simultaneously at high speed. The faster the dubbing speed, the lower the fidelity. This should be familiar to anyone who's made double-speed cassette-to-cassette copies on their home stereo. You will notice a loss of fidelity and additional hiss at only two times the normal speed. Usually, full-length records are transferred at 32 times the normal "reel" speed.

The other drawback is that the record heads of the cassette machines that are recording the music often fall out of alignment. The duplication house is supposed to align them daily, but there are usually hundreds of them, and whoever is in charge tends to slack off. This leads to poor cassette reproduction, which, unfortunately, represents a little over a third of the artist's sales. (According to the RIAA, in 2001 U.S. artists sold roughly twice as many CDs as cassettes.)

There is little anyone can do about this, because record companies won't pay for slower "real-time transfers" of the album due to the added cost. This is why your homemade "bootlegged" tapes of CDs often sound better than the official commercial ones.

CHAPTER TWENTY-ONE

⊘Marketing Mishigas

After the record is completed, the marketing department gets their crack at figuring out how to best represent the artist to the public. Most of the time it's of benefit to the artist. But sometimes . . .

This section looks at the strengths and weaknesses of the marketing process.

⊘ Lots of Airplay Assures Big Record Sales

Hopefully. While there *is* a direct correlation between radio play and sales, it would not be uncommon for a song to become a "radio hit." The term has an obvious meaning. It's when a song gets put on many playlists—either because the label has promoted it to many stations or because the station manager likes and believes in it—but the record stores can't seem to sell the record. This happens a lot with *sophomores* (an artist who has a great first record but a less than successful second record). The radio will play it to death, but the airplay won't translate into record sales.[1]

Then there are the classics like "Wild Thing," which is still played over and over on the radio but sells barely any records. Or more commonly, dance records,

[1] Unless it's part of a compilation album.

which do well in the clubs and on the air but don't translate into big sales at the stores as one would think.

The reverse can be true. Just because the radio doesn't play a record doesn't mean that it isn't selling. *Enigma* got very little radio play comparatively but sold over a million copies.

❷ "We Get to Say What Our Album Cover Will Look Like"

Are you sure? Read your contract carefully. If it says, "The artist will be consulted for final approval," that means all the label has to do is ask you what you think; it doesn't mean that they have to take your advice. If it says, "The artist will contribute to the cover art design," that means that you can submit something, but again they don't have to use it.[2] Whatever way you think you can get control of this, there is usually a loophole that will let the label get around it. Labels rarely, if ever, give up the right to decide how to package a new artist. Deal with it, and try to rationalize that they want you to sell the most records that you possibly can, so they're on your side even if it seems they're not.

2 See "Legalese?," page 193.

❷ The Virtual Record Store— Will Music Be Sold over the Internet?

It has become a popular and sexy concept: downloading recordings into your personal computer after shopping for them online. The dream of instant access to millions of buyers has everybody buzzing about the Internet's potential. But will it become reality?

Although the technology exists to download a CD from the Internet to a home CD burner, at the moment online record stores still deliver the actual CD via normal United States snail mail. This may change as data compression algorithms improve, making downloading faster, but will this affect record sales substantially? The first edition of *Confessions* (which was published in 1998) was criticized for its pessimistic predictions about the proliferation of the "information superhighway." Now, several years later, what was published in 1998 is still true. Pioneers of the virtual future have yet to overcome several obstacles.

Despite the proliferation of home PCs, still relatively few people can take advantage of all the new bells and whistles. Less than 15% of the globe even owns a telephone, let alone a personal computer along with a modem, a high-speed Internet connection, and a CD burner. One area that has been conquered is the cost of the media; blank CDs now cost less than a buck if you buy in bulk. But the still-long downloading time—plus the fact that the RIAA has pushed the authorities into arresting a few college students for "pirating" music—has cast some doubt over the feasibility of the Internet as a delivery system for paying music customers. Companies like Napster and MP3.com seemed like paradise at first, allowing people to download just about any song, *for free*. That is, until they were bought up by Big Fives and re-groomed as subscription-based services. In these services you generally have to give your name, address, and credit information and fill out marketing surveys before you get your "free" records. The jury is still out on whether this model will stand muster. In the long run, all these prerequisites may be a huge deterrent when compared with the ease of going to the record store and buying the CD for $12-$15.

RIPPIN', BURNIN', DOIN' TIME

You're not going to believe this one. The Recording Industry Association of Amerika (RIAA), asserting their position that all "file sharers" should get nothing less than capital punishment, tipped off a district attorney about a 19-year-old student who was "sharing" Pink Floyd's *Dark Side of the Moon* (a record just about everyone owns anyway) with about 3,000 other fellow students. The goat was a graphics-design freshman at Oklahoma University. The DA, seized his computer and placed him under arrest. The student pleaded no contest to a misdemeanor charge of "unlawful advertisement or offer to distribute sound recordings" and was fined $5,000. He also had to forfeit his computer, monitor, and hard drives so they could be destroyed.

The irony is that while another college student was heralded on the cover of *Time* magazine for creating Napster, the ultimate file-sharing system with millions of users, this art student—with only a campus-full of exposure—will now have a criminal record. Can somebody explain this to me so that it makes sense?

In addition to the problem of fast and affordable technology, there is the problem of how to make sure the artist and record companies get paid from this downloading deal. Doesn't a digital transmission constitute making a copy or a performance and therefore require a royalty? The answer is, despite new laws that have been written over the past three years, no one really knows at this time. Congress and special-interest lobbyists are presently sorting out the details about who should be paid what, and this will go on for years to come.

Before online music can be properly regulated, each artist and each CD will have to be encoded to verify that the downloads are official and licensed. The cataloging of hundreds of thousands of albums to make this possible is something no major label seems eager to undertake at this time. Besides, Hollywood spy flicks have fostered paranoia that no system is safe from hackers stealing their masters.

One probable solution will result from the AOL/Time Warner merger of 2001. This may be the single greatest thing for the consumer while also being the single worst thing for the artist. The merger combines one of the world's largest music catalogs with the world's largest Internet service provider. This marriage means AOL can implement a complete delivery, watermarking, and accounting system without getting approval from the rest of the Internet industry. Their 30 million users would create a de facto standard that would catapult Internet music delivery into an instant reality. The down side is that in all likelihood they will be giving away a lot of music to attract new members. Once again, music will become the "free" item used as a lure. (See "Sponsors," page 150.) These giveaway items will likely fall under the heading of "free goods." (See "Packaging Deductions and Giveaways," p. 57.) This means that the artist will not be paid for those downloads, even though the ISP/record company gets a direct benefit.

Despite the realities above, no amount of logic seems to stop trade mags and TV news shows from selling us the idea that the brave new frontier of interactive sales is about to put new dollars into artists' pockets. Remember when you read these articles that most of those magazines are supported or outright owned by the same companies that own the major labels, and that "new and improved" always creates a buzz compared to the boring and traditional. The Internet has served marketers well in this respect.

Will the artist of tomorrow be seeing a quarterly statement showing "download sales" as a substantial portion of their revenues? Well…maybe the artist of the day after tomorrow.

The Internet does, however, seem to have a more immediate function as a promotion tool rather than a distribution tool. Web sites keep fans informed of their favorite artist's movements and their touring schedule. Never before could one person with a computer reach hundreds of thousands of fans instantly. Most major label deals make the artist give up the right to own and maintain their own website, but the power has provided the smaller independents and individual artists the means to sell their music to millions of potential record buyers. Up until now, that privilege has been one that only major labels have enjoyed. In this respect the Net gives indies an edge over majors—the ability to stay connected to their market.[3]

❯ Record Industry Slumps Are the Direct Result of Poor A&R Decision-Making

Every time the record industry has a bad year, the rhetoric is the same. "It's because the labels have lost touch with their market. They don't know good music when they hear it." I disagree.

In most cases these stories are generated by music journalists who have an ax to grind with major labels. Often the records that they give poor reviews to sell the most. Conversely, the records they give the best reviews to often go nowhere. Who can say why?[4]

In the years that record sales have been universally deflated there is usually an outside force that interfered. In 1996 every major paper ran a story stating that were it not for Alanis Morissette and Hootie and the Blowfish, the industry would have sold almost no records. Journalists seem to overlook the coincidence that 1996 was also the big boom year for home computers and the public's fascination with the Internet. Also, for the first time in recent years, television hit with shows that grabbed a young audience (*Friends* and *X-Files* to name two).

The record industry functions on surplus income. That's why it markets itself mostly to the under-20 crowd; they have no mortgages or child support payments and plenty of cash for fun stuff. The last great upset in record sales came in the early '80s. Critics once again claimed that it was because record companies were putting out junk. This was also the same time that Baby Boomers (who fueled record sales throughout the '60s and '70s) were now buying homes and having babies of their own. Coincidence?

The good news is that pendulums swing, trends come around, and for every bad year there usually follows a year of "great growth." The executive turntable rotates and the new generals take the credit for what is, by and large, the natural ebb and flow of commerce. There's no business like show business.

[3] In a lame attempt to tailgate this trend, some major record companies have taken to hiring young computer jockeys to stay online generating a false buzz on their newest corporate virtuosos. Give me a break.

[4] For some odd reason, good reviews in the mainstream papers and magazines seem to be the kiss of death for an album. Underground reviews apparently carry more weight. This is probably because most young record buyers don't trust mainstream media's taste in "good music."

CHAPTER TWENTY-TWO

⊝Getting Credit Where Credit Is Due

O
n major-label albums credit is more coveted than people realize. A&R people typically want executive producer credit. Engineers and writers typically want coproducer credit. Key musicians hired for overdub sessions have often argued that their contributions to the material constitute a coproduction or cowriter credit. DJs, who are part of rap groups, have hired lawyers claiming that the turntable they "play" is a musical instrument and therefore they should be paid a union wage for session work and credited for it. Singers whose vocals have been sampled and used for other records have sued if they didn't get credit on the sampled record. Studios have bargained with producers to include them as the studio of record on an album just so they can tell their clients that "this hit was recorded here."

It can get brutal. Here are a few guidelines to credit—how to get it and when to watch your back.

⊝ Look for the Union Label

My first paying job in the music industry was as a sideman playing on the soundtrack of a motion picture. I was only 17, and as you can imagine I was quite excited; it was my first recording session, and it was at Sigma sound, where Billy Joel and Aerosmith were recording their albums at the same time. I was put in a glass booth and did my thing. It was cool.

When the session was over, I was asked to sign a piece of paper that required me to join Local 802 of the AFM (see "The Musicians' Union," page 36). The dues would have cost me everything that I earned for doing the session. But aside from that, I didn't want to join a union that I knew would do nothing to get me work. I declined to join, as did many other first-timers on the session.

ROCK AND TUNA TEKI ROLL

n the mid-'80s I was working for a Japanese production company owned by one of the major distributors. We manufactured karaoke music.

They had set up shop in a midtown studio in Manhattan and were hiring union musicians left and right for sessions, but were paying them only $20 per hour. (And believe me, they worked them.) Twenty dollars an hour doesn't even come close to the union minimum scale of about $300 for a three-hour session. But the company didn't care. This was their deal, and they weren't putting a gun to anyone's head to take their money.

I can recall many top musicians coming through those doors for work every day—musicians who play in TV bands and on commercials for thousands of dollars were showing up at this company to pick up an extra couple of hundred off the books for pocket cash.

The AFM. eventually found out and paid the studio a visit to speak to the Japanese project director. The conversation was very short. The director screamed to the union representative in Japanese and broken English that he didn't care about their "fucking union," and to "get the fuck out" or he would have him "arrested for trespassing."

The union threatened to pull the cards of anyone who worked for this company again. So from then on, the musicians used fake names on their invoices. Since they weren't getting credit on a karaoke record, they didn't care.

The law of supply and demand will always prevail over organized policies.

When the record came out, I ran to the record store and bought the album. I couldn't wait to see my name on a record, especially such a popular one. But when I ripped open the cellophane and looked at the liner notes, I saw that my name wasn't mentioned. In fact, the credit for the work that I had done had been given to someone else.

Imagine my disappointment and anger.

I called the production company and spoke to a woman that I had become friendly with. She did some inquiring and told me that since the recording sessions were union sessions, only union people were allowed to get credit. The person listed where my name should have been was a union session player who never even set foot in the studio with us.

In retrospect, I should have joined the union, because the credit was more important than the money, and the union does guarantee certain rights. This was not explained to me at the time, however. But the idea of only giving credit to union players is not uncommon. In fact, most major labels insist that their recording artists join the union. And, by agreement with the union, any player who doesn't join will not receive credit on the record, even if they're part of the established band.[1] Sometimes the joining dues are paid for out of the artist's advance, sometimes not, but for this reason alone the union gets members. No one wants to pass up a major label credit for a few hundred bucks.

[1] The established band is really the band as a corporate entity, see page 190.

This insistence that starving musicians spend hundreds of dollars to join an organization that offers little by way of health benefits and does not guarantee work is one of the last old-economy rituals to fade away and also shows the callousness that big business takes toward labor. At the same time, record companies offer even less by way of pension plans, or any form of assistance in helping the artists they exploit. So unfortunately, even though the union may not be the musician's best friend, it's the musician's only friend.

Incidentally, indie labels don't usually engage in this kind of extortion, and it's my guess that majors will stop soon. The connections between unionized labor and corporate management are thinning day by day in this country. As the connection thins, so does the union's power. One particularly colorful example of the thinning process is illustrated in the "Rock and Tuna Teki Roll" sidebar.

In the area of Latin music this matter of credit has become a major cancer. Most albums that are recorded on major labels' Latin imprints are not done under a union contract. So a musician getting proper credit as well as proper pay is an uphill battle.

⊘ Major Label Philosophy on Giving Credit to Sidemen and Engineers

Musicians are protected to some degree by the fact that they have a union. Unfortunately, they're the only group in the music industry that has this privilege. Engineers, producers, recording studios, programmers (sometimes classified as keyboard players), DJs (who claim the turntable as a musical instrument), and writers are not unionized and have no voice to assert their right to be credited for work; they are at the mercy of the record labels.[2] Unfortunately, unless the producer submits the credits, the label often doesn't make any effort to discover who actually worked on the record.

As you might guess, producers don't consider policing their underlings' credit

[2] Writers receive protection from credit fraud because miscrediting the writer of a song can have serious consequences. (See "The Myth of Copyright Protection," page 159.)

"WE'LL FIX YOUR CREDIT ON THE NEXT PRINTING"

On one record that I engineered early in my career, the producer forgot to include my engineering credits on two songs. Since both songs charted, I was anxious to get my name where it belonged. I called the label, but they wanted proof that I had worked on the record. My next step was to call the producer. He swore that he submitted my name; the label said otherwise. The producer wrote a letter to the label asking that my credit be added in the next printing. I also had the recording studio where we cut the record fax the session reports to the label. I had to sign those reports—*indisputable proof that I did the work.* The assistant to the A&R director finally said that they would change the liner notes in the next printing. They never did. Even if the assistant was being sincere about changing the notes in the second printing, turnover in the record biz is so high that in all likelihood he probably quit or was fired shortly afterward. The new person would not have been left a memo to deal with such an insignificant problem, so it would get shoved under the rug forever.

The record to date has over sold several million copies.

---

a high priority. Producers generally like to take credit for as much as they can. There are exceptions, and it is important to quickly ascertain what type of producer you are working for and deal with your credit from there.[3] I have been shafted so many times on this issue that the exact spelling and description of my credit is outlined *in my contracts.*

3 See "Control Freaks," page 28.

Labels complain that record buyers don't read credits and that they take up too much space, costing the artist money for the additional panel of the packaging jacket. Labels will use this as leverage to get the artist on their side of the argument, but it's total bullshit. It doesn't even cost a penny to put an extra panel on a CD. The unspeakable fact is that labels and producers just aren't that enthusiastic in general about giving credit. Believe it or not, giving credit means exposing themselves to liability.

How, you ask? It's simple but sad. When a record is a hit, everybody who was even in the neighborhood when it was made comes out of the woodwork to say that they had something to do with it. People will even try to claim that they cowrote the song. Obviously, if they have a credit on the record, the label can't say they never heard

SONGWRITERS' CREDIT

Writers are, under most circumstances, protected under the law against fraudulent credit being assigned to their song. However, there are cases where songs are done as a work for hire and the employer puts their byline on the song and doesn't include the original writer's credit. I believe that there's something evil about this, but apparently it's legal.

In fact, one very large entertainment company has been known to ask the writer of a song to sign over the complete copyright and byline even if the writer does not work for the company and the song pre-existed the film project it's being bought for. The legality of claiming that a pre-existing song could be work-for-hire is, at the moment, questionable and will remain so until someone takes this company to court. This is not likely to happen for two reasons: (1) the company is extremely powerful, and (2) a copyright infringement case would be held in federal court—lots of time and money and no punitive damages even if the songwriter prevails.

of them, so they are forced to deal and settle with the individual. This doesn't happen a lot, but it happens often enough to make labels wary about giving credit indiscriminately. As a result, proper credit for the talent on great records is not given, or worse yet, is stolen. It's not uncommon for credit to be given as a favor in exchange for a favor that is owed.

❷ How To Get Even

Legally, there is little anyone can do to get record companies to print complete or even accurate credits in the liner notes of records. When my credit was omitted from that multiplatinum record I mentioned in the side bar, I went to an attorney to discuss my options. According to him I could have sued the record company for "publishing false information." This would have to be done as what's called a *class action suit.* This means I would be filing suit in the name of every person who bought a record and was potentially misled by the information the label falsely printed.

As you can imagine, this would be hard to prove, and wouldn't do much for my reputation either. Plus, a victory wouldn't necessarily amount to much money for me.

A personal civil suit, my other option, would have required me to prove that the omitting of my credit cost *me* money personally. Even though it might seem obvious to most that not having a major label credit could cost an up-and-coming professional money, proving it in a court of law is another matter. So I let it go.

But, I discovered through the process that there is one way around the system, but you have to be ballsy and sneaky. However I have been advised that I must tell you **NOT TO DO THIS. THIS IS WRONG. IT IS BAD. DON'T DO IT. I AM NOT RECOMMENDING THAT YOU DO THIS. THE PUBLISHERS DO NOT RECOMMEND THAT YOU DO THIS. THE BOOK STORE WHERE YOU BOUGHT THIS BOOK DOES NOT RECOMMEND THAT YOU DO THIS.**

But in case you're still interested here's how it goes . . .

Record companies hate to redo the printing plate of the liner notes (known as the *mechanical*) once it has been approved. The liner notes are all drawn by the art department, which is part of the production department at the label. (Note: "Production department," when used to describe a part of a record company, has nothing to do with the production of the recording. It's just the department responsible for the final assemblage of the CD and its packaging.)

If you have friends who work in the company that is putting out the record that you want credit on, have them find out who is the artist drafting the mechanical.

It may be more than one person, but it doesn't matter—the more there are, the better it is for you. Just find one of them. These people are usually paid very little, and they are easily bribed with concert tickets or free goods. However, no amount of money will bribe them unless there is a way for them to cover their ass in case of discovery.

This can be handled simply by faxing a memo with the letterhead of a management agency directly to the art department. The memo should be marked with an important person's signature forged on it and should state the credit that must be added. Example:

To: **Lori Rubinstein (low-paid employee/conspirator**
    in the art or production department)
From: **Gleason Management Inc./Jason Gleason**
    (important name that everyone will recognize)
Re: **Addition to liner notes for Johnny Rock Star album**
    Give Me a Break

Please be advised that the name Moses Avalon should be added to the
    engineering credits.
                    —Jason Gleason/Management for Johnny Rock Star

Your conspirator will add the credit and then give the entire mechanical to the head of the production department, as usual, for their approval. The head of production in a major label will, in all likelihood, not even question the addition, because such last-minute changes are done frequently and he or she will have five projects going at a time, all with deadlines. If they do question it, Lori, the fictional conspirator, will show them the memo.

The VP of marketing is next in the approval process. They will have even less of an idea if it's right. If they do question it and call the management company, they will find out that it's a fraud. This could be a problem, but all that will happen is that they will delete the credit and you will be no worse off than you were before. Your friend will be covered, because a lowly mechanical artist would have no way of knowing if the memo was or wasn't real. With no one to blame, all departments will chalk it up to another prankster trying to get one over on a record label. But knowing human nature, and our natural tendency to do as little as possible to make waves, they will probably approve the final draft without even questioning the change. By the time anyone realizes that the credit is unauthorized, the CD will be on the shelves in the record store. If you've read my discussion of the way the distribution chain works, you should be able to guess why the record company will never recall the records for a liner note error. If you're laughing at this little plot, laugh at this: I am personally aware of over 20 situations that were resolved in exactly the manner I've just described.[4]

The lesson to be learned:

Low-paid employees make excellent spies.

❯ The "Coproduction" Credit

As bands gain more clout, they will want to produce their own recordings. It's not uncommon that the band and engineer end up doing most of the producer's work anyway. The riff goes something like this: The producer says to the engineer or artist, "I have to do some things. I'll be back in a couple of hours. Record the vocals, okay?" Of course, they will oblige. But what does "record the vocals" mean? If the engineer or artist must decide which takes to keep and which to do over, doesn't that mean they're doing the producer's job? The answer is yes, definitely.

It happens that way because snagging a major credited producer if you're not a top act is not all it's cracked up to be. Here's why:

If the producer they have seduced with a lot of money also has other acts that he or she is producing, the artist may find that the one really in charge of making the record is not the producer but the producer's assistant.

Big producers prioritize their jobs. They will give most of their attention to one big project but let their engineer or a protégé attend to the lesser ones. Only if the lesser act is lucky will the producer even take the time to personally okay the tracks before they go to the label for final approval.

But if the engineer or artist voices a dissenting opinion that they deserve recognition as a producer, they can generally be pacified with a coproducer credit.

Here's the catch. Coproducers are not listed on the *Billboard* charts as one of the producers of the song. (Nor do they get any points.) In essence, the credit serves only as a résumé builder (much like the vice presidency of the United States). What they should be asking for is a line that reads, "Produced by Joe Producer *and* Johnny Rock Star" (or "*and* Eddie Engineer").

CHAPTER TWENTY-THREE

⊘Industry Census

The ridiculous myth that everyone seems to accept at face value is that the record industry is a small place and everyone knows everyone. This is completely unfounded. The people who still say things like this are the ones that have been in the business for years or even a couple of decades. They deal with the same people constantly and think that it's a small community. Indeed, when they were starting out in the industry, it was much smaller. In the '60s there were only about 20 or so legitimate labels and about a hundred independents. There were maybe 30 A&R people worth talking to and only five national indie promoters.

Nowadays there are over three thousand labels in this country alone. About ten new ones spring up every week, as five others fade away. While it's true that the distribution pyramid is getting more bottom-heavy and the people at the top are therefore more elite, the structure of the industry has changed and made these people less significant than they might want to admit. Currently there are about 35 labels that could be called "majors," which would include several one-deeps that have made outstanding names for themselves, like Maverick, Mercury, and Verve. Combined, these 35 companies create seats for approximately 1,240 executives. Yes, we've grown quite a bit since the '60s.

But leaving these 1,240 folks aside, you no longer need a major label to break an act, as we saw in "The Vanity Label," page 131. Because the indie distribution channels are getting more effective by the day, the network of nepotism has expanded greatly, giving powerful jobs to a massive new base of people. The local college radio DJ now plays a more-than-insignificant role in breaking a record in a region as do writers of several websites that cover local music scenes. This means that when you size up the populace of the industry you have to include these people as well.

There is no way one can say this is a small industry when you include all of the people who contribute to the success of a record. If you include the indie promoters, the indie publicity people that the artist hires, the local and regional DJs and their program directors, the engineers and mastering house, and the secretaries and office support people who work for these entities, you can figure on well over 1,000 people who help contribute to the success of a record.

So while we're discussing the makeup of the industry I thought I'd give a few special interest groups something to chew on.

⊘ Are All the Powerful People in the Business Jews?

I have been witness to many a conversation with Jewish folk bemoaning the fact that they wish there were some truth to the stereotype: that there is a powerful network of Jews who hire each other and meet secretly to direct the major trends in the record business. But this is not true, and anyone who still believes it is the case hasn't done their homework. If one were to take the time to do any research, they would see that Jews are a minority in this and every other business, as they are a minority in the world (about .03% worldwide). It does, however, seem that there are an awful lot of Jews in the entertainment industry. Without going into a history of minority life in America, I offer this simplified explanation.

Most of the music industry revolves around New York and L.A. These two cities have the largest population of Jews in the world—even more than Israel. New York has about two and a half million Jews out of its eight million people. This means that the odds are about one in four that any person you meet, regardless of their profession, will be a Jew. But I can assure you that in places like Nashville (the other U.S. music industry capital), London, Munich, Chicago, Minneapolis, Seattle, Austin, Latin America, and Canada, the situation is quite different.

Also, one has to remember that the Jewish community in this country rose largely out of poverty, like most immigrant communities, and found it hard to get decent paying work. Because of discrimination, many Jews who made it out of the ghettos of New York (where over 90% of all Jewish immigrants entered this country in the late 1800s and early 1900s) started working in new industries where the status quo had not yet been established—like the entertainment industry. Over the years, as the community grew, so did its power base. Of the 35 major labels, and their 1,240 executive positions, about 20% are occupied by those of the Jewish persuasion. Most of them occupy positions in A&R and finance. On the surface this might seem like there are Jews everywhere. But one must also consider two other important factors. First, in the indie record world the ratio of Jews in the driver's seat is considerably smaller—less than 5% in the CEO positions. Also every Latin division of a major is Jew-free.

The other important thing to note is that most major record companies are owned by larger multinational holding companies. These companies do not directly decide which bands to sign, but they do determine if the president of the label will have his or her job next month. The boards of directors of these companies are the *real power* in the music industry. With the exception of Michael Eisner at Disney and Gerald Levin at Time-Warner, no chairman of the board or chief executive officer position in these companies is held by a Jew. And out of the 62-odd members of combined Board of Directors of the companies that own the Big Five, only 11 have names that even *sound* Jewish. (See "The Big Picture," page 237.)

❷ Are Women Discriminated Against in the Music Business?

It would be easy to jump on the activist bandwagon and talk about the discrimination that women face in business. But this is a book about naked truth, not political correctness, so I won't insult your intelligence by candy-coating this important issue.

The long hours required to excel in this industry make it hard for anyone who's planning a family to succeed, regardless of their sex. By way of a stereotype, since women tend to have a stronger instinct toward family, they are naturally going to be affected more by this than men.

While I'm sure that the lion's share of discrimination stories do have truth to them, I tend not to see big business discriminating against women specifically as much as I see it keeping down all contenders in general. I view it as more of a class struggle rather than a race or sex struggle. The fact of the matter is that record companies are so greedy for good product that if someone put a hit on their desk, they wouldn't care if it was produced by a woman, a man, or a chimpanzee.

When assessing the degree of effectiveness or presence that women have in the industry, it has to be remembered that women in the work force in general are quite new. It is only since the 1960s that women as a class have expressed an organized interest in forgoing the conventional roles of wife and mother and opting for the high-pressure, corrupt, power-hoarding careers that men have long enjoyed. Dismantling any power structure, especially the male-dominated workforce which has had over 10,000 years to evolve to its current standard, is a long process; in 1990 there were fewer than five women in CEO, COO, or CFO positions at the 35 major labels. But by 1997 that number climbed to 16[1] and has remained stable since then. Today almost 40% of the major labels have women in VP/national director positions, and more than a third of them have women as VPs of A&R. Of the 1,240 executive titles offered by the Big Five, 410 of them were held by women in 2001. That's approximately one in three executive positions held by the fairer sex. And if you look at two-deep labels, the percentage of women in the driver's seat increases. Compared to other industries, like finance, medicine, and law, the music industry—with its 30% ratio—is highly progressive.

As producers, women's struggle is harder. Even female A&R representatives tend to prefer a man in the producer's chair. I'm sure this will change as more women make the bid to be producers and it becomes less unusual to hire women for this position, but this will not be a battle that is easily won. Most artists are men (rather testosterone-driven ones at that) and will probably have trouble accepting a woman as having control over their record. No amount of social reconditioning is likely to change this attitude any time soon. If I may wax psychological for a moment, in my experience many women artists—for whatever reason—also seem to prefer men as the father figure in the studio.[2]

As managers, however, women seem to fare much better. The *Recording Industry Source Book*[3] shows that almost one third of the people who call themselves managers are women. And this percentage is climbing yearly.

[1] That's 16 out of the (approximately) 35 major labels, or roughly half the industry.

[2] If you think I'm full of it, look at the production credits on the jacket of any powerful female recording artist's CD. You'll be hard-pressed to find a woman's name credited as the producer.

[3] The *Source Book* is kind of a yellow pages for the music industry. It's a well-produced and useful publication, even though it still owes me some money.

CHAPTER TWENTY-FOUR

⊜The Big Picture,
or the Record Industry from the Point of View of the Rest of the World

N ewspapers love to print huge numbers describing the record industry's annual worth. Four billion a year, $8 billion a year, $12 billion a year. I've seen it go as high as $40 billion. But what real meaning do these numbers have? Unless you know the cost-to-profit ratio, they have zero meaning. A company can earn $1 billion dollars in one year, but if it cost $999,999,999 to run the company, then they made only a dollar. Think this is a far-fetched example? It's not. In 2001 Sony music took in almost $5 billion in sales. But after expenses, they were left with only $400 million—about 8 cents on the dollar.

So what does this have to do with getting a record deal? Nothing. This chapter has nothing to do with record deals. It's a bird's-eye view of the industry and will probably not have much to do with your day-to-day operations in music. So why is it in this book?

Obviously I think there is value in understanding the big picture of business and how our financially small but emotionally powerful industry fits into the global puzzle, so this chapter is more theory than anything else.

Santayana said, "To predict the future you must look at the past." I have my own interpretation of that: The key to making money is understanding trends. The key to predicting trends is understanding how big players interpret their past mistakes.

⊘ Do Record Companies Really Make Any Money?

The answer is not as obvious as you might think. If you look at entertainment shows, you'd expect that the music business is alive and healthy, with everyone making zillions of dollars. Careers are built and huge salaries paid to executives, artists, and other pros. But does it make money for the one entity footing the bill—the parent record label? This is a difficult question to answer, since we don't know exactly how much money they make after they pay out all those huge advances and salaries. But we can use some information that is public to build a gauge. For example, when MCA was sold to the Seagram beverage company for approximately $10 billion—a shockingly high price to those in the know—it sent ripples throughout the industry and gave other multinationals the expectation that they could sell their record divisions for high prices. EMI and WEA both restructured, trimming the fat to make them lean and attractive for hungry purchasers.

When the smoke cleared, there were none. EMI was considered substantially more successful than MCA, yet even at an asking price of only $9 billion ($1 billion lower than MCA's closing price) it could get no takers. For a company that's supposed to earn $7 billion a year, this is fairly pathetic.[1] What's the story?

The answer lies in how these companies fit into the portfolios of their parent companies and how they fare over the long haul. Observe:

MCA has been sold four times within 15 years for a cumulative price of over $18 billion. Yet it hasn't earned anywhere near that in the same time period.[2] If Seagram had an agenda other than profit for owning MCA, they may have not cared whether the company actually makes money by selling records. As history reveals, the position of MCA/Universal in Seagram's portfolio made them an attractive buy for media giant the Vivendi Corporation in 2001. They sold to Vivendi for a substantial bonus to the company's key players, even though Universal had not increased profits since they were originally bought by Seagram.

Whatever the financial details, the fact remains that record companies are not necessarily bought because they're profitable, as illustrated below.

Loss Leader

"Loss leader" is an old retail expression. Its roots come from the ploy of having a giveaway item that draws one into a retail store, after which the patron would be sold other things. A crude but simple example might be the "free" prize one finds in the bottom of breakfast cereal for children. (All right, I admit it, I still buy them, too.)

[1] A general rule of thumb in finance is that if the earnings of a company over a five-year period can surpass its sale price, it's a good buy. Thus, EMI would have earned $35 billion over five years, making the $9 billion asking price very attractive.

[2] This example is somewhat exaggerated to make a point. In truth, profits were earned upon each individual sale of the company. However, in the 1980s the value of many companies was based on estimates of their future earnings potential rather than their present actual earnings. Ofttimes estimates were a bit optimistic.

Several of the multinationals that used to hold major label record companies found that there was a synergy between record sales and other products they manufactured. For example, Sony and PolyGram (which was owned by Philips until 1999) co-own the patent on the compact disc. Every time a CD is manufactured they each enjoy a 2.5-cent royalty. It doesn't matter if the records sell in a store or online—they get the fee at the manufacturing end. By this gauge it could be argued that the artist and the musical content on the CD is a loss leader[3] (sometimes called, in the corporate world, a "support function") for generating activity in the CD-manufacturing business, thus earning money for the company's patent division. It is not surprising, then, that in 1999 Philips sold PolyGram. One probable reason is that the patent on the CD is soon to become public domain. Without patent royalties, Philips probably doesn't see the sense in keeping the company in its family.

Another example is RCA, whose record division in the 1950s lost money consistently and was kept running solely because RCA also manufactured record players.[4] Radio airplay stimulated sales of record players. This may seem far-fetched, but believe me, it isn't. Big business looks at the big picture. For example: A major book retailer claimed in a 1995 statement that book sales were hedging back and that the mainstay of their profit came from the sale of coffee to people browsing while in the bookstore. As a result, this particular chain of bookstores has become little more than a library that serves cappuccino.

Another wild example of loss leader comes from the movie industry. Theaters claim that they make little or no money on ticket sales, and that the $100 million blockbuster is just a loss leader, or support function, to bring in the crowds so they can sell popcorn and soda.

In the retail world of record sales, Virgin Super Stores provide an indication that CDs alone cannot justify the cost of building a large outlet. They feel they have to offer the buying public a "shopping experience" to get them in the mood. Tower Records, HMV, and Specs have all experienced financial hardship in recent years. A partial solution has been to start carrying merchandise other than music: T-shirts, posters, CD-ROMs, even Calvin Klein cologne.

Does all this mean that movies are just two-hour commercials for selling junk food? That books are bait for selling coffee? Or that great recording artists are just an excuse to sell T-shirts and collect patent royalties? On a personal level I would like to think not, but the naked truth is, it depends on how your bread is buttered.[5]

As far as music retail goes, in the future you will probably see multi-media stores replace old-style record stores. You will have a sort of supermarket of entertainment. The evidence for this comes from the megatrends in the global economy. Enter-

[3] There is an odd similarity between the expression "loss leader" and the expression "lost leader." The latter is an audio term. It comes from the protective length of paper or plastic film at the beginning and the end of reel-to-reel recording tape. The film is called "leader" because it leads the way for the rest of the tape through the transport mechanism. The actual leader tape is considered worthless. Bad recordings are still cynically called lost leader even though in digital technology there is no actual tape.

[4] Originally called Victrolas; way back then, the Radio Corporation of America merged with the Victor record company to form RCA Victor.

[5] Wouldn't it be really wacky if it turned out that breakfast cereal was the loss leader/support function and that the manufacturer's real intention was to sell the little cheap toy inside? Keep a sharp eye out for the realities of this joke in the next few years.

tainment companies are merging into fewer but larger incarnations of themselves. In the final analysis the entertainment supermarket will probably emerge for no other reason than it will make financial sense to do it.

Here's a more modern and relevant example: According to the annual report of Internet giant AOL/Time Warner, in the fiscal year 2000 their record division earned about $4 billion. But after expenses WEA, the distribution company owned by AOL/Time Warner was left with only a measly $500 million. And from that they had to pay taxes. That sucks—especially when compared to the Internet portion of AOL/Time Warner, which earned $7.7 billion and managed to keep about a third of it. Now, do you think AOL is considering increasing their record division's budget next year or cutting it? Here's a clue: AOL's interest in buying Time Warner was for their music catalog and cable TV distribution. Perhaps they plan to offer subscribers free downloads from the entire roster of WEA artists as an incentive to join America Online. If so and the record division loses money, who cares? It's about subscribers. Does this affect how you go about shopping for a label? You betcha.

Looking at the business this way allows you to rephrase the question that leads off this section. The question shouldn't be, "Do record companies really make any money?" but rather, "How does owning a record company help make money for its owner?"

Bertelsmann AG
(Approx. Annual Sales: $22 billion)

Publishing ($7.73 Billion)

Gruner + Jahr AG & Co
G & J U S.A. (US version)
American HomeStyle & Gardening
Child Magazine
The Family Circle
Fast Company
Fitness
inc.com
Parents Expecting
Parents Magazine
Rosie (formally McCall's)
Women's Magazines Group

Random House
Alfred A. Knopf Inc.
Ballantine Books
Bantam-Dell Group
Crown Publishing Group
Doubleday
Random House Adult Trade
Fawcett Books
Fodor's Travel Pub.
Beginner Books
Pantheon Books
Schocken Books
Times Books
Villard Books
Adapt Electronic Publishing
Bonanza Books
Harmony Books
Julian Press
Portland House

Clarkson N. Potter Inc.
BookSpan
Dell Publishing
Delta
S.I.C.
Laidlaw Brothers Mfrs.
Sonopress Inc.
Transworld Publishers
Bantam Books
Corgi Books
Broun Printing Co.
BCA
Mondadori S.p.A.
Springer-Verlag GmbH & Co
Mosaik Verlagrisma Verlag
Reis-und Verkehrs Verlag
Schulverlag Vieweg
Bertelsmann Lexikothrk
Bertelsmann Club
Albrecht Knaus Verlag
Wilhelm Goldman Verlag
Friedich Vieweg & Sohn
Westdeutscher Verlag
Deutscher Pree Verrieb
Buchhasa
Manager Magazin
Verlagagesellschaft
Morgenpost Druck &
Vertagsanatalt

TV & Radio ($10.5 Billion)

Ufa Film und Femseh
RTL Group
TV
Channel 5 (London)
Fun TV
RTL TV
TMC
TPS
Teva
VCF
Multivision
Premier
RTL Radio
Atlantic 252
Bandit 105.5
Berliner Rundfun
FM Radio Network (Germany)
Fun Radio
Klassik Radio
NSR
104.6 RTL
Radio Hamburg
Radio NRW
Bel RTL
Radio Contact
DTS
ENEX
Infomedia

BMG Music ($4 Billion)

BMG
BMG Classics
Bluebird
Catalyst
Conifer Classics
Deutsche Harmonia Mundi
ECM
Greatest Hits
Living Stereo
Melodiya
Novus
Buddha
BMG U.S. Latin
AME
Ariola
Arista Latin
Barco
Milan Latino
NCR
Palma
Premium
RCA
CMC International
Damian Music
Dancing Cat
J Records
Y Clef
Logic
Milan / Jade
MusicMasters
New Amer. Music
Push
Razor & Tie Ent.
Continental
ATO
Babylon
Blue Dog (UV Records)
Iron Music Group
Melisma
Sanctuary Records Group

RCA
RCA Nashville
Arista Nashville
BNA
Windham Hill
BNA
Beyond
Restless
Robbins Ent.
Time Bomb
Trauma
V2 / Gee Street
White Label Music
Wind-up Ent.
Zomba
Battery
Benson
Brentwood
Dangerous Music
Essential
Jive
Music For Nations
Reunion
Sickwidit
Silvertone
Sound Mex
Verity
Volcano

Arista
Bad Boy Ent.
Arista UK
Grateful Dead

Internet ($0.34 Billion)

CDNow
Barnsandnoble.com
Napster.com Inc.
MyPlay Inc.

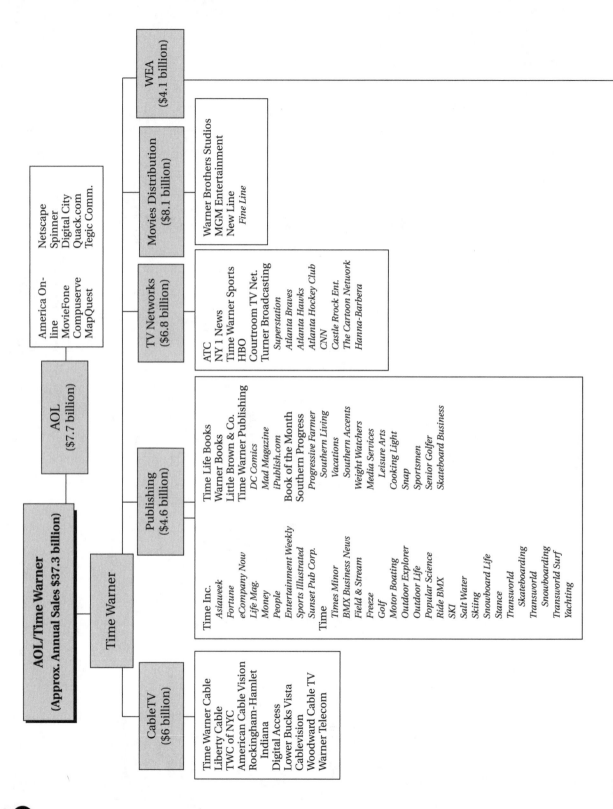

AOL/Time Warner
(Approx. Annual Sales $37.3 billion)

AOL
($7.7 billion)

America On-
line
MovieFone
Compuserve
MapQuest

Netscape
Spinner
Digital City
Quack.com
Tegic Comm.

Time Warner

Cable TV
($6 billion)

Time Warner Cable
Liberty Cable
TWC of NYC
American Cable Vision
Rockingham-Hamlet
Indiana
Digital Access
Lower Bucks Vista
Cablevision
Woodward Cable TV
Warner Telecom

Publishing
($4.6 billion)

Time Inc.
Asiaweek
Fortune
eCompany Now
Life Mag.
Money
People
Entertainment Weekly
Sports Illustrated
Sunset Pub Corp.
Time
Times Minor
BMX Business News
Field & Stream
Freeze
Golf
Motor Boating
Outdoor Explorer
Outdoor Life
Popular Science
Ride BMX
SKI
Salt Water
Skiing
Snowboard Life
Stance
Transworld
Skateboarding
Transworld
Snowboarding
Transworld Surf
Yachting

Time Life Books
Warner Books
Little Brown & Co.
Time Warner Publishing
DC Comics
Mad Magazine
iPublish.com
Book of the Month
Southern Progress
Progressive Farmer
Southern Living
Vacations
Southern Accents
Weight Watchers
Media Services
Leisure Arts
Cooking Light
Snap
Sportsmen
Senior Golfer
Skateboard Business

TV Networks
($6.8 billion)

ATC
NY 1 News
Time Warner Sports
HBO
Courtroom TV Net.
Turner Broadcasting
Superstation
Atlanta Braves
Atlanta Hawks
Atlanta Hockey Club
CNN
Castle Rrock Ent.
The Cartoon Network
Hanna-Barbera

Movies Distribution
($8.1 billion)

Warner Brothers Studios
MGM Entertainment
New Line
Fine Line

WEA
($4.1 billion)

Warner Bros.

Warner Urban Music
Warner Bros. Jazz
Warner Australia
Warner Canada
Warner Music International
Blanco y Negro Delicious Vinyl
London-Sire
Maverick
Warner Bros. Nashville
4 AD
Asylum
Big Screen Music
Dark Horse
Earthbeat!
Giant
Reprise
RuffLife
Ruffhouse
RuffNation
Slash
Nashville
Ruffworld
Silverlight
WEA Latina
Avenue
Breaking
High Tone
Humility
Kinetic
Nonesuch
Pyramid
Quinlan Road
Robert Vale
Vapor
Zebra
Emerald Forest
Foodchain
London-Sire
Hybrid London UK
Qwest
Music For Little People
ADA (dist.)
Warner Music Canada
Ground Swell
Stony Plain
Warner Music Australia
Massive Recording
Warner/Chappell
Warner Bros. Pub

Atlantic Records

Atlantic UK
Atlantic Christian
Children's Group Atlantic
Classics
Erato
Nonesuch
Teldec
Atlantic Nashville
Blackbird
Big Beat
Curb
Caliente
Eardrum
Es Paranza
Finnadar
Blackbird
First Priority
Modern
Rhino
Kid Rhino
143 records

Elektra

Aquemini
EastWest
Flavor Unit
Flip Flipmode Gold Mind
Keia
Monami
The Music Company

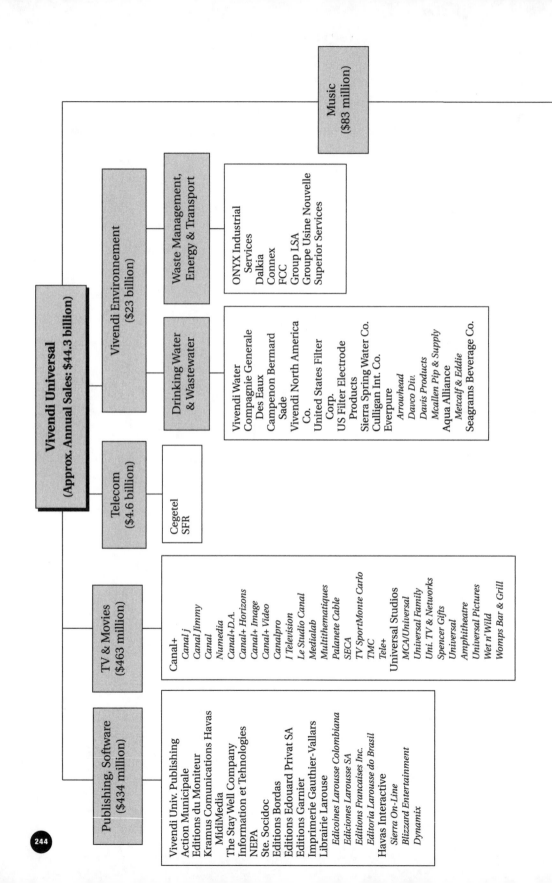

Vivendi Universal
(Approx. Annual Sales: $44.3 billion)

Publishing, Software
($434 million)

Vivendi Univ. Publishing
Action Municipale
Editions du Moniteur
Kramus Comunications Havas
MidiMedia
The Stay Well Company
Information et Tehnologies
NEPA
Ste. Socidoc
Editions Bordas
Editions Edouard Privat SA
Editions Garnier
Imprimerie Gauthier-Vallars
Librairie Larousse
Edicoines Larousse Colombiana
Ediciones Larousse SA
Editions Francaises Inc.
Editoria Larousse do Brasil
Havas Interactive
Sierra On-Line
Blizzard Entertainment
Dynamix

TV & Movies
($463 million)

Canal+
Canal J
Canal Jimmy
Canal
Numedia
Canal+D.A.
Canal+ Horizons
Canal+ Image
Canal+ Video
Canalpro
I Television
Le Studio Canal
Medialab
Multithematiques
Palanete Cable
SECA
TV SportMonte Carlo
TMC
Tele+
Universal Studios
MCA/Universal
Universal Family
Uni. TV & Networks
Spencer Gifts
Universal
Amphitheatre
Universal Pictures
Wet n'Wild
Womps Bar & Grill

Telecom
($4.6 billion)

Cegetel
SFR

Vivendi Environnement
($23 billion)

**Drinking Water
& Wastewater**

Vivendi Water
Compagnie Generale
Des Eaux
Campenon Bernard
Sade
Vivendi North America
Co.
United States Filter
Corp.
US Filter Electrode
Products
Sierra Spring Water Co.
Culligan Int. Co.
Everpure
Arrowhead
Davco Div.
Davis Products
Mcallen Pip & Supply
Aqua Alliance
Metcalf & Eddie
Seagrams Beverage Co.

**Waste Management,
Energy & Transport**

ONYX Industrial
Services
Dalkia
Connex
FCC
Group LSA
Groupe Usine Nouvelle
Superior Services

Music
($83 million)

Universal	MCA	Island Def Jam Music Group	Interscope / Geffen / A&M	
Universal Classics & Jazz	**MCA Nashville**	Def Jam	A&M	Mercury Nashville
Archiv	*Curb / MCA*	*Def Soul*	Geffen	Curb / Mercury
Argo	**MCA Records**	*Roc-A-Fella*	Interscope	Nashville
Decca	*Chess*	Island	*Aftermath*	Recognition
Deutsche Grammophon	*Coral*	Mercury	*B-Rite*	RMM
Gimell	*Duke*	*Blackheart*	*Barak / Goodvibe / Jcor*	*Merengazo*
Imaginary Road	*Peacock*	*Casablanca*	*Booga Basement*	*Soho Latino*
Mercury Living Presence	*Vocalion*	*Tone-Cool*	*Coolsville*	*Tropijazz*
Penguin Classics	*Curb*	Rounder	*Flip*	Thump
Philips	*Drive Thru*	*Bullseye*	*Goodvibe / Jcor*	*Thump Street*
Point	*Experience Hendrix*	*Easy Disc*	*Gospo Centric*	*Jimmy & Doug's*
Universal Music Latino	*Jersey*	*Heartbeat*	*Jake*	*Farmclub.com*
Bohemia	*Radioactive*	*Philo*	*Jcor*	Lideres
Discos Rocio	*Refugee*	*Zoe*	*Lil' Man*	Lost Highway
Karen	*Silas*		*Nothing*	
Magic Music			*Organized Noise*	
Melody			*Prawn Song*	
Mercury			*Rock Land*	
Platano			*Ruff Ryders*	
Protel			*University*	
Rodven			Abkco	
Universal			Ark 21	
Abrupt			*Bliss*	
Biv 10			*9th Floor*	
Cash Money			*Recordz*	
Crazy World Entertainment			DreamWorks	
Deston Entertainment			*Def Squad*	
Mojo			*DreamWorks*	
Motown			*Nashville*	
Polydor			Hollywood	
Republic			*Lyric Street*	
Universal			*Mammoth*	
			Surf Dog	

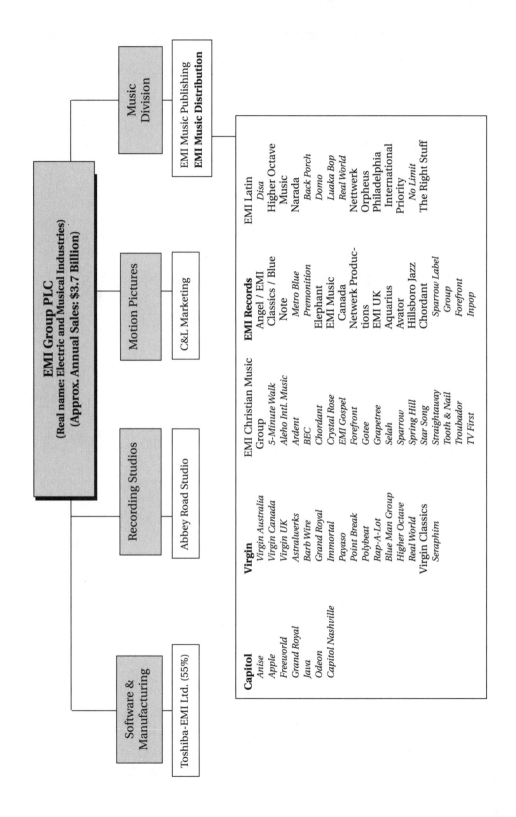

EMI Group PLC
(Real name: Electric and Musical Industries)
(Approx. Annual Sales: $3.7 Billion)

- Software & Manufacturing
  - Toshiba-EMI Ltd. (55%)
- Recording Studios
  - Abbey Road Studio
- Motion Pictures
  - C&L Marketing
- Music Division
  - EMI Music Publishing
  - **EMI Music Distribution**

Capitol
Anise
Apple
Freeworld
Grand Royal
Java
Odeon
Capitol Nashville

Virgin
Virgin Australia
Virgin Canada
Virgin UK
Astralwerks
Barb Wire
Grand Royal
Immortal
Payaso
Point Break
Polybeat
Rap-A-Lot
Blue Man Group
Higher Octave
Real World
Virgin Classics
Seraphim

EMI Christian Music Group
5-Minute Walk
Aleho Intl. Music
Ardent
BEC
Chordant
Crystal Rose
EMI Gospel
Forefront
Gotee
Grapetree
Selah
Sparrow
Spring Hill
Star Song
Straightaway
Tooth & Nail
Troubador
TV First

EMI Records
Angel / EMI Classics / Blue Note
Metro Blue
Premonition
Elephant
EMI Music Canada
Netwerk Productions
EMI UK
Aquarius
Avator
Hillsboro Jazz
Chordant
Sparrow Label Group
Forefront
Inpop

EMI Latin
Disa
Higher Octave Music
Narada
Back Porch
Domo
Luaka Bop
Real World
Nettwerk
Orpheus
Philadelphia International
Priority
No Limit
The Right Stuff

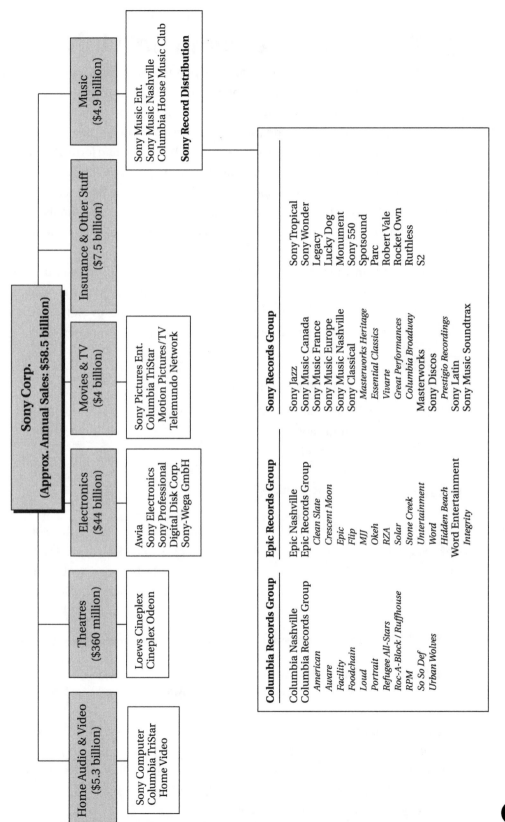

➤ A Map of the Financial Universe

How does the record industry look from the point of view of the parent holding companies? Look at the family trees on the previous pages and you'll get an idea of the big picture. Notice that the record division in most cases brings in the lowest, or close to the lowest, amount of revenue and profit compared to other holdings.

If the trees above are a bit confusing, check it out in a more fluid form. Below is a breakdown of the parent company portfolios that hold the major record distributors. This oversimplified chart shows how the money trickles down. All of the figures, taken from publicly available data, are for 2001. In the Appendix there are the same family trees as they appeared in 1998. Look how the industry has changed and who owns what today as opposed to just three years ago.

None of the companies breaks out record sales alone, excluding other items like music publishing. Even so, the figures should give you a picture of what's going on. The set of numbers represent the total amount of money earned by the division and the amount left over after that division paid its operating expenses (excluding taxes, etc.)

Quick Key:

WEA belongs to AOL/Time Warner.

MCA, UNI, and Interscope belong to Vivendi Universal.

BMG belongs to Bertelsmann AG.

Sony owns itself, as does EMI.

AOL/Time Warner Inc. ($37.3 billion)

	Total earned	After expenses	Cents on the dollar
American Online	$7.7 billion	$2.3 billion	30 cents
Cable	$6 billion	$2.8 billion	47 cents
Movies	$8.1 billion	$800 million	10 cents
Networks	$6.8 billion	$1.5 billion	22 cents
Publishing	$4.6 billion	$700 million	15 cents
Music	$4.1 billion	$500 million	12 cents

Vivendi Universal ($44.3 billion)

	Total earned	After expenses	Cents on the dollar
Telecommunications	$4.6 billion	$1.1 billion	24 cents
Internet	$42 million	<$162 million>	-3.8 cents
TV & movies	$7.8 billion	$682 million	11 cents

Environmental Services	$23 billion	$3 billion	14 cents
Publishing	$3.1 billion	$434 million	14 cents
Music	$5.8 billion	$1 billion	17 cents

Sony Corporation ($58.5 billion)

	Total earned	After expenses	Cents on the dollar
Electronics	$44 billion	$2.0 billion	4.5 cents
Games	$5.3 billion	-$400 million	-7 cents
Movies & theaters	$4.4 billion	$30 million	.67 cents
Insurance	$4.3 billion	$100 million	2 cents
Other small stuff	$3.2 billion	$100 million	3 cents
Music distribution	$4.9 billion	$20 million	<.5 cent

Since Bertelsmann AG and EMI Group are not public companies, only total earnings numbers are available.

Bertelsmann AG ($21 billion[6])

BMG Entertainment (film, TV)	$10.5 billion
Music distribution	$4.0 billion
Publishing (magazines, newspapers, books)	$7.7 billion
Dot-coms	$0.34 billion

[6] This number is from the annual reports of these companies. It may or may not match the calculations to the right.

EMI Group PLC (formerly Thorn EMI PLC) ($3.7 billion)

(Electric and Musical Industries)

EMI Music	$3.7 billion

The Walt Disney Company ($27.4 billion[6])

Walt Disney is not a major label; it is listed here purely out of respect for the 300-pound indie giant.

Theme parks and resorts	$6.8 billion
Broadcasting	$9.1 billion
"Creative content" (including films, records, and consumer products)	$9 billion (33%)

(Note: Estimated annual sales for Walt Disney Records were $50 million.)

What Does the Above Teach Us?

It costs a typical major label about $8.50 in overhead to make a single dollar. Because the record industry is probably really worth about $10 billion a year in before-expense sales, that may sound like an idle complaint—but consider the alternatives: paper, oil, gas, military contracting and other commodities. These industries are worth $15 to $50 billion a year *after expenses*, and they don't have anywhere near the same overhead that the music industry does. What all this means is that at the end of the day it costs more to make less in the record game.

This is nothing new; the profits in music have always been questionable. But in the past there was always a secondary business to offset the losses. Things are different now, because most large companies have sold off the unprofitable parts of their empires in the mergers and acquisitions of the 1980s. Those who bought the record divisions rationalized that they could make these enterprises work if they could just keep their overhead down—something they have been unable to do. When the reality of this settles in, the corporation will look to sell.

What keeps the record game going is the allure. Crown jewels like U2, Bob Dylan, the Rolling Stones, Madonna, and other cash cows attract large multinationals to gobble up what they think are money-making ventures; the sale is made, and lots of new money flows. Then, after several years, the attractiveness of owning a glamorous liability wears off. During this phase a new mentality emerges: "Sign hits or get the ax." Naturally one can't sign hits every day, so the policy mutates into one of damage control—giving away as little as possible to each signed act. This also means paying off as few people as possible and cutting out the middlemen, like producers and managers, whenever possible.

In time, the budgets shrink, favors are hard to come by, and eventually the record company is sold off, starting the process all over again. In the interim more artists, producers, executives, and lawyers make their mark while Papa Bear holding company figures out how to get out of the mess it bought into.

But can this kind of game continue? Eventually, won't everyone know that big profits in the world of major labels is somewhat of a fallacy? The answer is yes, they already do. But major labels are presently trying to redefine their roles in the brave new digital future and are experiencing the most far-reaching transformations that they have ever known in their 50-year history. When the restructuring is over, there will likely be fewer jobs in middle management (like A&R, artist relations, and promotions) at big record labels and more splinter record labels (which many call indies and I refer to as one-deep and two-deep labels) with ties to Big Five distribution.

⊘ Family Tree of Big Five Distributors as of January 2001

BMG

Arista

    Bad Boy Entertainment

    Arista UK

    Grateful Dead

Beyond

BMG Classics

    Bluebird

    Catalyst

    Conifer Classics

    Deutsche Harmonia Mundi

    ECM

    ECM New Series

    Greatest Hits

    Living Stereo

    Melodiya

    Novus

BMG Special Products

    Buddha

BMG U.S. Latin

    AME

    Ariola

    Arista Latin

    Barco

    Milan Latino

    NCR

    Palma

    Premium

    RCA

BMG Video

CMC International

Damian Music

Dancing Cat

J Records

    Y Clef

Logic

Milan / Jade

MusicMasters

New American Music

Push

Razor & Tie Entertainment

RCA Label Group / Nashville

    Arista Nashville

    BNA

    RCA Nashville

    Windham Hill

Restless

Robbins Entertainment

Time Bomb

Trauma

V2 / Gee Street

White Label Music

Wind-up Entertainment

Zomba

    Battery

    Benson

    Brentwood

    Dangerous Music

    Essential

    Jive

    Music For Nations

Reunion
Sickwidit
Silvertone
Sound Mex
Verity
Volcano
Continental
ATO
Babylon
Blue Dog (UV Records)
Iron Music Group
Melisma
Sanctuary Records Group

EMD

Angel / EMI Classics / Virgin
  Classics
    Seraphim
Blue Note
    Metro Blue
    Premonition
Capitol
    Anise
    Apple
    Freeworld
    Grand Royal
    Java
    Odeon
Capitol Nashville
EMI Christian Music Group
    5-Minute Walk
    Aleho International Music
    Ardent
    BEC
    Chordant
    Crystal Rose
    EMI Gospel
    Forefront

Gotee
Grapetree
Selah
Sparrow
Spring Hill
Star Song
Straightaway
Tooth & Nail
Troubador
TV First
Higher Octave Music
Narada
    Back Porch
    Domo
    Luaka Bop
    Real World
Nettwerk
Orpheus
Philadelphia International
Priority
    No Limit
The Right Stuff
Virgin
    Virgin Australia
    Virgin Canada
    Virgin UK
    Astralwerks
    Barb Wire
    Grand Royal
    Immortal
    Payaso
    Point Break
    Polybeat
    Rap-A-Lot
    Blue Man Group
    Higher Octave
    Real World
EMI

Spitfire

Vital Sounds

Sanctuary Records Group

  North America

Elephant

EMI Music Canada

     Netwerk Productions

EMI UK

Aquarius

Avator

Hillsboro Jazz

Chordant

    Sparrow Label Group

    Forefront

    (Chordant/EMI)

    Inpop (Chordant/EMI)

EMI Latin

Disa

SONY MUSIC

Columbia Nashville

Columbia Records Group

American

Aware

Facility

Foodchain

Loud

Portrait

Refugee All-Stars

Roc-A-Block / RuffHouse

RPM

So So Def

Urban Wolves

Epic Nashville

Epic Records Group

Clean Slate

Crescent Moon

Epic

Flip

MJJ

Okeh

RZA

Solar

Stone Creek

Entertainment

Word

     Integrity

Hidden Beach

Legacy

Lucky Dog

Monument

Sony

Sony Classical

    Masterworks Heritage

    Essential Classics

    Vivarte

    Great Performances

    Columbia Broadway

Masterworks

Sony Discos

    Prestigio Recordings

Sony Latin

Sony Music Soundtrax

Sony Tropical

Sony Wonder

Sony Jazz

Sony Music Canada

Sony Music France

Sony Music Europe

Sony Music Nashville

Spotsound

Parc

Robert Vale

Rocket Own

Ruthless

S2

UNIVERSAL

Abkco

Ark 21
    Bliss
    9th Floor Recordz

DreamWorks
    Def Squad
    DreamWorks Nashville

Hollywood
    Lyric Street
    Mammoth
    Surf Dog

Interscope / Geffen / A&M
    A&M
    Geffen
    Interscope
        Aftermath
        B-Rite
        Barak / Goodvibe / Jcor
        Booga Basement
        Coolsville
        Flip
        Goodvibe / Jcor
        Gospo Centric
        Jake
        Jcor
        Lil' Man
        Nothing
        Organized Noise
        Prawn Song
        Rock Land
        Ruff Ryders
        Shady
        University

Island Def Jam Music Group
    Def Jam
        Def Soul
        Roc-A-Fella

    Island

Mercury
        Blackheart
        Casablanca
        Tone-Cool

    Rounder
        Bullseye
        Easy Disc
        Heartbeat
        Philo
        Zoe

Jimmy & Doug's Farmclub.com

Lideres

Lost Highway

MCA Nashville
    Curb / MCA

MCA Records & Affiliated Labels
    Chess
    Coral
    Duke
    Peacock
    Vocalion

MCA Records Distributed Labels
    Curb / MCA
    Drive Thru
    Experience Hendrix
    Jersey
    Magic Johnson Music
    MCA UK
    Radioactive
    Refugee
    Silas

Mercury Nashville
    Curb / Mercury Nashville

Recognition

RMM
    Merengazo
    Soho Latino

Tropijazz

Thump

Thump Street

Universal Music Group

Universal Music Group
Canada

Merderecords

True North

TVT Canada

Universal Classics & Jazz

Archiv

Argo

Decca

Deutsche
 Grammophon

Gimell

Imaginary Road

Mercury Living
 Presence

Penguin Classics

Philips

Point

Universal Music Latino

Bohemia

Discos Rocio

Karen

Magic Music

Melody

Mercury

Platano

Protel

Rodven

Universal

Abrupt

Biv 10

Cash Money

Crazy World

Entertainment

Deston Entertainment

Mojo

Motown

Polydor

Republic

Universal

ZTT

Universal Music Enterprises

AVI / Excello

Chronicles

Geffen Goldline

Hip-O

Universal Special
 Products

UTV

Varese Sarabande

Fuel 2000

Verve Music Group

Blue Thumb

GRP

Impulse!

Verve

Walt Disney

Buena Vista

Video

DreamWorks Home Video

Lion's Gate Films

Playboy Home Video

Universal Family &
 Home Entertainment

Universal Home Video

EMC

3:33 Music Group

Flyte Tyme

JTJ Empire

Mammoth

PRA

Threshold

Tone-Cool

WEA

Atlantic

    Atlantic Classics

        Erato

        Nonesuch

        Teldec

    Atlantic Nashville

    Big Beat

    Curb

    Eardrum

    Es Paranza

    Finnadar

    First Priority

    Modern

Elektra Entertainment

    Aquemini

    EastWest

    Flavor Unit

    Flip

    Flipmode

    Gold Mind

    Keia

    Monami

    The Music Company

Emerald Forest

Foodchain

London-Sire

    Hybrid

    London UK

Rhino

    Kid Rhino

    Music For Little People

Warner Bros.

    Warner Urban Music

Warner Bros. Jazz

Warner Australia

Warner Canada

Warner Music International

Warner Bros. Records

        Nashville

    4 AD

    Asylum

    Big Screen Music

    Dark Horse

    Earthbeat!

Giant

    Giant/ Nashville

Maverick

Qwest

Reprise

RuffLife

RuffHouse

RuffNation

RuffWorld

Nonesuch

Pyramid

Quinlan Road

Robert Vale

Vapor

Zebra

Silverlight

Slash

    Warner Archives

Warner Bros. Nashville

Warner Bros. Canada

    Stony Plain

Warner Reprise Video

Warner Western

WEA Latina

⊘Record/Pause

A s a closing summary I've composed a checklist of every pitfall I could think of that a recording artist, producer, or small label owner could encounter. It's the Murphy's Law of the recording industry, if you will, and it's compiled from listening to 15 years of fuck-ups and fish stories. Remember, the wise man learns from other people's mistakes. If you can make it through this list, you're assured to make mountains of money and have lots of great sex.

⊘ Checklist for Disaster

(Note: Each of these things is guaranteed to have actually happened more than once.)

√ **Band members can't get along.**
√ **No consistent direction in the band's music/no good material.**
√ **Can't get a manager/producer interested in working with you.**
√ **The manager/producer working with you dies and ties up your contract in probate court.**
√ **The lawyer handling the negotiating of your record deal gets fired or moves, leaving your contract in limbo.**

√ The advance from the label doesn't cover the cost of making the record.

√ The studio you're recording in has a flood and it destroys your masters. Oh, yeah, and they recently canceled their liability insurance.

√ The label's distributor moves warehouses and loses your stock of CDs.

√ The A&R person who signed you is fired or dies and the new person filling their shoes is less than interested in you.

√ After two years of recording your masterpiece album, it is finally released and it sounds two years old.

√ The radio station that your label had a great relationship with changes its format.

√ Long hair is back and you just got a buzz cut to be hip.

√ The record is doing well, but the lead singer wants to do a solo project next.

√ While on tour the entire group is arrested by a local sheriff for DWI and knocking up his underage daughter.

√ The producer won't deliver the master to the record company until he gets more money.

√ The artist won't show up for a session or photo shoot until they get more money.

√ One or both of the above delay the record's release and the marketing window closes.

√ The single that the record company picks is the most atypical song on the record. It's a hit and the band's credibility is destroyed.

√ The label goes into Chapter 11, tying up your royalties and contract in bankruptcy hearings.

√ The artist, after one record, decides that they can produce the next record themselves. Oh yeah, and they don't need a manager telling them what to do, either.

√ You sold over 20,000 CDs through your local record store, but they have no receipts and it didn't show up on SoundScan.

√ Some Internet cyber-dweeb puts your single on an online bulletin board and everyone's downloading it, royalty-free.

√ You've sold a million records, but the label's cost for promotion was so high that you still owe another half a million dollars before you get royalties.

√ Your label merges with its parent distributor and trims the fat off their roster—you're on the cutting room floor.

√ Your indie label can't pay you because their distributor won't pay them, or went out of business.

√ You get a letter from the lawyer of some drunk you hung out with one night, and he's decided he helped you cowrite that new hit song of yours.

√ Some other band with the same name decides to sue you for trademark infringement.

❷ Final Word

In closing this book I would like to leave you with a somewhat philosophical thought: We are perched at a new age of our industry. Technology has lifted the veil of secrecy from record sales and has made it possible for anyone with a phone line to reach thousands with their message. New laws will alter the way artists will be paid, and electronic media may permanently change the way we buy and listen to our favorite songs.

There is something odd about change. We talk passionately about wanting it until it starts to become a reality. Then a deep-rooted fear of the unknown sets in as our status quo dissolves. We hope it's for the better.

Regardless of corporate influence, pop music responds to the values and needs of each new generation. If we look at modern music in this way, we must conclude that it is not just a "business." It is a key barometer of how our culture evolves. If we agree with that statement, then those who commit to music as a career accept an important contract with their fellow human beings—the power to influence.

If you've read this book carefully, you have more information and tips than over 90% of most people when they started out in this business. Use your new knowledge wisely. Make a difference. The movers and shakers who have had ongoing hits in this industry are constantly evolving and keeping on top of what's fresh. This is important. Do not lose touch with the market. Whether you're a producer, manager, lawyer, A&R person, label owner, session player, sideperson, engineer, or writer, remember:

Half of being smart is knowing what you're dumb at.

While you grow older, your client,
the record buyer, is forever young.

Peace.

➤ Appendix A: Family Trees of Big Six Distributors as of January 1998

Compare these charts showing what the industry looked like a few short years ago to the current status as shown starting on page 241. See how the industry has changed and who owns what now versus then.

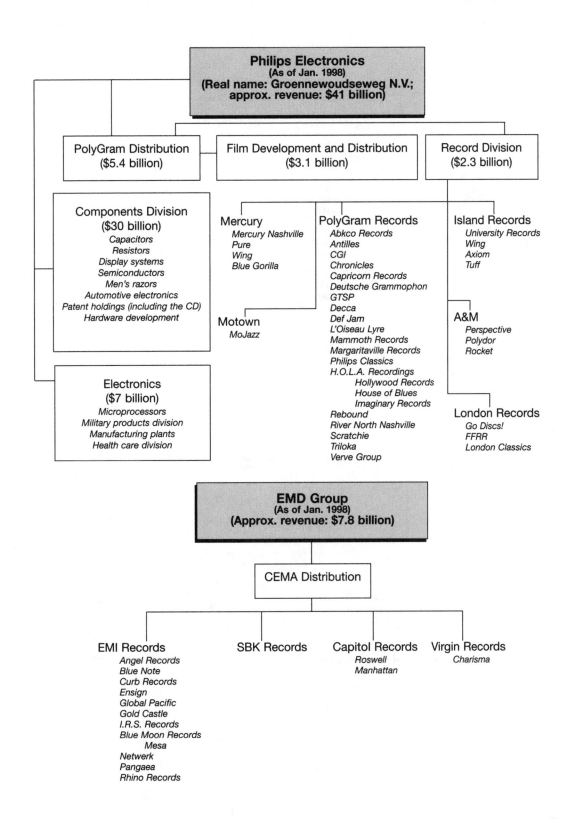

Philips Electronics
(As of Jan. 1998)
(Real name: Groennewoudseweg N.V.;
approx. revenue: $41 billion)

PolyGram Distribution
($5.4 billion)

Film Development and Distribution
($3.1 billion)

Record Division
($2.3 billion)

Components Division
($30 billion)
Capacitors
Resistors
Display systems
Semiconductors
Men's razors
Automotive electronics
Patent holdings (including the CD)
Hardware development

Mercury
Mercury Nashville
Pure
Wing
Blue Gorilla

Motown
MoJazz

PolyGram Records
Abkco Records
Antilles
CGI
Chronicles
Capricorn Records
Deutsche Grammophon
GTSP
Decca
Def Jam
L'Oiseau Lyre
Mammoth Records
Margaritaville Records
Philips Classics
H.O.L.A. Recordings
Hollywood Records
House of Blues
Imaginary Records
Rebound
River North Nashville
Scratchie
Triloka
Verve Group

Island Records
University Records
Wing
Axiom
Tuff

A&M
Perspective
Polydor
Rocket

London Records
Go Discs!
FFRR
London Classics

Electronics
($7 billion)
Microprocessors
Military products division
Manufacturing plants
Health care division

EMD Group
(As of Jan. 1998)
(Approx. revenue: $7.8 billion)

CEMA Distribution

EMI Records
Angel Records
Blue Note
Curb Records
Ensign
Global Pacific
Gold Castle
I.R.S. Records
Blue Moon Records
Mesa
Netwerk
Pangaea
Rhino Records

SBK Records

Capitol Records
Roswell
Manhattan

Virgin Records
Charisma

Bertelsmann AG
(As of Jan. 1998)
(Approx. revenue: $14 billion)

BMG Music
$5 billion

BMG
- *Reunion*
- *Time Bomb*
- *Bad Boy*
- *Career Records*
- *Private Music*
- *RLC*
- *The Children's Group*
- *CMC International*
- *Critique*
- *Logic*
- *Miramar*
- *Musicmakers*
- *Restless Records*
- *Robbins Ent.*
- *Wind-Up Ent.*
- *V2*
  - *Gee Street*
- *Volcano Recordings*

RCA Records
- *Beggars Banquet*
- *Big Time*
- *Bluebird*
- *Dedicated*
- *Grunt*
- *LMR*
- *Milan*
- *Nashville*
- *Novus*

Windham Hill
- *Windham Hill Jazz*
- *Dancing Cat*
- *High Street*
- *Hip Pocket*
- *Open Air*
- *Rabbit Ears*

Arista Records
- *LaFace*
- *Bad Boy*
- *Career*
- *Dedicated*
- *Rowdy*
- *Time Bomb*

Imago Entertainment Group

Gruner+Jahr Publishing
($7.3 billion)
- *Baby Care*
- *Home Video*
- *Family Circle*
- *McCalls*
- *Doubleday*
- *Dell Publishing*
- *Transworld*
- *5% of America On Line*

Sony Corporation
(As of Jan. 1998)
(Approx. revenue: $43.3 billion)

Sony Electronics
($10 billion)
Aiwa

Telecommuncations
($3.5 billion)
Semiconductors
Logistics services

Sony Entertainment
($4.6 billion)
Columbia Pictures
Tri-Star Pictures
The Peter Guber Co.
Barris Productions

Research
($2 billion)
Thinfilm coating
Etching systems
High purity metals
& materials

Ceramics
($6.2 billion)
Hightech very pure ceramic easings for electronics

Sony Music
($2.9 billion)

Sony Records

Chaos	*Hall of Fame*	***Columbia***
Soundtrax	*Heartcry*	*Def Jam*
Sony 550	*Higher Ground*	*Relativity*
Crescent Moon	*Hoppoh*	*So So Def*
OKeh	*Hudlin Brothers*	*Sony Discos*
Tri-Star Music	*Immortal*	*Sony Tropical*
Sony Classical	*Independent*	*Stonecreek*
Soho Square	*Lucky Dog*	*Word Gospel*
Sony Wonder	*Myrra*	*Word Nashville*
Chrysalis	*New Deal*	*Yab Yum*
Big Cat	*Q Division*	***Epic***
Crave	*Ruffhouse*	*Lifestyle*
Creation	*Slam Jamz*	
Flavor Unite		

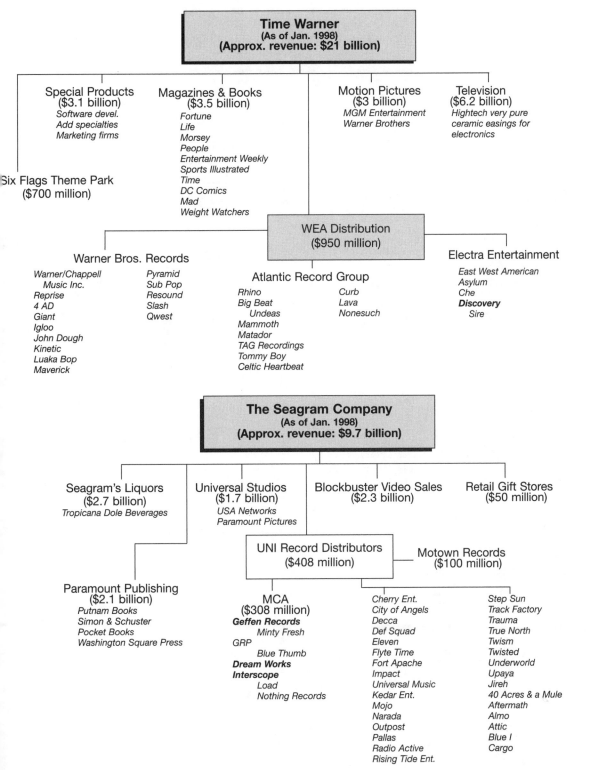

Time Warner
(As of Jan. 1998)
(Approx. revenue: $21 billion)

Special Products
($3.1 billion)
Software devel.
Add specialties
Marketing firms

Magazines & Books
($3.5 billion)
Fortune
Life
Morsey
People
Entertainment Weekly
Sports Illustrated
Time
DC Comics
Mad
Weight Watchers

Motion Pictures
($3 billion)
MGM Entertainment
Warner Brothers

Television
($6.2 billion)
Hightech very pure
ceramic easings for
electronics

Six Flags Theme Park
($700 million)

WEA Distribution
($950 million)

Warner Bros. Records

Warner/Chappell
*   Music Inc.*
Reprise
4 AD
Giant
Igloo
John Dough
Kinetic
Luaka Bop
Maverick

Pyramid
Sub Pop
Resound
Slash
Qwest

Atlantic Record Group

Rhino
Big Beat
*   Undeas*
Mammoth
Matador
TAG Recordings
Tommy Boy
Celtic Heartbeat

Curb
Lava
Nonesuch

Electra Entertainment

East West American
Asylum
Che
Discovery
*   Sire*

The Seagram Company
(As of Jan. 1998)
(Approx. revenue: $9.7 billion)

Seagram's Liquors
($2.7 billion)
Tropicana Dole Beverages

Universal Studios
($1.7 billion)
USA Networks
Paramount Pictures

Blockbuster Video Sales
($2.3 billion)

Retail Gift Stores
($50 million)

UNI Record Distributors
($408 million)

Motown Records
($100 million)

Paramount Publishing
($2.1 billion)
Putnam Books
Simon & Schuster
Pocket Books
Washington Square Press

MCA
($308 million)
Geffen Records
*   Minty Fresh*
GRP
*   Blue Thumb*
Dream Works
Interscope
*   Load*
*   Nothing Records*

Cherry Ent.
City of Angels
Decca
Def Squad
Eleven
Flyte Time
Fort Apache
Impact
Universal Music
Kedar Ent.
Mojo
Narada
Outpost
Pallas
Radio Active
Rising Tide Ent.

Step Sun
Track Factory
Trauma
True North
Twism
Twisted
Underworld
Upaya
Jireh
40 Acres & a Mule
Aftermath
Almo
Attic
Blue I
Cargo

The Seagram Company

(Consolidation of Seagram & PolyGram as of Jan. 1998)

(Approx. revenue $15.1 billion)

See other holdings previous page

UNI Record Distributors — Motown Records

PolyGram Diversified Ent.
(Approx. revenue $2.3 billion)

Film Development slated to be sold

Records

MCA
Geffen Records
Minty Fresh
GRP
Blue Thumb
Drean Works
Interscope
Load
Nothing Records

Cherry Ent.
City of Angels
Decca
Def Squad
Eleven
Flyte Time
Fort Apache
Impact
Universal Music
Kedar Ent.
Mojo
Narada
Outpost
Pallas
Radio Active
Rising Tide Ent.

Step Sun
Track Factory
Trauma
True North
Twism
Twisted
Underworld
Upaya
Jireh
40 Acres & a
  Mule
Aftermath
Almo
Attic
Blue I
Cargo

Mercury
Mercury Nashville
Pure
Wing
Blue Gorilla

Motown
MoJazz

PolyGram Records
Abkco Records
Antilles
CGI
Chronicles
Capricorn Records
Deutsche Grammophon
GTSP
Decca
Def Jam
L'Oiseau Lyre
Mammoth Records
Margaritaville Records
Philips Classics
H.O.L.A. Recordings
  Hollywood Records
  House of Blues
  Imaginary Records
Rebound
River North Nashville
Scratchie
Triloka
Verve Group

Island Records
University Records
Wing
Axiom
Island Black Recor
Tuff

A&M
Perspective
Polydor
Rocket

London Records
Go Discs!
FFRR
London Classics

ACKNOWLEDGMENTS

The music industry is a place that attracts many who claim to be of high moral character. I have been fortunate to know some of the few who really live up to that claim. The making of a book like this does not come without great personal sacrifice. I would first like to thank all of those who, despite potential derision, supported and applauded this effort. They deserve my eternal thanks and the appreciation of all who enter the business of music.

First and foremost a good friend, Pat Cameron, who, along with Matt Kelsey at Backbeat, had the vision and bravado to give this project a chance. Jim Aikin, my editor, for his talent in turning a phrase and whose irritating demand that I back up every fact in this book will probably keep me out of court. Renee, my research assistant, who spent tireless hours in the public library looking up names, dates, and obscure elements of copyright law. Richard Wolf, a barrister of undying righteousness who found time for me. Matt at Grubamn/Indursky and Rick at Warner Bros., the two most honest lawyers in the business, who helped keep me honest when entropy proposed otherwise. Holly, at Polly, who still returns my calls via her assistant. My first agent, Donald. Dick Gabriel, and his desire to make a difference. R.B., a royal pain in the butt who gave a smart-ass engineer a shot and taught me that Allah loves all. My engineering mentor, John H., who showed me how to set up a mike, and that new does not necessarily mean improved. Doug, who looked at my early scribbling and thought I had something worth pursuing. Shasti, my spiritual sister, whose illustrations do not appear in this book. Brian, my oldest friend, who indulges me in the sport of arguing (I have that $20 I owe you). Additional thanks go out to the following for their uncompensated contributions to keeping this book accurate: John Luongo for his keen eye and math skills; JM at Middle Ear; Lauren, my buddy on the inside; Jennelynd, wherever you are—you started all this; Josh at Intouch; Dean—please resurface; the two dudes at SpinArt; Mike Baker; Stan Soocher; JJ French; Steve Addabbo; Bruce the gnome; all the affiliates of www.MosesAvalon.com; the educators at music schools everywhere who do not get enough credit; and anybody whose name I've forgotten. Thanks to all.

Finally, my mother, who raised me right, teaching me to tell the truth, the whole truth, and nothing but the truth. And my wife and best friend, whose support and inspiration make every day worth living.

You are all a credit to the human race.

ABOUT THE AUTHOR

Moses Avalon earned his kudos in the music business by producing and engineering records in New York City for Warner Brothers, Atlantic Records, and BMG as well as many independent labels. His work with Grammy-award-winning recording artists has earned him five Platinum records and several Ampex Golden Reel awards. As a composer, his soundtracks have been used by Citibank, AT&T, Levi Strauss, and Pepsi, as well as in several independent films that have won outstanding achievement awards at Cannes, The New York Expo, and WorldFest.

Moses started as an assistant engineer in a small eight-track recording studio in the late 1970s. His consulting company presently assists artists, managers, lawyers, labels, film production companies, and investors interested in the music business.

Readers can contact the author by e-mail via: www.MosesAvalon.com

ABOUT MOSESAVALON.COM AND THE MOSES AVALON COMPANY

www.MosesAvalon.com

Launched in September 2000, MosesAvalon.com has become the premier portal for inside information on the music industry—everything from newsletters to an interactive **Royalty Calculator,** where the value of any record deal can be instantly assessed free of charge. Mr. Avalon started the website to give musicians, songwriters, artists, managers, and others information useful in making career decisions in the world of music. A popular feature has been **"the $10 consultation."** In this service Mr. Avalon or a person from his advisory board will answer via e-mail any single question regarding the music business. The site also offers books and other products to aid the music industry professional.

The Moses Avalon Company

The Moses Avalon Company specializes in commercial consulting services regarding any matter related to record companies or the music industry. Services include: music licensing, negotiations of major label recording contracts and publishing deals, and expert witness testimony. In the near future the company will begin hosting educational seminars and study-at-home courses aimed at expanding understanding of the music business for attorneys and musicians.

INDEX

n: indicates footnote

A

accounting statements, 136

act(s)

  buzz with, 113

  cost effectiveness of, 108

  dressing up, 92

  first look with, 214

  hot sheets and, 113

  under indie or major labels, 116

  labels signing bad, 212–213

  managers and up-and-coming, 211

  signing of, 24

  soundtrak scams/CD samplers and, 180–181

ADA (Alternative Distribution Alliance), 49

advances, 54*n*1, 55, 73, 185

  administrative expenses and, 71–72

  against future royalties, 55

  recoupment formula for, 71

advice ,of lawyers, 7

AFM (American Federation of Musicians),
  36–38, 89, 226

agreement(s). *See also* contracts

  breach of, 202

  first draft of, 189–190

  informal, 128–129

  legal-ease in, 193–197

  management, 129

  online indie, 185

  production, 129

  reserve clause in record, 61

  revisions in, 189–190

  slimebag, 193, 198

  verbal, 190

  virtual terms in, 184–185

  work-for-hire, 27

airplay

  on radio, 20, 101–105

  record sales and, 219

  stimulated sales of record players, 239

albums. *See* records

All-In Deal, The, 25, 78, 83

  all-in budget in, 78

alternative rock, 94, 108

A&M, 47*n*1, 261, 264, 268

America Online, 47*n*1

AMRA (American Mechanical Rights Agency), 42

AOL/Time Warner, 47*n*1, 222, 235, 240,
  242–243, 248

A&R (Artists and Repertoire) people, 113,
  128–129, 174, 185, 190, 214, 233, 235

  assistant, 10

  charts and, 100

  executive producer credits and, 225

exposure of band and, 210–211

future of, 250

humbling facts about, 11

  at Indie level, 10, 11

kickbacks and, 84, 213

mercy signing and, 213–214

musicians as, 17

passing over tapes by, 211–212

promotional kits and, 209–210

record labels and, 9–10

revolving door and, 65

salaries of, 10

sending second demos to, 211

singles and, 105

tenuous footing of, 10

thrill of chase and, 210–211

typical day of, 10

women and, 9, 9*n*2

A&R label, 49*n*4, 50*n*7

Arista, 47, 47*n*1, 50, 52, 262, 267

arrangement(s)

  protecting, 141

  of songs, 19

  update of law with, 19

arrangers/cowriters, 20

artist/producer production deal

  joint venture and, 126

  mini-record deal and, 124–126

  work-for-hire deal and, 126

artist(s). *See also* musicians

  album covers and, 220

  approval, in contracts, 196

  audit, 179

  break-even equation, 115

  and business savvy, 25

  buyouts and, 138

  commercial viability of, 93

  and compromising values, 24

  controversial qualities of, 23

  deductions and, 89

  disaster checklist for, 257–259

  distributing own records, 124

  download sales and, 222

  earnings, 148–150, 152

  end-zoning their producers, 128

  income, 25

  independent record deal for, 115–121

  informal agreements with, 128–129

  ISP record companies v., 222

  joint venture with producer, 126

  kickbacks and, 82

  letter of direction (LODs), 146

  like movie actors, 26

love/hate relationships with producers, 80

major label deal, 53–55

and management contracts, 129

mercy signing of, 213–214

overrides and, 137

pay from downloading and, 222

performance royalties and, 35

poor representation of, 23–24

producer conflict, 75–78, 77*n*2

producer production deal, 123–127

and producers, 26*n*12

promoters and, 103, 103*n*10

record deals and, 24

record royalties, 148

recording advances, 148

samples and, 175, 175*n*6

second records and, 120

side chain letter and, 125

as sophomores, 219

sponsors and, 95–96

suing record companies, 116–117, 117*n*4

union scale and, 79*n*9

unions and, 227

work for hire agreement and, 27

from working class backgrounds, 23

working for label, 202

ASCAP (American Society of Composers, Authors,
  and Publishers), 35–36, 85, 85*n*13, 104*n*11, 149, 169

Atlantic Records, 47, 47*n*1, 64, 243, 256, 263, 265.
  See also Warner Bros.

attorney(s), 173

  blackballing of, 168

  and both sides of a lawsuit, 9

  career goals and, 8

  on commission, 162

  conflicts of interest with, 8–9

  contraceptive contracts and, 129

  contracts and, 184

  copyright protection and, 159

  as crusaders, 7–8

  ethical, 9

  fees for, 6, 184

  finders fees and, 129

  general partners and, 187–188

  humbling facts about, 9

  letters of misdirection and, 189

  litigation, 161

  logic, 7

  negotiation fees for record deals, 55

  new, 7

  as rainmakers, 6–7

  record deals and, 6

  record labels and, 8–9

Serious Players.

The Music Player Network is for serious players. From guitars, bass, keyboards and recording to computer music culture, dance, trance and more. • Our industry-leading magazines, *Guitar Player, Keyboard, Bass Player, Gig, MC², Rumble, EQ* and *Extreme Groove*, take the art of playing music seriously. And so does our leading portal website, MusicPlayer.com. • Our editors and writers are experienced musicians and engineers with special insights and hands-on experience that only comes from real-time playing. • If you want to get serious about your playing, check us out at your nearest newsstand or visit MusicPlayer.com on the web.

WHEN IT COMES TO MUSIC WE WROTE THE BOOK